Winds of Exile

Te reconozco viento del exilio
saqueador de jardines
errante con tus látigos de polvo.
Me persiguen sin tregua tus silbidos
y borras mis pisadas de extranjero.

LIBRO DEL DESTIERRO, V

WINDS OF EXILE

The poetry of Jorge Carrera Andrade

by

Peter R. Beardsell

The Dolphin Book Co. Ltd.
Oxford, 1977

*This book is published with the financial
assistance of the University of Sheffield*

Published in Oxford by The Dolphin Book Co. Ltd., and
distributed by The Dolphin Book Co. (Tredwr) Ltd.,
Llangranog. Llandyssul, Dyfed SA44 6BA, Great Britain.

Printed in Spain

ISBN 0-85215-062-8
Depósito Legal: V. 2.730 - 1977 ISBN (Spain) 84-399-7424-8
Artes Gráficas Soler, S. A., Jávea, 28, Valencia-8.

ACKNOWLEDGMENTS

I wish to express sincere thanks to the University of Sheffield Research Fund and the University Grants Committee for facilitating a vital period of study in Ecuador; to the Special Collections Library of the State University of New York at Stony Brook, Long Island, for permission to consult their material on Jorge Carrera Andrade (and in particular to the Librarian, Evert Volkersz, and his secretary, for generous assistance and hospitality); to the Leverhulme Trust, for a fellowship which enabled me to work on this topic in London; to the Director-General of Canning House and his staff for their help and hospitality in London; to the staff of the Casa de la Cultura in Quito for their enthusiastic assistance; to colleagues who have constantly encouraged and guided my interest in Latin-American Studies, in particular Giovanni Pontiero and Frank Pierce; to the students of my Spanish-American poetry group at the University of Sheffield; to my wife, for her moral support and patience, and to Jorge Carrera Andrade himself for his generous and unhesitating cooperation. I am also grateful for the financial support of the University of Sheffield and the enthusiasm of the publisher, both of which have made the publication of this book possible.

The book is broadly based on a thesis approved for the degree of Doctor of Philosophy at the University of Sheffield in 1974.

P.R.B.

CONTENTS

Symbols used in page references   8
Preface   9

PART I: ECUADOR AND EXILE

I.   A life of exile and returns   15
II. The prose works   36
III. Ecuador   49

Initial discontent, 49. — Early impressions of the countryside, 51. — Metaphors, 54. — Social criticism, 60. — National themes, 72. — Influences of Ecuador on Carrera Andrade, 78. — Ecuador as the virginal land, 82. — Ecuador as childhood, mother, self, 86. — Ecuador as light and key, 90.

IV. Foreign lands   99

The lure of foreign lands, 99. — Impressionist scenes, 103. — Solidarity with the European proletariat, 108. — Cities and manufactured landscapes, 113.

PART II: A QUEST FOR MEANING

V.   Ontological problems   123

Solitude, 123. — The anguish of modern man, 130. — Transitory life, 136.

VI. Solutions   152

The role of nature, 154. — The eternal present, 171. — Universal unity and solidarity, 193.

VII. Exile as a poetic theme   204
VIII. Conclusion   223
Appendix. Chronological summary of Jorge Carrera Andrade's career   236
Bibliography   240
Index of works and poems   249

SYMBOLS USED IN PAGE REFERENCES

POETRY

Symbol   Edition

ROL   *Rol de la manzana,* Espasa Calpe, Madrid, 1935.
REG   *Registro del mundo. Antología poética 1922-1939,* Segunda
        edición, Editorial Séneca, México, 1945.
PE   *Poesías escogidas,* Ediciones Suma, Caracas, 1945.
AYE   *Aquí yace la espuma,* Editorial Presencias Americanas, Paris,
        1950.
EP   *Edades poéticas (1922-1956),* Casa de la Cultura Ecuatoriana,
        Quito, 1958.
MVP   *Mi vida en poemas,* Ediciones Casa del Escritor, Caracas, 1962.
PU   *Poesía última,* Las Américas, New York, 1968.
OPC   *Obra poética completa,* Casa de la Cultura Ecuatoriana, Quito,
        1976.

PROSE

CE   *Cartas de un emigrado,* Editorial Elan, Quito, 1933.
LAT   *Latitudes,* Editorial América, Quito, 1934.
MT   *Mirador terrestre,* Las Américas, New York, 1943.
RC   *Rostros y climas,* Ediciones de la Maison de l'Amérique Latine,
        Paris, 1948.
CS   *El camino del sol,* Casa de la Cultura Ecuatoriana, Quito,
        1958.
GMI   *Galería de místicos y de insurgentes,* Casa de la Cultura Ecua-
        toriana, Quito, 1959.
VPL   *Viaje por países y libros,* Casa de la Cultura Ecuatoriana,
        Quito, 1961.
PEV   *Presencia del Ecuador en Venezuela,* Editorial Colón, Quito,
        1963.
IH   *Interpretaciones hispanoamericanas,* Casa de la Cultura Ecua-
        toriana, Quito, 1967.
VC   *El volcán y el colibrí (Autobiografía),* Editorial José M. Cajica
        Jr., Puebla, México, 1970.
SAP   *Reflections on Spanish-American Poetry,* State University of
        New York Press, Albany, 1973.

A complete list of Carrera Andrade's books is given in the Bibliography.

PREFACE

I n 1970 Jorge Carrera Andrade published an extended poem, 'Libro del destierro', [1] which, without introducing any radical change in his themes, contributed a vital perspective to his poetry to date. Carrera Andrade assures his readers that he wrote the work 'in Paris under adverse conditions. The banishment was real and not metaphysical'. [2] Yet one can be in no doubt, on reading 'Libro del destierro', particularly in conjunction with other works by this author, that the theme of exile transcends the literal reality and acquires metaphysical dimensions; exile serves the poet, moreover, as an image for expressing associated themes. What Carrera Andrade's words serve to emphasise, however, is that the web of interrelated themes has at its hub a genuine experience of exile. More significantly, this is an exile which had endured — with only brief interruptions — for over forty years. It is proposed to demonstrate the great impact on Carrera Andrade's themes of his preoccupation with his homeland and his life abroad. It is intended to evince the special interrelation of his themes, and in particular to show the fundamental importance of homeland and exile as determinant factors on the overall structure of Carrera Andrade's poetic world. The division of the book into two parts is contrived to accentuate the chief features of the interrelationship.

Critics are strongly influenced by the essays that Carrera Andrade has written from time to time to interpret his own poetry. In the four main autocritical essays [3] he has empha-

---

[1] First published separately in *Papeles de Son Armadans*, CLXIX, 1970, pp. 35-48, and later included as a section in *Misterios Naturales*, Centre de Recherches de l'Institut d'Etudes Hispaniques, Paris, 1972, pp. 21-37. It a so appeared as a bilingual edition (Spanish and French) published by the University of Dakar (Senegal), Dakar, 1970.

[2] 'Decade of my Poetry', *Reflections on Spanish-American Poetry*, State University of New York Press, Albany, 1973, p. 65.

[3] 'Edades de mi poesía', preface to *Edades poéticas (1922-56)*, Casa de la Cultura Ecuatoriana, Quito, 1958; 'Mi vida en poemas', preface to *Mi vida en*

sised the development of his themes in relation to events in his life, drawing attention to his pervasive attempt to explore the various concrete phenomena of the world, and adducing the formula life=journey as the guiding principle underlying his verse: 'Soy un hombre del Ecuador, que ha tratado de conocer el mundo para desenvolver en él su vida como un viaje'. [4] Clearly, his own statements have been a welcome guide, and the present writer must acknowledge a debt to them. It would seem, however, that the emphasis of the formula should undergo a subtle but important change in the light of the new significance found for exile. In place of life = journey the present writer would substitute life = exile.

A full study of Carrera Andrade's poetic technique does not lie within the scope of this book. Points on technique are made, however, as appropriate within the framework of themes, especially in the sections on metaphors, impressionist scenes, animism, light and universal unity.

Until recently the reader of Carrera Andrade's poetry was faced with the problem of difficulty of access to certain texts. He had published mostly in small collections of verse and in limited editions; his books had appeared, moreover, in places as far apart as Quito and Paris, New York and Tokyo. The numerous anthologies helped to give an overall picture of his production, but inevitably left important gaps. [5] *Registro del mundo, Edades poéticas (1922-1956)*, and *Poesía última* must be regarded as key editions since they were fairly complete at the time of their publication in 1940, 1958, and 1968. [6] With the appearance of his *Obra poética completa* in 1976 [7] the principal difficulties were removed; in the present work page references will be given for this edition. It should be noted, however, that certain poems from the

---

poemas, Ed. Casa del Escritor, Caracas, 1962; 'Decade of my Poetry', *Reflections on Spanish-American Poetry*, State University of New York Press, Albany, 1973, pp. 58-67; and 'Poetry of Reality and Utopia', *ibid.*, pp. 68-84.

[4] 'Mi vida en poemas', *loc. cit.*, p. 9.

[5] By far the most useful anthology is the bilingual edition: *Selected Poems of J. C. A.*, Edited and Translated with an Introduction by H. R. Hays, State University of New York Press, Albany, 1972.

[6] *Registro del mundo, Antología poética. 1922-1939*, Ediciones del Grupo 'América', Imprenta de la Universidad, Quito, 1940; second edition by Editorial Séneca, México, 1945; *Edades poéticas (1922-1956)*, Casa de la Cultura Ecuatoriana, Quito, 1958; *Poesía última*, Las Americas Publishing Company, New York, 1968.

[7] *Obra poética completa*, Casa de la Cultura Ecuatoriana, Quito, 1976.

earlier books appeared in an amended version in *Edades poéticas* and are reproduced in this modified form in *Obra poética completa.* Since I have preferred to give quotations from the original version, page references to one edition besides *Obra poética completa* are included wherever significant variants occur in the lines quoted. References make use of the system of codes listed on page 8.

PART I

ECUADOR AND EXILE

I

A LIFE OF EXILE AND RETURNS

AFTER spending the first twenty-five years of his life in Ecuador, Jorge Carrera Andrade had been in almost permanent residence abroad until his return in 1976. Though his returns to the homeland have been numerous, they have also been relatively brief. Clearly, once he had chosen a diplomatic career a life overseas was always a probability; it will be recognised, however, that the very choice of this career corresponds to an underlying attitude to his country and to his life. The inherent contradictions of his position may be summarised by the statement that his career has been in the service of his country, while his life has been that of an exile.

A crucial moment for Carrera Andrade was the first departure from Ecuador, in 1928. In the pages of his autobiography, *El volcán y el colibrí*, devoted to the years prior to that date he stresses the extent of his involvement in the contemporary political events. [1] This emphasis is repeated by critics such as René Durand and H. R. Hays; [2] even Enrique Ojeda, who is more concerned with literary affairs, also attaches importance to that aspect of his life. [3] There can be no doubt that the poet did indeed become considerably embroiled in the movement for social justice and in the opposition to an unjust régime.

---

[1] *El volcán y el colibrí. (Autobiografía)*, Editorial José M. Cajica Jr.. S. A., Puebla (México), 1970, pp. 12-55. All subsequent references to this book will be made within the text by the symbol VC followed by the page number.

[2] René L.-F. Durand, *Jorge Carrera Andrade* (Présentation, choix de textes, traduction, bibliographie), Éditions Pierre Seghers, Paris, 1966, pp. 9-12; and H. R. Hays, *Selected Poems of Jorge Carrera Andrade*, State University of New York Press, Albany, 1972, pp. ix-xi.

[3] Enrique Ojeda, *Jorge Carrera Andrade. Introducción al estudio de su vida y de su obra*, Eliseo Torres, New York, 1971, pp. 63-4 and 93-4.

His social conscience was born early. During the days
of his adolescence his mother and her elder sister — Isolina,
the nun referred to in two of his poems [4] — exerted on him
a conservative type of influence, and encouraged a proximity
to the Church. He attended, for example, the religious
institution, the Colegio de la Merced, where the austere but
peaceful and refined atmosphere rendered him drunk with
incense and oblivious of the suffering outside (VC 25). It also
incurred, eventually, a spirit of rebellion. [5] But his father, by
contrast, was a Liberal of some repute. His influence ran
counter to that of mother and aunt, and he it was who
arranged for Carrera Andrade to be transferred to a secular
school: the Instituto Nacional 'Mejía'. In addition to parental
views and pressures, the contemplation of the world outside
his house left a profound impression on the boy. His house
lay on the border of two social classes: the whites and mes-
tizos of the city itself, and the Indians who inhabited the
hill known as the Panecillo. [6] He grew up, he recalls in
his autobiography, inwardly reconciling the two worlds
(VC 13). One of the political events to have most impact on
him was the downfall of the Liberal president, Eloy Alfaro,
in August 1912, particularly because of the violence of the
street scenes. Then, during the period immediately following World War I, Carrera Andrade and his friends
underwent a profound influence from writers such as Jacob
Von Uexcull, Ortega y Gasset, Haldane, and Spengler, whose
ideas contributed to his concepts of the decline of the West,
the beginning of the machine age, and a need for social
change and economic democracy (VC 29-30). This led in
turn to an awareness of the unjust system which existed
in Ecuador: the low wages of Indian agricultural workers
and of the working class, the competition among only a
small middle class for public office, and the control exerted
by the landowning and banking oligarchy over the political
and economic affairs of the country. Carrera Andrade

---

[4] 'Isolina' (OPC 106), and 'Evangelio de la Sor' (OPC 109).
[5] See Ojeda, op. cit., p. 26. It is not a question of rebellion against the
Church specifically, but against the Establishment generally.
[6] To the south of the centre of Quito rises a high hill which, through its
physical resemblance to a loaf of bread, has been given the name of 'el Panecillo'. The hill is of historical significance to the indigenous people.

therefore joined student groups (becoming particularly associated with one known by the name 'Renovación'), and took
part in politically-motivated campaigns proclaiming the
slogan: 'Tierra, pan y alfabeto para todos los ecuatorianos'
(VC 30).

His political agitation began to reach the point where he
was seen as a trouble-maker by Ecuador's régime. He helped
to organise lightning demonstrations and became editor of
a newspaper popular with the students and the working
class: *Humanidad*. On one occasion he set out on a campaign
to whip up the Indians' awareness of social and political
affairs in the nearby village of Guápulo (VC 38). During
his period in Guayaquil he managed to avoid trouble when
a demonstration was violently suppressed by the army (15
November 1922), but, for his part in a planned uprising in
favour of the left-wing presidential candidate, Juan Manuel
Lasso, he was imprisoned in a notorious, minute cell known
by the ominous nicknames of 'infiernillo' and 'ataúd de pié'.
His ardour intensified by these events, he continued to
publish the newspaper despite threats from the military,
and he wrote a few revolutionary poems such as 'Lenin ha
muerto' and 'Campanas del Kremlin' which were well received by the workers (VC 51). Not long after the formation
of Ecuador's Socialist Party, recognition of his activities came
with his election to the post of General Secretary. When the
fifth International Conference of Socialism was due to take
place in Moscow he was named, in 1928, delegate of his
country's Party. Mere fulfilment of this function may seem
in itself sufficient to account for his first departure from
Ecuador. But in the light of his active opposition to the
government one must agree with H. R. Hays that he also left
the country 'partly because the government was beginning
to look askance at his activities'. [7]

It would not be accurate to call this a case of political
exile. In the first place, there was clearly no question of a
formal banishment. Not only that, risky though his position
may have been, he was not bound to leave in order to

---

[7] Hays, op. cit., p. xi.

protect his skin. It is worth pointing out that he was not
in the conspicuous position of belonging to a minute group,
for socialism had indeed become something of a trend by
this time. The Liberal rule of Eloy Alfaro had, despite its
ambiguous character, helped to instil some sense of democracy in the education system, and had introduced certain
limited reforms. The middle class began to grow, political
awareness increased, while in Ecuador, as throughout the
continent, Marxist ideas found ready listeners among the
working class. To these factors one might add the appearance
of a number of sociological works, and the attempts to form
workers' and peasants' unions. In the opinion of Hernán
Rodríguez Castelo, 'Una naciente intelectualidad política de
signo socialista había dado caracteres críticos y hasta con-
vulsos al vivir ecuatoriano de los años veinte', and the poets
of Carrera Andrade's generation who turned inwards and
away from politics were the exceptions. [8] In such circumstances it does not seem likely that external political pressures played as great a role in his decision to leave as his
own inner dissatisfaction with the political life of his country,
his discouragement with the lack of clear progress achieved
by the Socialists, and — more positive and constructive — a
desire to study political affairs in Europe, Russia, and other
foreign lands. His own recollections of that decision substan-
tiate this argument: 'Acepté mi nombramiento de Delegado,
con intención de estudiar de cerca la complejidad de la experiencia soviética y recorrer algunos países de Europa,
sobre todo Francia, cuyo pensamiento ejercía sobre mí una
poderosa influencia' (VC 54).

One account of Carrera Andrade's life in those years
leading up to his departure from the country relegates political activity to secondary importance. Since he was a col-
league of the poet, Hugo Alemán must be considered as
an authority to heed. [9] For him, what seems most worthy of
recollection is Carrera Andrade's search for private pleasure.

---

[8] Hernán Rodríguez Castelo, *Gangotena, Escudero, y Carrera Andrade. Tres cumbres de nuestro postmodernismo*, Clásicos Ariel, Guayaquil/Quito, 1972, p. 1 of typescript. I am grateful to the author for permitting me to consult this work before its publication.

[9] Hugo Alemán, *Presencia del pasado*, Casa de la Cultura Ecuatoriana, Quito, vol. II, 1953, pp. 88-140.

It is not intended to debate here the relative importance of his public and private affairs, [10] but it is essential to expose the evidence for arguing that when he set sail for Europe private considerations, besides his political activities, were an important factor.

Carrera Andrade had a comfortable, secure childhood. As a schoolboy he was a hard worker and had a passion for learning. In his enterprises during early manhood there are signs that he was not without success (his contributions, for instance, to the magazines *Vida Intelectual, La Idea, El Crepúsculo, Frivolidades*). But it would appear that there was a growing sense of dissatisfaction. In part this was a nascent metaphysical anguish, arising from meditation on the themes of human love, the fragile nature of life, and the omnipresence of death (VC 27-8). In the search for an answer to such eternal problems, his reading played an important role. From André Gide's *Les Nourritures terrestres* (1897) — which he considers to have been of especial significance — he selects as a key quotation the following advice: 'Nathanael, que la importancia esté en tu mirada y no en la cosa que mires' (VC 28). As his poetry shows, he developed the technique of close observation of minute things. More immediately, however, consolation for his anguish and a substitute for the metaphysical inquiry — indeed, a possible answer to it — was offered by an epicurean indulgence in the delights of the various senses (ibid.). A restlessness is discernible in his activities of that period: abandoning the study of law at the University, he moved temporarily from Quito to Guayaquil. His friend of those years, Hugo Alemán, witnessed the change in him: 'Su vida, prematuramente empañada de cansancio, busca sorpresas'. [11] In the coastal city, away from the circle of family and acquaintances, he could freely seek sensual pleasures, including the taking of drugs. [12] When he returned, after a few months' journalism, to the capital this bohemian way of life continued: 'Comprometía febrilmente

---

[10] Although one is prepared to trust the facts that Alemán remembers, there seems reason to be cautious before accepting that his emphasis is also accurate. His book hardly does justice to the well-known facts about Carrera Andrade, being more concerned with the revelation of buried details.

[11] Alemán, op. cit., p. 97.

[12] Ibid., p. 98.

su tiempo la voluntad de asir, perennemente, la guirnalda
del ensueño.... Su angustia se quemaría en la marmita cre-
pitante de "los diablos azules" '. [13] Carrera Andrade's autobiography is understandably quiet about his personal life in
those years, but according to Alemán, who is engagingly
frank in his supply of details, the poet became embroiled
with a licentious, scandalous woman. He wrote a poem based
on this affair, intending that it should be kept private, but
some of his friends acquired it, passed it around, and permitted it to become widely known. In the scandal that ensued,
Carrera Andrade lost a number of friends in polite circles
and was confronted with the indignation of his family, who
refused to admit him to his home until he recanted pub-
licly. [14] Although he did perform this reconciliatory act, his
life continued 'inconforme' and 'desordenada' [15] up to the
moment of setting sail for Europe. He was causing disapproval, censure and discredit among the middle-class society
to which his family belonged, and — doubtless with some
exaggeration — Alemán gives the impression that the whole
of Quito was hostile to him.

On a personal level, therefore, it is clear that Carrera
Andrade was developing a sense of dissatisfaction with his
life and beginning to search for a solution. In epicureanism
he did not find complete satisfaction; journeys within his
own country were inadequate to fulfil his need. His home
society disapproved of his way of life, and he was unwilling
to conform to the local standards. A sharp, complete break
— however temporary — was essential, and the journey to
Europe provided the means.

An assessment of Carrera Andrade's activities and mo-
tivations during the years 1917-1928 could not fail to take
into account a third vitally important aspect: his poetry. The
literary environment in Quito both helped to mould his own
form of writing and instilled a sense of discontent and rebellion. All critics agree that *modernismo* had arrived late in
Ecuador. The key date is 1910, for although there were some

---

[13] Ibid., p. 100.
[14] Ibid., pp. 112-3.
[15] Ibid., p. 124.

poets who had already been writing *modernista* verse it was from that year that young writers grouped together to publish the new aims in newspapers and magazines and set out in consort to apply the principles to their poetry. [16] In Quito, Arturo Borja (1892-1912), Ernesto Noboa y Caamaño (1891-1927), and Humberto Fierro (1890-1929) were the representative figures, and *Letras* (1912-17) their principal organ, while in Guayaquil Medardo Angel Silva (1898-1919) was the main poet of the generation, and *El Telégrafo Literario* (1913) and *Renacimiento* (1917) the important organs. Carrera Andrade had meanwhile begun to write verse in 1917. He made an early entrance on the literary scene in Quito with *Vida Intelectual,* the traditional magazine of the Mejía college, of which he was to become editor, and *El Crepúsculo* (1917) which he founded with Augusto Arias and Gonzalo Escudero, also in the Mejía college. In the same year he was one of the editors of *La Idea* (1917-19), a journal which is now recognised by Ecuador's literary historians as an important event in the renovation of the country's literature. [17] It was in *La Idea* that he printed several of his earliest poems, but by 1922 he had published *El estanque inefable,* and by 1926, *La guirnalda del silencio.* In this way he became one of the figures in Ecuador's movement away from *modernismo.* Although it could not be described as a sudden or violent break with the previous generation, it constituted a step or two forward: the crumbling of the ivory tower, whispers of social awareness, transcendence of the purely subjective, and an extensive use of metaphor — all features that were eventually to develop into a new epoch in Ecuadorian letters. [18]

Something the *modernistas* had in common was a strong reaction against the social milieu: 'Evadirse, salir fuera del ambiente mezquino, era el vago anhelo que los conducía a la ensoñación. No tenían voluntad para obligarse en la lucha, sino la debilidad de la desesperanza', writes one of the

[16] See Isaac J. Barrera, *Historia de la literatura ecuatoriana,* Casa de la Cultura Ecuatoriana, Quito, 1960, p. 1103; Benjamín Carrión, *Indice de la poesía ecuatoriana contemporánea,* Ediciones Ercilla, Santiago de Chile, 1937, p. xiv; Augusto Arias, *Panorama de la literatura ecuatoriana,* Casa de la Cultura Ecuatoriana, Quito, Quinta ed. revisada, 1971, p. 257.
[17] 'Llegó a hacer época en los anales de la literatura ecuatoriana', Olmedo del Pozo, quoted in Arias, op. cit., p. 268.
[18] See Carrión, op. cit., p. xix.

most notable of the literary historians. [19] It was an outlook
partially inherited by Carrera Andrade, for a mood of disenchantment continued to pervade the world of letters in
Quito; but he, in contrast with their resignation, proved
himself capable of active struggle. Later he felt compelled to
remove himself from that environment. One is bound to add
that Carrera Andrade cannot have been impressed by the
speed with which new literary trends were introduced.
Despite the advances made by his own group the avant-
garde, with its extremes of innovation, did not arrive for
some time. Indeed, some *modernismo* persisted as late as
1930. [20] In this and other respects Ecuador remained an
unfavourable literary climate for a budding poet. Educated
people showed disdain for new writers, and tended to lack
interest in cultural occasions. [21] News of cultural events in
foreign lands was slow to arrive. Granted the difficulty in
obtaining foreign books, Carrera Andrade had read as widely
as possible and like most young writers of his period sensed
the necessity of visiting Europe, where the environment was
deemed to be more encouraging to the creative powers. [22]

Clearly Carrera Andrade's motives for setting sail for
Europe in 1928 were multiple, and their respective importance is difficult to assess. It would not seem accurate, in
the final analysis, to emphasise the political reasons too
strongly at the expense of the others, even though he
considers them — in retrospect — to be the reasons most
worthy of mention: 'En mis años mozos creí que yo estaba
pre-destinado para realizar un cambio revolucionario en la
estructura socio-económica de mi país y redimir a mi pueblo.
Viajé primero para instruirme y observar los movimientos
sociales de distintos lugares de la tierra' (VC 10). Circumstances in his private life made a change of environment
desirable if not essential. Literary growth and fulfilment
required a visit to Europe. In addition, he had the natural
eagerness of a young man to travel and to see new things.

---

[19] Barrera, op. cit., p. 1110.
[20] Ibid., p. 1126.
[21] Alemán, *op. cit.*, p. 97.
[22] The topic of Latin America's erstwhile unfavourable literary environment
is resumed in the Conclusion.

His departure was a response both to external pressures and to inner needs. It meant, ultimately, the opportunity to search for answers to political, social, literary, and personal problems which were incapable of resolution in Ecuador. This is where the emphasis properly lies: he left Ecuador not as an act of evasion but, essentially, as one of quest. The three outstanding aspects of his life hitherto — politics, poetry, and private experience — which had never been completely separable in any case, were fused in that single action. At this stage there can be no question of his realising that his quest would lead him into a more or less permanent state of exile.

Although his decision to leave was a free one, there seems little doubt, to judge from his autobiography, that some political figures in Ecuador had been manoeuvring to encourage his departure, or at least were pleased to see him go (VC 62). Once in Europe he had the sense of being abandoned. He was without money; and his Party published a newspaper article in Ecuador announcing his death at sea (VC 59). Even in 1929, after recovering from his first hardships, he wrote of this abandonment to Juana de Ibarbourou, in Montevideo: 'Mi pueblo me abandonó y me faltó suelo en qué apoyarme. Yo quiero identificarme con mi pueblo, ser su voz y su conciencia. Fisonomía propia y sensibilidad universal'. [23] It was what would seem to be a justifiable sense of pique at the absence of help (especially financial) from those whom he was supposed to be serving, but to this one must add the inevitable effects of distance from his homeland, difficulty of communication, and strangeness in foreign countries. His initial experience in Hamburg and Berlin was bound to instil in him a feeling of uneasiness and imprisonment (VC 62). Penniless, not understanding or speaking German, suffering from the unaccustomed severity of a cold winter, unable to accomplish his mission as Secre-

---

[23] Letter to Juana de Ibarbourou, 1929. Only an extract from the letter is preserved. It may be consulted in the folder entitled *Correspondencia* and bearing the dates 1929-49 in Box 8 at the Special Collections Library of the State University of New York, Stony Brook, Long Island. There was no pagination or index system when the correspondence was consulted in July 1972. Subsequent references to the correspondence will be made with the name of the person to whom a letter is addressed, the date, and the Box in which the appropriate folder may be found.

tary of the Socialist Party, [24] he was compelled to make a
vain search for manual labour, and to mix with the hungry
masses at the start of the great Depression. All this ensured
that Ecuador was never far from his thoughts. Gradually his
situation improved: he sold deaf-aids, became Secretary of
the Asociación General de Estudiantes Latinoamericanos,
travelled to Paris, Marseilles, and Barcelona, met Haya de la
Torre, César Arroyo, and Benjamín Carrión, spent a period
in residence with Gabriela Mistral, was given editorial work,
saw his *Boletines de mar y tierra* well received, and found
some success — and earnings — in journalism. It is clear from
the *Cartas de un emigrado* (1933), from *Latitudes* (1934),
and from his unpublished correspondence that while he
was very much alive to the contemporary realities of the
Europe he witnessed every day, his own country constantly
surged to the foreground of his thoughts. In several letters
there is political comment on European countries; but in
several Ecuador also occupies his attention. A good illustration is a letter of 1929 in which, while explaining how
Germany impressed him for its technological and social advances, for the dignity shared by all men of the nation, he
instinctively feels the need to draw contrasts with Ecuador,
characteristically evincing his profound distress at the plight
of the Indian:

> Vi que el hombre en la Mitteleuropa era el 'factor hombre', es decir
> un ser cuya sola condición humana merecía ya respeto. Me acordé
> entonces con dolor del aborigen ecuatoriano, del indio, cuya exis-
> tencia es igual a la del semoviente y que no tiene amparo alguno
> en nuestra tierra, donde le explotan y maltratan el Cura, el Teniente
> Político y el hacendado. *¡Sin embargo es también un hombre!* y to-
> dos los espíritus libres y generosos del Ecuador deben contribuir a su
> dignificación. Es ya tiempo de liquidar para siempre la esclavitud en
> nuestro país, porque así lo demandan el siglo y la humanidad. [25]

---

[24] In a letter to the editor of *El Día*, Quito, in 1933 (Box 8), he gives three
reasons for not being allowed into Russia: (i) he was a friend of a bourgeois
civil servant, (ii) his papers had a late date, (iii) he spoke French (the language
of spies). In VC he gives different reasons: he arrived after the Conference had
finished, and he requested entry on notepaper from Ecuador's Consulate in
Hamburg. The conclusion is the same in both accounts: he was suspected of
being a government agent.

[25] Letter to Manuel Salguero, 4 November, 1929 (Box 8).

And yet, though preoccupied with the problems of his country, and though tempted to return home, he took the advice first of César Arroyo and later of Benjamín Carrión that the situation in Ecuador had not improved, that there was no hope yet, and that he would do better to stay in Europe and to decide again when things were more favourable. It is manifest in his correspondence of those years that he was dismayed by faults in his country's political system, which permitted a few leaders to dispose of the nation's destiny, without consulting the people. There is some bitterness also in his attitude towards the people of Ecuador who acted like a flock of sheep, nobody protesting against injustice. The young intellectuals kept quiet in order to ensure their public employment. [26] Absence from the homeland permitted him to avoid such a climate, and enabled him freely to express his opinions — a freedom of which he took abundant advantage in his letters. He believes, indeed, that he was living in Barcelona to serve his country (VC 78).

His absence was weighing heavily on his conscience, however. The letters collected for publication in Quito in 1933 — after his return — bear a title indicative not of the attitude of a mere traveller, not of a visitor to foreign lands, but of one for whom the residence seems more permanent, the rupture with the homeland more complete: *Cartas de un emigrado*. Retrospectively, Carrera Andrade employs the term of 'exile' rather than 'émigré': in *El volcán y el colibrí* he recalls that those walks in Barcelona through the parks and by the sea, when his mind was full of thoughts of Ecuador, were 'erranzas de desterrado' (VC 83).

What had begun as a journey abroad had now become a form of exile. By this time he had already encountered much of the essence of exile as it was to manifest itself in his life. Ecuador's political system was alienating; its social system was not providing justice for the Indian; its people were passive; and there was even a suspicion that the country (or his Party) did not desire his return. Other lands, in contrast, offered him advanced technology, social progress,

---

[26] See his letter to Alex Gastelú, 26 November, 1929 (Box 8).

freedom of speech, a politically-educated working class, and cultural facilities. One thing that did not foreshadow later developments was that his written comment at this point in his life tended to find little but fault in Ecuador, and little but good in Europe. As was to happen many times in his life, however, this did not prevent homesickness — 'La nostalgia de la tierra natal me corroía hasta el fondo del ser' (VC 86) — and in due course the desire to return proved stronger than the dissatisfaction with the homeland: in July 1933, with a third-class passage, he humbly made his way back to Ecuador. It is worth adding that by this time his behaviour had undergone a change. [27] In his search for an answer to his needs and a meaning to his life the bohemian existence and the epicureanism had long ago proved negative.

The years 1933-4 are also crucial in their decisive moulding of the pattern to be followed by his life. It is clear that he had been considering the possibility of a diplomatic career since at least as early as the years in Barcelona, where he attended University courses in Diplomacy. [28] On his return to Ecuador he accepted the post of Pro-Secretary of the Senate. This was a position which — as he himself recognises — would inevitably keep him on the fringe of political affairs (VC 88). Although his political beliefs were fundamentally unchanged it appears that he was unwilling to become involved in the agitation of that period, and preferred to maintain his political independence. More precisely, it may be said that he was a moderate, reluctant to find himself embroiled in the various forms of extremism prevalent in Ecuador's contemporary affairs. As early as 1931, writing from Barcelona on Ecuador's politics, he made clear his opposition to both fascism and communism: 'Bonifaz ha dicho: "Ni Roma ni Moscú"; y esto lo encuentro muy acertado y digno de elogio'. [29] The divisions between socialism and communism, he argued elsewhere, should be forgotten, and a United Socialist Party should be formed for both

---

[27] See Ojeda, op. cit., p. 130.
[28] Ibid., p. 129.
[29] Letter to General Leonidas Plaza, November 1931 (Box 8).

working class people *and* those middle class people also wanting social reform. [30] Now, with a University group, he founded a new party: the Social Agrarian. But by this time it would appear that he was losing hope of directly participating in any radical change in Ecuador. In the Introduction to his autobiography he confesses that although at first he travelled to learn about movements abroad, he soon realised he could not be an actor in the universal transformation but simply an alert and knowledgeable witness (VC 10). That transformation from actor to witness was already beginning to take place. His consular posts clinched it. In 1934 he obtained a temporary posting as Interim Consul in Paita, Perú, where, despite his 'corazón de desterrado' (VC 101), and his feelings of 'un solitario en el exilio" (ibid.), he entered a competition for admission to the diplomatic service in Europe. On winning the competition he was assigned to Le Havre. 'Tal hecho produjo un cambio radical en mi vida. El político activo que había en mí cedió el paso al funcionario del Estado y al hombre de letras, porque comprendí que había varias maneras de servir a la patria y al pueblo' (VC 104).

Two points are particularly significant in these words: one is the express wish to ensure for himself the opportunity to write; the other is the belief that his major causes might be served in a diplomatic career. His correspondence plainly implies that he received a good deal of criticism for allegedly compromising his political principles by acting in consular posts on behalf of régimes which on some occasions at least were alien to his own policies. Over the course of many years his defence has been consistent: in 1935 he wrote: 'Yo sirvo en el Consulado, como podría servir en cualquier empresa, o casa comercial, o fábrica o taller'. [31] Several years later he explained why it was possible to serve as Consul even under a government of which he disapproved: 'No me siento ni nunca me he sentido ligado a ningún régimen sino a la Patria'. [32] It is an attitude compati-

---

[30] Letter to Enrique Teñón, 7 July 1932 (interpolated in the above-mentioned letter).
[31] Letter to Luis Alberto Sánchez, 8 October 1935 (Box 8).
[32] Letter to his father, 20 June 1944 (Box 8).

ble with his move away to the fringe of political events.
Unwilling to associate himself directly with a form of extremist ideology or activity — either to the Right or to the Left —
he felt nevertheless that a complete withdrawal constituted
defeatism. It has always been essential to him to be in some
way useful to Ecuador. In the case of a few governments,
however, he has found no alternative but to hand in his
resignation. He resigned from a diplomatic post in Venezuela
in 1946, for example, when his conscience would not permit
him to fulfill a command by the President of Ecuador, Velasco Ibarra. [33]

With the crucial issues already decided, the main features
of the course of Carrera Andrade's life were already mapped.
A diplomatic career would mean inevitable wide travel and
long absence from his home country. Between 1928 and 1976
one can find recorded a total of only some fifty-one months
spent in Ecuador. Of the eight returns that had punctuated
his life, five would appear to have occurred in response to
an invitation or summons, and three alone through a completely free choice. Such evidence does not suggest, therefore,
that life in his country has had a compelling attraction for
him.

It is not that Ecuador has no advantages. He has always
been attracted by the purity and freshness of its natural
environment. Quito's sun and light have been welcome on
his returns from abroad (VC 308). When he arrived from
Barcelona in 1933 it was the countryside that lured him
most (VC 87, 92, 93), and it has always been his ultimate
refuge. During a visit of two months in 1958, he recalls, 'mi
permanencia en el Ecuador se redujo como siempre a un
recorrido de las altas Sierras y una visita a los volcanes, en
una repetición del culto de mis antepasados' (VC 223-4).
The countryside helped him, indeed, to see his country as a
refreshing symbol of primitive simplicity and innocence in

---

[33] See his letter to Raúl Andrade, 14 May 1946 (Box 8), and VC 171-2.
Velasco Ibarra had violated the Republic's Constitution; he then demanded that
Carrera Andrade should deny the reports and criticisms of this event in the Vene-
zuelan press.

contrast with a supercivilised world dominated by cynicism, hatred and materialism (VC 223). [34]

Of the places he has visited, the European nations and the U.S.A. seem to be most representative of this vision of the world at large. In the U.S.A., for example, he learned that no service is rendered free of charge: his correspondence during the period of residence in San Francisco in 1942 shows clear evidence of this. Even poetry itself seemed to be treated as though it were a commercial product; refusing to be abused, he adapted himself to the system and began to play it. Thus, in a letter concerning the translation into English of some of his verse, he fought for his financial due: 'Tal vez se sorprenderá usted de mi exigencia acerca de los honorarios. América del Norte ha sido una buena lección para mí, en lo que se refiere al lado práctico de la vida. Nadie hace aquí nada gratuitamente. Toda labor, por humilde que sea, tiene una retribución económica. Y yo no creo en la inferioridad de la labor poética...'. [35] Although he does not reveal in his letters and autobiography (or in the poetry, for that matter) the blatant *antiyanquismo* of a Pablo Neruda or a Nicolás Guillén, his attitude has undergone a certain hardening process in recent years. The Americans' role in the Second World War met with his approval; but he has been disturbed to notice more recently evidence of that very anti-democratic character against which they had earlier fought: 'Ahora veo, con pena, que esa gran Nación está en peligro de caer en manos de un neo-Nazismo más poderoso aún que el germánico ya extinguido. Mi única esperanza es la juventud norteamericana y el triunfo de la "América sensata" que restaure la tradición de libertad'. [36]

His European experience, however, seems to have produced an even more profound despair and bitterness. In 1951 he began what was to become a long period of absence from Ecuador when he took up the post of his country's permanent delegate at UNESCO in Paris. Although he resigned this post on the accession to power of Velasco Ibarra (for the

---

[34] A detailed study of the expression of these attitudes in his poetry and prose will be made below.
[35] Letter to Lloyd Mallan, 13 November 1942 (Box 8).
[36] Letter to the author, 3 August 1972.

third time) he remained in Paris, doing editorial work for
UNESCO. He was appalled by the materialism of the country in which he was residing, by the alienation he was suffering, and by the spiritual impoverishment of the French:
'Siempre he lamentado la "soledad de las ciudades", pero
nunca me ha parecido el mundo más desolado que en el
París existencialista, escéptico y groseramente materialista
de estos años. El francés no sabe otra cosa que odiar y
traicionar'. [37] It would be unjust to attribute all his antipathy
for this society to a single country; it was not merely France
but the whole of Europe that dismayed him: 'En Europa,
mi querido Mariano' — he wrote to Picón Salas — 'hay mucho
orgullo, mucho menosprecio del hombre, mucha codicia'. [38]
There is little doubt that his feelings in those years were
intensified by a sense of living in exile. 'Nueve años de exilio'
is his choice of title for the chapter covering that period in
his autobiography (VC 210-26). He turned his attention to
Ecuador's history, unable to serve the homeland in any official capacity. In 1958 he felt compelled to make a two-
month visit to Quito. But after returning to Paris, his health
deteriorated and a nervous depression beset him, neces-
sitating a spell of repose with relatives in the U.S.A.

Yet it is some indication of the predicament in which he
found himself that during those very years in which Europe
proved a repellent environment he should write of aspects
of life in Ecuador with the same degree of antipathy. His
principal objections were those he had expressed in the
twenties and the thirties: the unjust social and political system, the pettiness of human relations, the lack of will and
concern among the people. Replying to Ricardo Descalzi,
he confessed: 'Le comprendo en su "vuelta a la soledad" del
Ecuador. Nunca se siente el hombre más solo que en esa
"Capital de las Nubes", pequeña e inhumana, donde no su-
perviven sino las mezquinas pasiones y triunfan los menos
dotados . . . . En cuanto a mi viaje al Ecuador, creo que no
se realizará por el momento . . . . Esperaré a que la gente
despierte y a que se respire un nuevo hálito de esperanza

---

[37] Letter to Dorothy E. Harth, 28 February 1957 (Box 12).
[38] Letter to Mariano Picón Salas, 9 January 1957 (Box 13).

para el Ecuador . . .'. [39] In 1972, even with Velasco Ibarra
ousted from his fifth period in power, Carrera Andrade once
again gave political motives for remaining in voluntary exile:
'No regresaré a mi país mientras no se normalice la situación
política, aunque noto signos de avance en las reformas sociales'. [40] It was not until 1976 that he felt able to return.

To judge from *El volcán y el colibrí*, Carrera Andrade's
first return to the homeland was not all a question of ex-
uberance. On the one hand, renewed contact with his native
countryside invigorated him (VC 92). But on the other hand
this pleasure was modified by disappointments. Everything in
Quito struck him as being small: the parks and buildings
for example; and even more significant, there appeared to
be a pettiness in the 'dimensiones espirituales' (VC 87) — 'Las
relaciones humanas, la amistad, el amor, la vida social, el
trabajo diario estaban entorpecidos por una maraña de intri-
gas y mezquindades' (ibid.). What may be noticed here is
that his feelings about Ecuador's shortcomings are not confined to political circumstances. He also reacts — quite naturally — on the level of amenities and personal relationships,
things affecting his personal life. Besides, he has never been
secret about regarding one drawback of life in Quito to be
its impoverished cultural ambience. It seemed a literary
backwater not only in the twenties but also in the fifties. On
setting out for the UNESCO post in Paris, he left his native
land with mixed feelings in which regret was a dominant
element. He would have preferred, he recalls, to have spent
the whole of his life in Ecuador, but it was a country where
the writer could not earn a living from his craft, a country
without readers (VC 207).

On the termination of his posting in London, in 1949, he
was given an appointment in Cuba. The letter that he wrote
to the new President of Ecuador, Galo Plaza, is highly
illuminating for what it reveals concerning his motivation. [41]
A move to Cuba, he objects, would constitute a step down
the diplomatic ladder, whereas if he has served well in

[39] Letter to Ricardo Descalzi, 5 May 1955 (Box 13).
[40] Letter to the author, 3 May 1972.
[41] Letter to Galo Plaza, 14 February 1949 (Box 8).

previous appointments he deserves promotion. Besides, he argues, he has spent eight years in America (i.e. Latin America and the U.S.A.), three in Japan, and only two in Europe, 'y para emparse en las aguas lustrales de la cultura occidental es menester residir en los países europeos un tiempo más largo'. He requests, in order of preference, Paris, Rome or London. There is no question of any antipathy for Cuba itself, or for Latin America, for that matter. Nor do political considerations appear to be uppermost in his mind. Two things make a further period in Europe so desirable: the career advancement inherent in a prestigious diplomatic post, and — at least equally important — the advantageous conditions for his ambitions as a writer. In Europe, and particularly perhaps in France, he has found a kind of peace and a suitable environment for writing poetry. When he arrived at Le Havre in 1934 with his first consular post in Europe, 'El puerto normando me brindó un refugio, un abrigo, un remanso favorable para la creación poética' (VC 106). Despite those reservations about the materialism, cynicism and inhospitality of France discussed above, there is no doubt about his ultimate fondness of the country — one might almost call it a sense of attachment or belonging. It was in Le Havre that he met his first wife; when he remarried, in 1951, he again chose a French bride. To land at Orly Airport, as Ambassador to France in 1965, was as though to return home (VC 208). With its large Latin American community, moreover, Paris has always provided excellent literary stimulus besides increasing that sense of being at home: 'Aquí, en París, me siento más sudamericano que en Quito y respiro el "aura" intelectual de nuestro Continente'. [42]

Other foreign lands have also attracted Carrera Andrade, without attaining quite the significance of Europe. The U.S.A., for example, has not only caused his aversion. He has been deeply impressed by New York (VC 116), fascinated by San Francisco (VC 117), full of admiration for the U.S. Second World War effort (VC 150-1), pleased by the climate, scenery and people of California, [43] and revitalised by the interest in

[42] Letter to Mariano Picón-Salas, 20 April 1956 (Box 13).
[43] See his letter to José Camacho Lorenzana, 28 February 1941 (Box 8).

culture shown by San Francisco's inhabitants.[44] He has maintained contacts, made non-professional visits to the country (1959, 1975), served in New York as Ecuador's delegate at the United Nations (1960), and held the post of Visiting Professor at the State University of New York at Stony Brook, Long Island (1969-71). Japan, where he spent three years of rich experience (1938-40), left him with a favourable impression of its customs, its colour, its cleanliness, and with the feeling that it has something in common with the Andean countries through the characteristics of the people and the sound of their language (VC 119). Periods of residence in Latin American countries are remembered with pleasure. Paita (Peru, 1934) seemed a paradise because of its scenery and its remoteness (VC 101). Venezuela (1944-7 and 1961-3) treated him well and respected him both as poet and diplomat (VC 158); its countryside inspired his production of poetic images (VC 172). In Nicaragua too (1963-4) the natural scenery and creatures impressed him greatly, producing a notable influence on his poetic inspiration (VC 280).

There is clearly a fundamental dichotomy in his view of Ecuador. To have spent most of his life in exile has, the poet confesses, left him with some regret: 'Sí, siento pesar por mi ausencia del Ecuador que nunca fue realmente voluntaria sino determinada por las condiciones especiales de mi vida. Mi primer viaje fue en cumplimiento de una designación del Partido Socialista y los viajes que le siguieron fueron en busca de trabajo o dentro del Servicio Diplomático...'.[45] It will be noticed that he stresses the involuntary nature of his absence from Ecuador. Although this would seem — in the light of the discussion above — an over-simplification of the issues, it is significant that he prefers to feel that his exile has been something over which he has been unable to exert control. There are no grounds for doubting his loyalty to Ecuador, and his life has clearly been permeated with a sense of nostalgia for it. Not only this: his life, though spent mainly in exile, has been devoted to his homeland's cause.

---

[44] See his letter to Bolívar Paredes, 2 May 1941 (Box 8).
[45] Letter to the author, 27 February 1973.

In cultural, social and political terms, however, Ecuador has not attained the standard required of a land he could call a home. When all the factors are placed in the balance it transpires that he has actually preferred to live abroad (especially in Europe), partly to serve his country in a way for which he is well equipped, it is true, but also to benefit from the improved amenities for his private life and his literary career.

In the final analysis travel itself is seen to have had a vital function. Since his youth he has sought new sights and new experiences by travelling whenever possible. In 1922 he moved temporarily from Quito to Guayaquil, prompted by a mixture of political, journalistic and personal motives. After returning to Quito, and taking a post with *Humanidad*, he would make mysterious journies away from the capital. [46] The initial journey to Europe, which began — ostensibly — with a clearly-defined aim and a specific destination — soon evolved into a series of visits to different cities and countries: Hamburg, Berlin, Paris, Marseilles, Barcelona.... On his transfer from Le Havre to Yokohama (1938) he made brief tours of New York and San Francisco. During his three years in Japan he took advantage of the chance to see other parts of the country at week-ends. In fact, wherever he has been posted he has not been content to remain in the city of his consular assignment, but has sought always to familiarise himself with the country as a whole. He has taken particular pleasure in going into the countryside, as much when abroad as during periods of return to Ecuador.

His own assessment of the role of travel in his life suggests a change of emphasis over the years: 'Viajé primero para instruirme .... Después, el viaje se hizo la razón misma de mi vida' (VC 10). It is evident, however, that even at first his travelling was essentially a response to the mystery of life. Dissatisfied with the familiar things and searching for better, burning with an intellectual curiosity and an adventurous spirit, he has always been travelling to satisfy some inner need. The early journeys created a momentum which has

---

[46] Alemán, op. cit., p. 104.

carried him forward in ceaseless motion. In such circumstances a diplomatic career has only partially answered his need, for besides granting him the opportunity of moving from place to place it has also enabled him to perceive the absence of a final goal in any of the stages of the journey. It is possible to interpret his last return to Ecuador as a recognition of that fact. The career, the homeland, and foreign countries are vital factors; but they act, ultimately, only as exteriorisations of inner motives, as symbols of the poet's ontological preoccupations. Like his writing, his diplomatic career and his travels have expressed the need to search for the meaning of existence; they have been in themselves an attempt to give meaning to his life.

II

THE PROSE WORKS

It has been usual for critics to ignore Carrera Andrade's prose, whether because it lies almost wholly in the category of non-fiction, because it is not considered of sufficient merit to warrant attention, or because it does not appear to contribute to an understanding of his verse. There are few grounds, admittedly, for claiming that the prose deserves to be studied in its own right, but a full impression of the poet's intellectual activity is an essential condition for a thorough comprehension of his themes. The relationship between the overall pattern of a man's life and the main themes of his poetry can be appreciated only if the areas of interest reflected in his prose are taken into account. As will be shown, Carrera Andrade's prose both clarifies certain issues arising in the verse and contains important differences, which place the poetry in its true perspective.

The works are of five types: —

(a)   essays (or letters) on current affairs *(Cartas de un emigrado; Latitudes)*;

(b)   surveys of literary trends and figures *(Guía de la joven poesía ecuatoriana;* chapters of *Rostros y climas; Galería de místicos y de insurgentes; Viaje por países y libros; Radiografía de la cultura ecuatoriana; Interpretación de Rubén Darío; Retrato cultural del Ecuador; Interpretaciones hispanoamericanas; Reflections on Spanish-American Poetry)*;

(c)   impressionistic word-pictures of places visited *(Latitudes; Rostros y climas; Viaje por países y libros)*;

(d)   accounts of Ecuador's history *(Mirador terrestre; La tierra siempre verde; El camino del sol; Presencia del Ecuador en Venezuela; El fabuloso reino de Quito)*;

(e)   autobiographical and autocritical comment ('Edades de mi poesía'; 'Mi vida en poemas'; *El volcán y el colibrí;*

two chapters of *Reflections on Spanish-American Poetry*).[1]
The most ambitious and substantial is his history of
Ecuador: *El camino del sol*. It comprises two parts. 'Libro I',
entitled 'El fabuloso reino de Quito' (published as a separate
volume in 1963), traces the development of civilisations in
Ecuador from the earliest Indian tribes through the Inca era
to the invasion of the *conquistadores*. 'Libro II', entitled 'La
tierra siempre verde' (published as a separate volume in 1955)
continues the historical account during the centuries of
Spanish colonial rule until the first signs of Independence.
The product of several years' work, *El camino del sol* draws
on a great number of sources (mostly in the Bibliothèque
Nationale in Paris) which are listed in the extensive bibliography of 225 entries dating from 1534 to 1957). But this is
not essentially an academic work, for though basically an
historical account the book has many pages of imaginative
reconstruction. Carrera Andrade brings to life moments of
great importance and situations of great pathos by turning
from bare factual remarks to narration of scenes and episodes,
evocation of mood, and description of the setting. Most of
the book is written in a prose style which, while elegant in
rhythm and diction, is clear and unadorned; but there are
many passages of sheer creative writing where the style, at
worst, becomes florid and, at best, adds to the interest and
pathos. It is also worth noticing the scarcity of dates. What
interests him is not a mere chronological outline of major
events in Ecuador's history, but impressions of situations,
scenes, eras and moments, their interpretation, and an imaginary insight into the minds of the figures involved.

This was not intended primarily as a standard history of
the country for the people of Ecuador. During the years 1951
to 1958 he was firmly based in Paris, isolated from his native
Quito. Such an extended absence both increased his nostalgia
and facilitated an understanding of the outsider's view of his
country. He was struck by the scant knowledge of Ecuador
in Europe. Although the pre-hispanic era of the Kingdom of
Quito was already recorded in the chronicles and reports

---

[1] In subsequent page references to these books the system of symbols listed
on page 8 will be used.

made by colonial missionaries and magistrates, nobody had yet gathered all the information together, arranged it in chronological order, and presented it in a pleasant and readable form (VC 220). His work was to be pleasant to read; he would take a partisan approach ('*reescribir* la historia con amor por el país'); [2] and above all, he was to write in order that Ecuador be better known and understood abroad. *El camino del sol* therefore responded to a desire to promote the interests of Ecuador in foreign lands.

These motives, which underlie his career as a diplomat, have prompted many other pages of his prose. Not all such works, however, are thorough, substantial, and valid for their own sake. Sometimes they amount to a crude exposition of elementary facts, and are better classed as propaganda than as art. (*Mirador terrestre* is such a book.)

Another aspect of this desire to provide basic information about Ecuador is the enthusiasm he has shown for writing surveys of his country's culture. The fullest account is *Galería de místicos y de insurgentes,* in which he was faced with the formidable problem of compressing Ecuador's intellectual life from 1555 to 1955 into 190 pages. The book is concerned with not only the novel, theatre, poetry, and essay, but also the evolution of scientific and political thought. It examines one writer, or movement, or group of figures in each chapter. Though intended as a source of information for the foreigner, in the paucity of dates this work differs from most histories of literature: it is a series of brief sketches, with biographical data plus, at times, personal impressions of works. With its vast coverage, there is insufficient depth to capture the reader's curiosity in any one author or political figure, and the book lacks overall cohesion and shape, failing to suggest general trends and outstanding features. *Retrato cultural del Ecuador* constitutes a different and more satisfying approach. Instead of information we find interpretation. Carrera Andrade notes the determining role of the mixed Indian and Spanish heritage of the people. Their writing has been inspired by an epigramatic nature, by a sense of humour,

---

[2] Ibid.; Carrera Andrade's italics.

intellectual curiosity, the love of nature, and a taste for the precious and exquisite. The argument is convincing in its main points. Originally an address to the Institut d'Études Hispaniques in Paris, the work is directed at a European audience and is intended to broaden knowledge of and assist understanding of the nature and culture of Ecuador's people.

Besides furnishing basic information, destroying ignorance, and encouraging an insight into Ecuador's culture, Carrera Andrade has sometimes written in order to defend an aspect of national interest. He strongly pursues, for example, the question of Peru's aggression against his country, even to the extent of including a catalogue of Peru's steady incursion into and expropriation of Ecuador's territory, in an essay of *Presencia del Ecuador en Venezuela* (PEV 13-38). After Ecuador had declared the nullity of the treaty signed in Rio de Janeiro in 1941 (by which Ecuador, under pressure from other American states, ceded the disputed territory) Carrera Andrade himself was assigned the diplomatic task of explaining his country's case in Chile, Argentina and Brazil (1960). The connection between this kind of writing and his diplomatic function is evident.

He has also sought to benefit his country by exalting its image, by singing its praises abroad. Its geographical realities, for example, are often the object of admiration; the merit of national writers and artists is frequently a subject. On certain occasions he has eulogised even his country's social development and political activity (in *El mirador terrestre,* for example). This surprisingly uncritical attitude is exceedingly rare in his prose; but that it should occur at all reveals how eager he is, when a foreign readership is envisaged, to uphold Ecuador's dignity and to advertise it to the world.

As a diplomat Carrera Andrade has sometimes found himself in the ambiguous position of serving his country even under regimes whose political views conflicted with his own. In his prose works the promotion of Ecuador corresponds to that role in his career: he has concerned himself not with the shortcomings of the particular parties in control but with the international prestige of the country as a whole. This has not prevented him, however, from consistently advocating certain political causes in his prose writing, not only in his journalistic period (i.e. until 1933) but in all periods.

Among these causes that of the improvement of conditions for Ecuador's Indians is predominant. In *El camino del sol* he presents the early Indian civilizations in idyllic terms. The detailed study of the Confederate Kingdom of Quito presents a picture of mutual aid, peace, and communion of man with nature. Although the advent of the Incas is seen as an intrusion, there is no comparison with the devastating effects wrought by the Spanish *conquistadores* on the Indian peoples in general. The Conquest is envisaged as the beginning of suffering for Ecuador's Indians, bringing them from a state of nobility to one of degradation. Without exaggerating the records, Carrera Andrade has selected and emphasised historical details which would serve to make out a case on behalf of the native peoples of Ecuador against the Spanish invaders. To his mind, moreover, the basic position of the Indians is unchanged even today. In 'Radiografía de la cultura ecuatoriana' he gives evidence that the Indians of Ecuador in pre-Conquest times lived better than those of today in terms of food, clothing, and leisure time (IH 114-7). Their original gaiety has yielded to fatalism, maturity and melancholy as a result of the life of a conquered people.

It is interesting to note here that Carrera Andrade once began work on a novel that would clearly have aimed at exposing the Indians' plight. One chapter, under the title 'Hombres en marcha', is all that was published. [3] The plot concerns a dispute over ownership of land between the peasants — who are shown to live in poverty and submission — and the local *hacendado* — who has most of the bad qualities imaginable (he is bullying, destructive, bad-tempered, inconsiderate, and haughty). When the peasants rise to protect their claim the *patrón* sends for troops. The soldiers arrive in force and immediately fire into the crowd of peasants, dispersing them and killing many, among them the mother of the narrator. It is an obvious case of social protest

---

[3] The chapter appeared in 1933 in *Cartas de un emigrado*, pp. 53-65.

literature, with ingredients typical of the Indianist novel. Though it anticipates by a year or two fellow Ecuadorian Jorge Icaza's *Huasipungo* (1934), one of the best-known and most extreme of these novels, its main theme and plot bear a close resemblance to various earlier works of the genre. Being no more than an unfinished part of an incomplete book, Carrera Andrade's narrative not surprisingly has little depth and compresses far too much into one chapter. But what is of interest is his aim: to expose the social injustice, especially the plight of the Indians, the brutality, greed and corruption of the landowner, and the connivance of the government.

This fragment of a projected novel was published in the same volume as a number of letters with political comment: *Cartas de un emigrado,* which discuss the position of the proletariat in Ecuador and the manoeuvrings of politicians. They constitute the most outspoken and the most detailed exposition of his views on the position of Ecuador's Indians. His arguments may be summarised as follows: —

1. There is inadequate provision for the Indian's needs (i.e. food and clothing) (CE 18);
2. The Indian is only nominally free; in reality he is a slave (CE 8, 20);
3. His situation has barely changed over the last century (CE 19);
4. The Church holds sway over his behaviour (CE 9);
5. Ecuador's laws guarantee him nothing (CE 32);
6. Nobody lifts a finger to help him (CE 19);
7. There is little in the way of medical care and education for Indian children (CE 40);
8. Ecuador's Socialist Party could help (CE 25-6);
9. If the Indians were converted into civilised men the whole country would benefit;
10. Agrarian reform must be introduced immediately.

Aphoristically condensing his proposals, he writes: 'EDUCA-CIÓN, TIERRA, TRABAJO necesita el proletariado ecuatoriano' (CE 32). [4] In this role of political campaigner it is

---

[4] Carrera Andrade's emphasis.

important to notice that he directs his argument at the
educated people, including and especially the politicians. He
does not incite the Indians to social revolution, or encourage
them to make their voices of protest heard. [5] Directing his
message to the people in power, he appeals for social reform
by an enlightened government. It is the kind of stance
adopted in his verse, as will be seen in the following chapter.
Other complaints that he has made against Ecuador have
occurred with less persistence and emphasis. The country's
imprisoning effect is a recurring criticism, whether it be a
stifling of intellectual freedom (CE 5) or a more general
spiritual experience (RC 164). He regrets the constant conflicts within the country, some caused by geographical divisions and others by class and racial barriers (GMI 12). He
sometimes censures the men in power — for their mediocrity
(CE 5), unwillingness to carry out proposals for improvement
(CE 5), lack of understanding (CE 5 and PEV 92-3), isola-
tionism, egoism, political intolerance and resentment (PEV
92-3). And the public as a whole are found guilty of indifference and pessimism (PEV 93). It amounts to a wide
range of adverse criticism, but it is diffuse, and only briefly
made. One fault alone is constantly stressed: the continuing
lack of progress in improving the Indians' position. In the
balance it becomes evident that he is more concerned with
praising and advertising his country than with writing books
of adverse criticism.

Carrera Andrade's attention to Latin America in the
prose concentrates almost exclusively on the poetry of the
area. There is no significant reference to social or political
affairs, nor are there many of the travel notes which — as
will be seen below — characterise his treatment of Europe
and the U.S.A. There are numerous brief, subjective studies
of individual poets: on Jaime Torres Bodet (in LAT), Nicolás
Guillén, Gabriela Mistral, César Vallejo (in RC), F. Lazo
Martí, José Muñoz Cota, Gabriela Mistral (again), Torres
Bodet (again), Sara de Ibáñez, Pálmenes Yarza, Carlos Augusto León (in VPL), Rubén Darío and José Asunción Silva

---

[5] Such revolution he seems to think doomed to failure and great bloodshed:
see *Hombres en marcha* and the poem 'Levantamiento' (OPC 174-6).

(in IH). And there are a few studies on the verse of individual countries: Mexico, Uruguay, Chile (in RC), and Nicaragua (in IH). But more frequently he groups the republics together in order to consider them as a collective unit. This is where his interest most fully lies: in the concept of a Spanish-American culture. Without doubting the validity of the collective concept (the terms 'Hispanoamérica' and 'hispanoamericano' are abundantly used), he analyses the salient features of Spanish-American poetry in comparison with the verse of Europe or the rest of the world. It is a product of his tendency to think in terms of world blocs.

The main survey-type essays on Spanish-American poetry are the following:

(a) 'El americano nuevo y su actitud poética' (RC);
(b) 'Medio siglo de poesía hispanoamericana' (IH);
(c) 'El poeta y el mundo material' (IH);
(d) 'Poetry and Society in Spanish America' (SAP); [6]
(e) 'Spanish American Originality' (SAP);
(f) 'Trends in Spanish American Poetry' (SAP).

To summarise the points made in these essays, we may begin with Carrera Andrade's view that a fundamental characteristic of Spanish-American poetry which distinguishes it from that of Europe is its reflection of man's telluric quality. Spanish-American man is aware of being surrounded by physical things; he is conscious of the elemental world (RC 102), and he draws from it not merely to express a thought or to study the meaning of life but simply to give the elements importance in their own right, 'sin reflejos lógicos ni metafísicos' (IH 268). Man acts in a way peculiar to that area of the world: he interprets the messages of the things around him and forms a relationship with them, 'un pacto de alianza con el universo' (IH 271). It will be noticed in subsequent chapters that his own poetry fully complies with this picture.

In the beginnings of social poetry, moreover, Spanish America led the world (with the exception of Russia, who anticipated by a few years). Carrera Andrade repeatedly

---

[6] First published in Spanish as 'Poesía y sociedad en Hispanoamérica', in *Revista Iberoamericana* No. 78, 1972, pp. 31-45.

argues that the Spanish-American poet always keeps in close
touch with his society; he has always been 'committed',
therefore, never an outsider in the sense of one who shuns
immediate social realities. He denies that poets such as Darío
ever wrote from an ivory tower (SAP 32). In Spanish America
'the poet is a social man who aspires to be a guide for his
people and who helps the collective effort by publishing his
works' (SAP 36). What the Spanish-American poet writes is,
he concludes, 'the offspring of collective tensions' (SAP 57),
with the result that when he uses a first person singular
pronoun he is in reality voicing the thoughts of a collective
'we'. This explanation of what he considers to be social or
committed poetry helps us to see how these terms may, in a
sense, be applied to his own verse.

Still generalising — though he might equally be referring
to himself in particular — he argues that the Spanish-American poet of the recent generation performs a service of
value to all mankind in that he defends humanistic values
against the threats of technological culture (SAP 57).

Finally, since Spanish America and Europe are at different
stages of evolution their thought and poetry are also at a
different point of development. While the continuity of
European culture over the ages has produced in Europeans
a sense of history, or 'historical emotion', as Carrera Andrade
calls it, Spanish Americans live with passion in the present
and keep an eye on the future (SAP 20).

In his own words, 'to sum up, an attitude exists in Spanish-
American man which is his own; this attitude concerns not
only the physical world but also the great concepts such as
time, love, religion, politics (SAP 20). Inevitably the European reader finds some of the views oversimplified, but few
would deny his basic point that the environment has some
degree of formative influence on the man, and that the
Spanish-American environment is greatly different from that
of Europe. That Carrera Andrade should make so much of
this point is derivative of an underlying attitude to the world:
there is a fundamental contrast between those countries
which are still elemental and those which have become
super-civilised (and decadent). His poetry constantly takes

up this theme. Insofar as he believes Ecuador to form part of the general geographical and cultural bloc, the republics of Latin America do not stand as foreign countries but as parts of his home area. It will be observed later that in his poetry he writes not only as an Ecuadorian but as a Latin-American envoy to an unhealthy technological world. [7]

Several of Carrera Andrade's books in prose are collections of essays on places visited, people met or admired, and books read. The places are greatly varied: the Caribbean, New Orleans, Berlin, Russia, Italy, Paris, Medan, Marseille, Barcelona and the rest of Spain (all in LAT); Japan, the U.S.A., Mexico, Uruguay, Chile (in RC); New York, England, Paris, Japan (in VPL); and Nicaragua (in IH). He has written complete essays on Georges Duhamel, Emilio Castelar y Ripoll (in LAT); Gandhi, Góngora, Milosz (RC); Baudelaire, Valéry (VPL); and Eliot (IH). [8] And among his surveys of trends in poetry abroad are those on Spanish writers of the late 1920s (LAT), on aspects of French poetry (RC), on United States poets of the twentieth century (RC), on the Japanese haiku (VPL) and the introductory sketches on the fifty-five French poets he has translated in *Poesía francesa contemporánea*.

What needs to be stressed is the personal nature of these works. The choice of topic does not conform to a strict plan, nor does the method follow anything but Carrera Andrade's whim. The essays are impressionistic notes. [9] 'Paseos literarios', the sub-title of *Viaje por países y libros*, is the term he applies to them. Noting their descent from the time of Rousseau, he sums up their characteristics as a 'combinación sugerente y amena de la descripción del paisaje con la alusión a lecturas útiles o deleitosas' (VPL IX). They spring from his creative urge no less than the poetry.

Most of Carrera Andrade's prose on Europe is contained in *Latitudes* (1934). Although the views expressed there cannot be assumed to hold true today, over forty years later,

---

[7] See chapter III, vi.
[8] This list excludes Spanish-American authors, who were dealt with above.
[9] i.e. notes based on his subjetive impressions. A more restrictive sense of the term 'impressionism' is used in chapter IV, ii, when the poetry is under discussion.

they do help in the understanding of some of the poetry of that period, particularly the poems of *El tiempo manual*. Among other things these essays indicate that the relatively small number of social poems written by Carrera Andrade hardly reflects the extent of his social awareness and the intensity of his concern. [10] In *Latitudes* he gives frank and powerful expression to his opinions on the Europe of the late twenties and early thirties.

In the essays on individual countries (Germany, Italy, France and Spain) he lends considerable emphasis to the social unrest. In the two essays which embrace Europe as a whole the picture is almost cataclysmic. It is the machine that he finds to be the prime cause of present troubles (LAT 94). The masses, moreover, have spoken out against the decadence of the West; messiahs, such as Mussolini and Hitler, have appeared and the masses, created by the machine, seeking justice, have turned to them (LAT 94-5). Europe is no longer fit to be the model for the rest of the world, as it was when it stood for moderation, love of truth, and justice (LAT 95). To his mind Europe is dying spiritually. It offers an historical and cultural heritage, outward signs of progress, moral emancipation, and man's taming of the physical world, but also widespread hunger, slums and ugly factories (LAT 97).

It helps us to see these views on Europe in perspective if we take into account the essay on Russia. He is disturbed by the poverty of the people, the perpetual tension, the feverish rhythm of life, the strong government based on a military which serves a minority of the population — the Communist Party. While the individual remains poor the State accumulates wealth and power; communism and capitalism, he argues, are similar expressions of different myths. However, Russia seems to him to represent the best example to date of new economic doctrines and new forms of social life. For this reason, despite its faults, he regards the country as a symbol and a hope for future advancement.

---

[10] See chapter IV, III.

The overall impression of Europe, then, in *Latitudes* at least is of countries in the throes of the Depression, in the ferment of social struggle, and in a feverish build-up of military power. With the environment dominated by machines, spiritual values are in jeopardy. These are precisely the themes of his verse in *El Tiempo manual* (1935). Since that poetry of the thirties what seems to have remained deeply engraved in his mind is the picture of a machine-controlled civilization; for this continues to be a major theme, a vital part of Carrera Andrade's overall vision of a sick modern world, and Europe is actually named in some poems as the epitome of it all.

In more recent prose writings he has tended to balance these views with the implicit acceptance that Europe is a great cultural area. Many of his pages are devoted to French authors, his greatest tribute being *Poesía francesa contemporánea,* an anthology 532 pages in length with translations of fifty-five poets and a brief introduction to each. In the final analysis, however, it is not the prime aspect of Europe to arouse his attention. Whenever he takes into account not only the great literary figures but also the new social trends his anxiety and disapproval are aroused.

In two essays on his own poetry Carrera Andrade attributes the growth of certain of his poetic themes to his experience in Japan. [11] The sense of the insecurity of the material world, and the 'cycle of disappointment and return' were induced by the sight of fragile dwellings at the mercy of the elements and the organisation of the countryside by man (SAP 73). There is little evidence in the poetry itself to suggest the impact of Japan. An essay on that country dating from the years of his residence there (1938-1940) only partially supports his point: 'Imagen real del Japón' reveals curiosity in the local scenes and customs, disappointment that this was not the land of fantasy that he had expected, and disapproval of the ultrafascist politics permitted by the people. But two essays of *Viaje por países y libros,* written some time later, are concerned only with attractive scenes and customs, while

---

[11] See 'Mi vida en poemas', which precedes the anthology of the same title, Ediciones Casa del Escritor, Caracas, 1962, pp. 7-44; and 'Poetry of Reality and Utopia', SAP, pp. 68-84.

his autobiography gives an admiring treatment of the country. Japan is not vital for an understanding of his verse; his visit there simply contributed to his inevitable arrival at a new stage in the evolution of his concept of the world.

Far more important is the impact of the U.S.A. In *Latitudes,* where the first relevant pages are found, the U.S.A. receives highly unfavourable comment. It is seen as a land where machines have an overpowering effect and where materialism is prevalent. He indicates the unjust social position and ill-treatment of the negro (LAT 52-7). These remarks, which are based not on first-hand acquaintance with the U.S.A. but on a new book by Georges Duhamel, [12] reflect preconceived notions of the kind widely expressed in essays by Latin Americans and in the socialist press. [13] Subsequent essays reveal on the whole a tolerant attitude towards the U.S.A. The scenery (both urban and rural), which is a favourite topic, impresses him greatly for its vast proportions and sometimes for its beauty; it is a land rich in things for a man to observe and discover. In fact, although the U.S.A. undoubtedly contributes to his concept of the modern technological civilization, which is to form a major theme of his poetry, the prose writings give greater emphasis to Europe as the basis of his impression.

One of the main points to emerge from Carrera Andrade's essays and histories is that although the range of vision is broad, there is little variation in the type of topic handled. The ontological themes which permeate his verse make no appearance here. The prose is virtually all on one or both of two themes: Ecuador and foreign lands. More clearly than the poetry, therefore, it evinces the tendency for Carrera Andrade's interest to polarise, and manifestly supports the argument that at the heart of all his preoccupations is the position of Ecuador in relation to the world, and his own place as an Ecuadorian in relation to other countries. In his poetry the pervasive concern with his country fuses with those other preoccupations and influences them.

---

[12] Georges Duhamel, *Scènes de la Vie future,* Paris 1930.
[13] See in particular José Martí, *Ensayos en los Estados Unidos* (1880-1895); Rubén Darío, *Cantos de vida y esperanza* (1905); and José Enrique Rodó, *Ariel* (1900).

III

ECUADOR

I. INITIAL DISCONTENT

A chronological approach to the study of Carrera Andrade's poetry, frequent among critics, has been stimulated by the poet's autocritical essays. [1] It is intended in the present work to depart form this norm by dealing with salient themes of the poetry as a whole, and by analysing their interrelationship. There undoubtedly is, however, a development in the poet's attitude to Ecuador, attributable in very general terms to events in his life. Certain important differences between the periods before and after his departure for Europe in 1928 make it essential that the initial attitudes be studied before attention is given to the main period.

When Benjamín Carrión set sail for Europe in the mid-1920s Carrera Andrade wrote a mildly envious poem, sardonically grimacing at the thought of being left behind: 'El camarada parte de la tierra natal' (OPC 101).

Significant advantages are foreseen for Carrión:

> ... La luz de otras ciudades
> le va a limpiar, por fin, la niebla de los ojos.
> El odre de su pecho se va a llenar de otro aire.

The physical effects of light, fog and air suggest abstract counterparts, as though Ecuador obscured and restricted man's cultural or perhaps spiritual vision, and as though a

---

[1] See Enrique Ojeda, *Jorge Carrera Andrade: Introducción al estudio de su vida y de su obra*, Eliseo Torres, New York, 1971; José Corrales Egea, 'Carta de París: J.C.A.', *Insula*, No. 96, 1953, p. 5; J. Palley, 'Temática de J.C.A.', *Hispania*, XXXIX, 1956, pp. 80-3; and the following essays by J.C.A.: 'Edades de mi poesía', in *Edades poéticas*, Casa de la Cultura Ecuatoriana, Quito, 1958, pp. IX-XIII; 'Mi vida en poemas', in *Mi vida en poemas*, Ediciones Casa del Escritor, Caracas, 1962, pp. 9-44; 'Decade of my Poetry' and 'Poetry of Reality and Utopia', in *Spanish-American Poetry*, State University of New York Press, Albany, 1973, pp. 58-67 and 68-84.

change of atmosphere, surroundings and attitudes were necessary for the recovery of health. Carrera Andrade then proceeds to spell out his discontent:

> Aquí nos quedaremos viendo la lluvia, con
> los ojos entornados y una paciencia de ángel.
> Nos hablará el vecino de siempre. Faltaremos
> a comer en casa alguna tarde
> por odio a la comida que dan todos los días ...
> De noche, nos pondremos a jugar a los naipes.

The Ecuador in which he must remain is melancholy, unstimulating, somnolent, burdensome, and monotonous, leading him to fill in time (and, possibly, to live in bohemian fashion). The term 'odio' stresses the extent of his feeling. A broadly similar impression is given in 'Canción breve del espantajo' (ROL 137-8; OPC 134), where a scarecrow seems to be an image of Carrera Andrade's feelings about his position in Ecuador: it is rooted to the spot, taunted by vain hopes of travel, mocked for its comic appearance, yet suffers nobly while fulfilling its humble rustic task. Powerful emotions are expressed in 'Mal humor' (OPC 97), an ill-tempered poem in which the city is treated as though it were responsible for the poet's mood. His soul, moreover, is compared to the chimneys: it sings, not of great, noble, eternal, and universal themes, but of small (perhaps petty) lives ('vidas pequeñas') and sad, thick matter; being sooty, it is unhealthy and functions badly, soiled by the very songs that it emits; and significantly — for this emphasises the poet's disgruntled mood — it does not *sing*, but *spits out* its matter. Summarising his view of Ecuador in this phase of his poetry in autobiographical notes, Carrera Andrade has admitted that his country seemed provincial, becalmed, while his feelings developed from tedium at the uniformity of everything to bitterness, thirst for the unknown, and anguish at being impotent to change things ('Edades de mi poesía', PE 17-20; EP IX-XIII). He draws attention to part of the first poem of *El estanque inefable* (1922):

> los pájaros de lluvia, eternos bebedores,
> hacen rueda a la cuba llena de agua verdosa.

Inclinan nuestros párpados los fracasos mayores.
Deja caer, ya inútil, la juventud su rosa.   (PE 18; EP XI) [2]

The choice of illustration is an apt one, for there is a clear
touch of bitterness in the lines, which insist on the repetitive
nature of melancholy rain, the idea of stagnation and im-
permeability to crises in the world at large, and a sense of
uselessness in this place that is the setting of his passing
youth.

Rather than constituting the main theme of the poetry of
those years, however, antipathy for his country's tedious,
provincial life is a central issue in only a handful of poems.
What may be said more accurately is that it determined the
underlying mood of many of them. It was, in fact, dwarfed
by another theme: that of the countryside, through which
Carrera Andrade expressed the various preoccupations that
beset him.

II.   EARLY IMPRESSIONS OF THE COUNTRYSIDE

Ecuador's countryside in itself was far from inspiring
antagonism. On the contrary, the city is seen as the villain,
as in 'Mal humor', where chimneys pour out hatred at nature,
and as in 'Han cerrado la escuela' (OPC 130), which evokes
a sense of the tedium of school and of yearning for freedom
through images juxtaposing urban and rural elements (especially the lines: 'Un vuelo de palomas/agita el cielo urba-
no'). Later, the theme of city versus country was to develop
into a major one under the impact of European and North
American cities, but it is worth noticing that the origins are
to be found in such poems as these where the immediate
source of inspiration was Quito.

From the earliest poems, Carrera Andrade reveals his attraction to the countryside. [3] Visual and aural impressions

[2] Entitled 'Epílogo' in OPC (57).
[3] The French poet Francis Jammes may well have had some impact on him,
encouraging his sensitive reaction to nature. See Enrique Ojeda, J.C.A. Introducción al estudio de su vida y de su obra, Eliseo Torres, New York, 1971, pp. 49,
66, and 67. One should not make too much of this, however, for Carrera
Andrade himself has confessed: 'Desgraciadamente, yo sabía muy poco de
Francis Jammes en esa época (i.e. that of La guirnalda del silencio). Apenas
había leído algunas traducciones en español y su novela Manzana de Anís ('Edades de mi poesía', PE 19; EP XI).

of local rural scenes are often evoked in his verse. In 'Sierra' (OPC 168) the poet's eye roams from one feature to another of a peasant village in the mountains: from corn-cobs hanging from rafters, to guinea-pigs, to a door blown roughly open by the wind, and finally to the approach and onset of rain which catches the Indian labourers out in the cornfields high up the slopes. 'Domingo' (OPC 167) reflects the poet's view of a country church as it chimes on a Sunday across the countryside. A rustic feast-day scene is the subject of 'Fiesta de San Pedro' (OPC 171), while an Indian community's time of refreshment is colourfully described in 'Corte de cebada' (OPC 173). More often than not, however, the rural scene in this early poetry includes no people. Seasons and the weather sometimes provide topics, as in 'Tormenta' (OPC 24), where a storm scene serves as a pretext for inventive metaphors, ingenious likenesses being found in turn for lightning, thunder, rain and rainbow. In 'Primavera & Compañía' (OPC 123) and 'Abril' (OPC 124) impressions of vigour and freshness are evoked as spring comes to the countryside. Creatures and plants are abundantly used as poetic material in this early poetry. Thus, in the two poems last mentioned Carrera Andrade refers to an almond tree, sparrows (twice), reeds, cherry trees, grass (twice), a fir tree, a swallow, and mosquitos. Frequently a creature or plant constitutes indeed the main theme of a poem, like the cricket in 'Vida del grillo' (OPC 125), the rabbit in 'La vida perfecta' (OPC 129) and the various subjects of the *microgramas*.

There is undoubtedly an element of the picturesque in this early verse such as is rarely encountered in poems written on the subject of Ecuador after 1928. Some poems do little more than reflect a scene, and indeed a few focus on a scene peculiar to Ecuador's own countryside (or, at the most, characteristic of the Andean republics). One of the forms taken by the *postmodernista* reaction throughout Spanish-American poetry was a return to simplicity (*simplismo* is a term often used to describe the trend), which besides its relevance to technique also meant an interest in simple themes, especially a 'return to the land', as Carrera Andrade puts it in 'Trends in Spanish-American Poetry'

(SAP 43). One should add to this the influence of the current vogue for *nativismo*, which placed emphasis on the colourful use of Indian themes. These local scenes, in poems such as 'Sierra', 'Domingo', 'Fiesta de San Pedro', and 'Corte de cebada' — all of which are mentioned above — do not constitute a lasting trend in Carrera Andrade's verse, where, on the whole, the regional ingredient is not obtrusive.

Indeed there are allusions to nature of such a kind that certain poems might equally have originated in a country other than Ecuador: in France, for example. The countryside in such poems is anonymous (e.g. 'Los amigos del paseo', 'Abril' 'Vida del grillo', 'Vida perfecta'). What ultimately matters on such occasions is not so much the countryside itself as the poet's reaction to it, or the poet's use of it as a vehicle for expressing his inner thoughts and feelings. Briefly anticipating Chapter VI, [4] we may state now that Ecuador's countryside helped to instil an attitude to nature that has lasted throughout his life. The landscapes, seasons, birds, animals, and insects of Ecuador were not merely a literary theme, but were capable of conveying messages and, therefore, of exerting influences over him. As René Durand observes, in this early period Carrera Andrade had already begun the 'Registro del mundo' which he was to continue abroad: 'L'inventaire du monde de Carrera Andrade a commencé par être jusqu'à son premier départ de l'Equateur celui de la province... et de ses horizons familiers'. [5]

In one sense it may be said that Ecuador's countryside was idealised by Carrera Andrade in his early verse: it was superior to the city, invoked inner responses, communicated messages, and taught him as an example. On the other hand, it would not be accurate to describe the landscapes as a whole as idyllic. Frequently what he presents is a countryside that is not beautiful to contemplate, one that does not inspire a sense of peace and harmony, one in which the reader would not like to find himself. All facets of nature are found in this poetry: the rain as much as the sun, the lofty

---

[4] See Chapter VI, I: 'The Role of Nature' for a full discussion of these topics.
[5] René L.-F. Durand, *J.C.A. Présentation* ......, Éditions Seghers, Paris, 1966, p. 34.

wilderness as much as the green valley. Ecuador may later
seem to him a land of light [6] but at this stage its countryside
is more often seen in muted tones or under cloud.
It was clearly not a question of resorting to themes of
the countryside in order to avoid painful topics. Nature
could certainly offer solace (as Chapter VI attemps to argue)
but it could also act as a reminder of human tragedy. A notable case is that of 'Episodio' (ROL 37; OPC 40), [7] where
a man's dead body lying in the midst of a countryside
teeming with continuing life illustrates the poet's anguish
over the paradox of life and death, of transitory man and
immutable nature. The theme of nature is, even in the early
poetry, a watershed in which a variety of themes have their
source. Looking back, more than forty years later, at that
period when he and his young contemporaries were emerging
as the new hopes in Ecuadorian poetry, he has given a
misleading emphasis to the national purpose which inspired
them: 'Nuestra preocupación fundamental era interpretar la
psicología del hombre ecuatoriano, pintar la tierra ecuatoriana, hacer la meta de nuestra obra la expresión del suelo
natal'. [8] Although, when one takes account of his activities
with the newly-formed Socialist Party, and his attention to
burning issues in his journalism, one is in no doubt that
this was indeed a passionate concern, the fact is that Carrera Andrade was not, *as a poet*, primarily concerned with
immediate national issues. He was chiefly concerned with the
universal and the eternal insofar as they were manifested
in the particular. And the particular was, inevitably, the
countryside (and society) of Ecuador.

III.   METAPHORS

The metaphor is the key to Carrera Andrade's technique
for expressing his attitude to nature. In singling out the use
of metaphor as an outstanding feature of his poetry, particularly of his early poetry, critics have sometimes stressed
the dexterity with which he creates these figures, at the

[6] See Section IX of the present chapter.
[7] The poem is entitled 'Tribulación de agosto' in OPC.
[8] Enrique Ojeda, 'Entrevista a J.C.A.', *Norte*, Año IX, 3 + 4, 1968, p. 91.

expense of their underlying significance. He has been called 'magician of metaphors'[9] and 'gran malabarista de la metáfora',[10] as though the virtuosity of the achievement were what counted rather than the effectiveness of the figures as vehicles for poetic expression. The vogue for striking metaphors, even for those meritorious in their own right, those created as an end in themselves ('autonomous' they are sometimes called) was especially associated with the avant-garde's impact on Spanish-American literature (beginning in earnest in the twenties), so that Carrera Andrade's skill was recognised as a major contribution to the renovation of Ecuadorian poetry.[11] But his use of metaphor is due only in part to a literary fashion; it is essentially the natural vehicle for him to use in the expression of certain innate attitudes to reality. Only the degree of excess that one finds occasionally in the earlier poetry is attributable to a vogue.

In a later chapter Carrera Andrade's metaphorical language will be examined as an element in impressionist poems written after his departure from Ecuador.[12] For the present it is intended to focus comments on his *Microgramas,* since, besides belonging to the period before 1928, they represent in crude form the basic structure of his metaphorical language of that period. The *microgramas* are essentially metaphors stripped of the framework of a poem.

It is possible to detect two main types of *micrograma,* corresponding to different stages of elaboration:

1. A creature (A) suggests something subjective (B) to the poet; the *micrograma* names A and links it with B, allowing the reader to dwell on the repercussions of the subjective comparison:

[9] H.R. Hays, 'J.C.A., Magician of Metaphors', *Books Abroad* XVII, 1943, pp. 101-5.
[10] Jorge Enrique Adoum, 'Las clases sociales en las letras contemporáneas de Ecuador', in *Panorama de la actual literatura latinoamericana,* Editorial Fundamentos, Madrid, 1971, p. 222.
[11] See, for example, the conclusion to the thesis by Fanny Casares Carrera, *J.C.A. y la nueva orientación poética en las letras ecuatorianas,* Colegio de los SS. Corazones de Rumipamba, Quito, 1962, p. 45.
[12] See Chapter IV, ii.

LO QUE ES EL CARACOL

Caracol:
mínima cinta métrica
con que mide el campo Dios (OPC 81).

In a variation of this type, the poet imagines A in action performing like B, still clarifying the link between the two by naming A (and using a colon):

MECANOGRAFÍA

Sapo trasnochador: tu diminuta
máquina de escribir
teclea en la hoja en blanco de la luna.   (OPC 82)

Sometimes A is named only in the title, as in 'Golondrina' (OPC 84).

2. In the second, more developed, stage, there is no preliminary naming of A outside the framework of the image. A is imagined in action performing like B, the two being fused in a single image and a single syntactic structure.

CHOPO

Moja el chopo su pincel
en la dulzura del cielo
y hace un paisaje de miel.   (OPC 85)

A first reaction to these metaphors may be surprise, or amusement, since the attributes that Carrera Andrade finds for the creatures are not those with which one normally associates them. To this extent reality seems transformed by the intellectual dexterity of the poet. On the other hand, it is not all playfulness. In each *micrograma* a minute form of life or a diminutive object is linked with thoughts of great proportions. A tree, part of a landscape, leads to a view of a complete landscape, while even more dramatically a snail, one of the smallest creatures, leads to associations with the whole countryside. Carrera Andrade takes observed reality as his starting-point, but suggests that each observed creature and object has something to say about the world in general.

The part is an image of the whole; every part is a manifestation of the universe. (In chapter VI, iii, the philosophical aspects of this concept are examined.) Once this is accepted as an underlying attitude the connections between object and image become less strained. Thus, a snail in all its humility may still seem to have a function in God's creation: as it performs its daily activity in travelling slowly across a minute area of land the vast proportions of the world's territory become apparent. Then a physical resemblance might even be found — retrospectively — between a measure and the coil of a snail's shell. If one starts from the premise that all phenomena of nature have a message for the poet (and man) to interpret, [13] then the toneless, repetitive croaking of a toad at night may be seen as a form of communication, and its association with a journalist working through the night on a typewriter gains credibility. In his introduction to *Microgramas* Carrera Andrade claims that these short poem-metaphors disclose the underlying reality of objects:

El micrograma no es sino el epigrama español, despejado de su matiz subjetivo. O más bien dicho, el epigrama esencialmente gráfico, pictórico, que por su hallazgo de la realidad profunda del objeto —de su actitud secreta— llega a constituir una estilización emocional; el epigrama reducido en volumen, enriquecido de compleja modernidad, ensanchado a todas las cosas que integran el coro vital de la tierra... Era menester añadir al humorismo el sentido trascendental, la vibración de la vida, la grandiosidad del mensaje de las cosas pequeñas. [14]

Without denying that transcendental meanings emerge, we may find it difficult to accept that the qualities disclosed are essentially the secret reality of the objects. They are surely the product of Carrera Andrade's subjective interpretation, the outcome of a thoroughly personal attitude to nature. A point that is worth stressing, however, is the 'graphic', 'pictorial' basis of these metaphors. In the *microgramas*, as in most of Carrera Andrade's metaphors, observed

---

[13] For further discussion see in particular Chapter VI, i.
[14] *Microgramas*, Colección del Pacífico, Ediciones "Asia América", Tokyo, 1940, pp. 1-2.

reality (a creature, a plant, an object, a scene) is the starting-point from which he develops a transcendental meaning. Ecuador's countryside thus provided inspiration, substance and pretext for his verse. If we find the earlier poetry less satisfying than that of *Biografía para uso de los pájaros* onwards it is perhaps because the basis is too firmly built on the world of nature, and the transcendental meaning emerges only from the subjection of that prime material to the dexterity of the intellect. Although the graphic quality remains in the later poetry, we find the metaphors more spontaneously serving the transcendental meaning.

Admitting the great impact of Góngora during his youth, Carrera Andrade has made a statement which reveals his own awareness of this shift of emphasis. The Spanish poet impressed him most for the ability to select the exact word, to express a concept in a compact, concentrated image (characteristics of the *micrograma*). He sympathised with Góngora's attention to the world of objects, his concept of the world as capable of efficient poetic expression through a system of images. But later he found, despite continuing admiration for Góngora, that this attitude placed excessive importance on images ('el mundo poético de la imagen no es el todo') and that he needed a human element, a preoccupation with mankind lacking in Góngora ('la palpitación humana', 'el hombre'). [15] In more general terms, replying (elsewhere) to a question concerning the relative importance of meaning and image in a poem, he has categorically affirmed the superiority of meaning (while not dismissing the validity of poems based purely on autonomous images):

> Estas dos categorías de poesía son altamente válidas. Sin embargo, mi preferencia es por la creación de un poema significativo, de un poema que imponga un significado y no sea sólo un juego estético producido por la gracia o luminosidad de una imagen. [16]

It is clear that he has been evolving towards a more thoroughly personal poetic expression.

---

[15] See Enrique Ojeda, 'Entrevista a J.C.A.', *Norte*, Año IX, 3 + 4, 1968, p. 93. See also his sonnet, 'Invocación a Góngora', in *Árbol de fuego*, 51, Caracas, 1972, p. 13.

[16] William J. Straub, 'Conversación con J.C.A.', *Revista Iberoamericana* 79, 1972, p. 311.

He was not alone in the 1920s, of course, in his enthusiasm for Góngora. Rubén Darío had for many years helped to renew interest in that poet. In Spain, on the 300th centenary of Góngora's death in 1927, a group of young poets (Gerardo Diego, Salinas, Alberti, García Lorca, Dámaso Alonso, Guillén among them) marked their respect by studying his work afresh and by seeking to diffuse knowledge of it throughout the country. [17] It is also valid to indicate the growing influence of avant-garde schools of poetry upon the climate in which Carrera Andrade wrote. But it is not possible to reduce the debt to any specific school, and the impact should not be overstated: 'Mis relaciones con el vanguardismo se redujeron a un ensayo que escribí sobre esta tendencia y no lo publiqué'; 'fue muy limitada la influencia del ultraísmo en mi país'; 'no creo tener afinidad con ningún poeta ultraísta'. [18] All he admits is to have points in common with the *creacionistas* [19] and to admire Huidobro. [20]

While writing of general influences on his metaphorical language one should pay tribute — as he does — to the role of the French Symbolists, and in particular Albert Samain, Tristan Corbière, Charles Baudelaire, and Paul Verlaine. [21] One might add that the *modernistas* also played their part in encouraging a taste for the image.

But this has now become a veritable ocean of influences, and there is little value in adding to it or exploring its depths. [22] Góngora, the Symbolist, *modernista* and avant-garde trends all served to produce a climate in which Carre-

---

[17] See Elsa Dehennin, *La Résurgence de Góngora et la génération poétique de 1927*, Didier, Paris, 1962, p. 244. To Góngora's impact on Carrera Andrade's use of the compact, concentrated image one might add the influence of Quevedo on the epigrammatic character of his *microgramas* (and on extended poems of a similar kind). In his introduction to *Microgramas* he modestly indicates this debt (ed. cit., p. 1). See also Giuseppe Bellini, *Quevedo nella poesia ispanoamericana del 900*, Viscontea, Milan, 1967.
[18] Straub, 'Conversación'......, loc. cit., p. 309.
[19] Ibid., p. 310.
[20] Ojeda, 'Entrevista' ......, loc. cit., p. 94.
[21] Ojeda, 'Entrevista' ......, loc. cit., p. 92.
[22] In an article on the widespread repercussions of Ramón Gómez de la Serna in Spanish-American poetry Richard L. Jackson finds that Carrera Andrade's metaphors single him out as one of the major poets to write in the manner of the *greguerías* ('Apuntes sobre la lengua greguerística en la poesía contemporánea hispanoamericana', *Hispanófila*, XXVIII, 1966, p. 57). Although a simple comparison is valid, it is doubtful whether any direct influence was involved. Carrera Andrade completed the *microgramas* and produced many poems with similar metaphors before visiting Spain; Gómez de la Serna's diffusion in Ecuador does not appear to have been extensive.

ra Andrade made his own experiments and followed his own inclinations. It would be erroneous to deduce that any literary influence actually determined his way of looking at reality; Góngora and others merely helped him to find a suitable form of poetic expression for that innate attitude. Carrera Andrade was profoundly attracted to nature. Moreover, he regarded the physical world as containing messages not only for the poet but for every man; [23] it was his natural tendency to study it, to make analogies, and to interpret. Weaving metaphors with the creatures, plants and objects around him was a way of discovering new (disguised, veiled) truths about them. It was also a product of his view that life becomes more intense, more substantial, and more meaningful when reality is closely observed and sharply experienced. [24] Finally, it was a manifestation of his eagerness to learn by exploration, another outcome of which was his travel in foreign countries and his writing of impressionistic poems. [25]

IV. SOCIAL CRITICISM

'Cuaderno de poemas indios' (OPC 165-76), written between 1927 and 1928 but published after Carrera Andrade's departure from Ecuador, is usually considered by critics to be his principal collection of Indianist poems. The poet himself has encouraged the view that all eight poems imply a degree of protest. Thus, in 'Corte de cebada' (OPC 173) he believes there is reference to the idea of exploitation of the Indian in the lines 'La loma estaba sentada en el campo/ con su poncho a cuadros'. His explanation of these lines is as follows:

> La loma es como un ser humano, y da una idea de una serie de cosas laterales. Por ejemplo, 'con su poncho a cuadros', es decir, con el recorte marcado por los sembrados que son más o menos geométricos en el campo sudamericano. Esto da idea del trabajo humano, y quien usa el poncho es el indio, lo cual nos lleva por una especie

---

de sistema analítico, automático a la idea de la explotación indígena y todo lo demás. [26]

Such an automatic analytical deduction can surely not be expected of all readers. Most would find in these two lines merely a visual impression and a use of animism. Granted the climate of Ecuador in the 1920s, it may well be that at that time and in that country any mention of the Indian in the fields inspired associated notions of social injustice and economic exploitation. But there is no guidance from the poet, no indication of attitude, with the result that this operates not as protest verse but more or less as *nativismo*.

It is essential to state from the outset, therefore, that not all poems by Carrera Andrade which deal with the Indian protest at his predicament in Ecuador's society. Most either give a picturesque treatment or depict him as a part of a rural Ecuador still close to nature. Some poems are concerned only indirectly with the Indian's plight, while a few — very few — make a strong, direct protest. The reasons for this circumstance will be discussed shortly; first the poems themselves will be studied.

Of the eight poems collected in the 'Cuaderno de poemas indios' four are best considered as picturesque impressions, mostly of Indian scenes, fundamentally uncritical of the scene they depict. These are: 'Domingo', 'Sierra', 'Fiesta de San Pedro' and the above-mentioned 'Corte de cebada'. There are indeed glimpses in the 'Cuaderno' of what seems to the outsider today to be a patronising attitude to the Indian, unconsciously acquired by Carrera Andrade from the customary speech-habits, and paying lip-service to the ingrained social attitudes of the white ruling class: for example, the use of the collective noun 'la indiada' or the use of a definite article followed by a proper name as in 'el Francisco', 'el Martín', 'el Juan'.

Protest is indisputably made, however, in the remaining four poems. Of these, three show disapproval of the Indian's conditions and suggest that he has cause for rebellion. 'In-

[26] Straub, 'Conversación'......, loc. cit., p. 313. In fairness to the poet it must be admitted that his explanation is chiefly concerned with the question of animism, not of social protest.

diada' (OPC 169) gives a sombre picture of Indians setting off to work in damp, chilly weather. The word 'protesta' in the following lines clearly indicates their attitude:

> La indiada lleva la mañana
> en la protesta de sus palos.

But no obvious social or political motive is introduced. 'Caracol' (OPC 170), while making no explicit link between the snail and the Indian, reveals compassion for a creature helpless and innocent, doomed to serve and to be sucked and crunched. In 'Tierras, bosques' (OPC 172) Carrera Andrade's position is detached, but he creates a scene in which farming people watch their land encroached upon by telegraph poles, symbols of modern civilization, and burned. Protest is made through the quoting of Indian voices:

> Matías dijo: Nos quitan nuestra tierra
> . . . .
> ¡Pisarán nuestro campo los postes sargentos!
> No más sor encina, no más fray manzano.

and through reference to a shaken fist. Anguish is in the hearts of the people.

But the poem most categorically sympathising with the Indians' plight and with the way they were treated in Ecuador is 'Levantamiento' (OPC 174-6). Carrera Andrade's own position is barely concealed behind a 'narrator' who remembers an uprising of 800 people to protest against the fencing-off of their territory by latifundistas. The 800, 'con un poncho de luz sobre los hombros' seem to be enlightened, acting as though under the protection of light (truth, justice). They have 'en la frente el mandado de la tierra', as though they were commanded by the earth, their act being as natural as other processes of Nature. The poem is characterised by a sense of profound grief at the tragic outcome: the death of most of the people from the rifles of soldiers. In order to de-humanise the soldiers, Carrera Andrade calls them 'ejercicios de puntería' and 'fusiles'. Clearly the poem arouses a sense of sympathy for the cause of the 'narrator' and his people. It is, significantly, one of the causes most frequently illustrated in Spanish American literature of social protest: the Indians' right to their land, the encroachment of large land-owners, the law's support for the latifundista, the instinctive rebellion of the Indian people, and their massacre by troops. Jorge Icaza's *Huasipungo* (1934) is a close parallel within Ecuador.

When Carrera Andrade's prose was examined in Chapter II the point was made that the Indian has been a constant concern throughout his life. In his poetry, campaigning on behalf of Ecuador's Indian goes little further than these few poems discussed, and indeed 'Levantamiento' is the only Indianist poem of his that is completely in the line of social protest poetry. One or two complete poems since 1928 have been dedicated to the Indian, however. 'Ocaso de Atahualpa' (OPC 459-60, 1963) pays moving tribute to the Inca civilization, which he pictures as peacefully building a simple world and devoting attention to everyday living off the land, while it is remorselessly crushed by the invading military machine of the Spaniards. Dwelling on impressions of spilt blood, Carrera Andrade arouses strong compassion for the Indians. Relevance to the contemporary scene may well be inferred by the reader. The pre-Inca tribes are invoked in 'Los antepasados' (OPC 462-3), a poem in which Carrera Andrade venerates the Indians for their message of peace and simplicity, for their life close to nature. 'Crónica de las Indias' (OPC 465-80), while strictly on a far broader plane than comment on the Indians' condition, nevertheless involves the theme of suffering millions who have lost their liberty and undergone injustice at the hands of Pizarro and the other *conquistadores*. A few other poems, moreover, contain passages concerning Ecuador's Indians of the twentieth century. In 'Alabanza del Ecuador', for example, a slightly oblique lament is made on behalf of their continued suffering:

> ... y la historia de un pueblo
> que gime hasta en la danza
> disparando su anhelo hacia las nubes
> en cohetes de fiesta,
> fuego que se deshace en lágrimas azules. (OPC 415)

And 'Hombre planetario' includes two passages clearly indicating how the Indian has suffered death at the hands of a ruthless enemy. The first alludes to the time of the Conquest:

> Contra las pobres flechas de los indios
> luchó con su arcabuz y su armadura
> y lanzó su caballo de batalla
> contra los pies desnudos.   (OPC 445)

The use of the word 'pobres', which in this context is not merely descriptive but also emotive, tends to stress Carrera Andrade's own sympathy. In the second instance within this poem a forthright attack is made against the ill-treatment, in the modern age, of peace-loving Indians whose only crime has been to seek freedom ('Hombre planetario' XVIII, OPC 449). Juan Cordero, the symbolic protagonist, lies dead, his grain-store burned down and his lands expropriated.

It is evident, then, that Carrera Andrade's poetry does at times reveal his indignation at the Indian's plight and evoke feelings of pity and horror in the reader. In some of his essays, as was observed in the preceding chapter, he has outlined certain remedies for this social problem. In verse he tends to communicate his message by implication rather than by explicit advice. It may be inferred from those poems under consideration above that the solution lies in harmonious living, an end to bloodshed, and fair and merciful treatment of the Indian by the authorities. In other words, the message — insofar as it may be said that these poems have a didactic sense — is directed at the ruling class, not the aggrieved. Carrera Andrade has written, however, a few poems in which he directly addresses the working class, and one of them, dating from 1924, is an appeal to the Indian labourers of Ecuador. Since it is vital for an understanding of Carrera Andrade's position, and since it is little known, I reproduce it in full here:

INVITACIÓN A LA PAZ

> Sobre la tierra hostil tiendo mi escala
> mientras gruñe la carne en su honda cueva
> y revelo una dulce verdad nueva
> a mis hermanos; la lección del ala.

Deben alzarse en huelga alas y armiños
contra el imperialismo de los muros.
Compañeros: labrad los campos duros
rociados por las risas de los niños.

Tapen gajos de frutas las trincheras
y la quijada de asno se abra en flores.
Cambien en humo todos los rencores
las fábricas, humanas gusaneras.

Hombres y niños, manos a la obra,
siglo es de construcciones y de inventos.
Demos nuestro puñado de lamentos
por el vino cordial de la maniobra.

Toque final de la hora de la espada,
primer minuto de la nueva hora.
Cien mil puños construyen con la azada
la montaña de trigo de la aurora.   (OPC 63)

The poet quickly establishes his solidarity with the labourers
suffering in a hostile working environment. But this is to be
no call for violent action: he writes of the '*dulce* verdad' and
of the 'lección del *ala*'. The walls of imperialism are to be
passed, by burrowing beneath them or by flying over them,
not brought down. Carrera Andrade urges the people to
work, to replace signs of war and discord with those of peace,
to transfer anger into a different kind of energy: constructive
work, the clenched fist laying aside weapons ('espada') for
tools ('azada'). All this is possible with a background of
gaiety, and the outcome will be a plentiful future for all. As
the title implies, peace is the object of Carrera Andrade's
appeal, not violent social revolution. He is, therefore, what
today would be called a 'moderate', or 'dove', in the jargon
of political journalists. His correspondence and prose works
have confirmed that this stand taken by Carrera Andrade in
the early years of his youthful socialism — desire for reform,
but by peaceful means within the existing structure of society
— has remained almost unchanged to this day.

In the short poem 'La extrema izquierda' (OPC 194) Carrera Andrade imaginatively and humorously attributes to a
cicada the qualities of a social rebel, humble, nonconformist
conspiring against a dictatorship ('la humana dictadura') and

spreading propaganda ('es˜ Secretaria de Propaganda'). The poem ends with the lines:

> Tienes razón, cigarra obrera,
> de minar el Estado con tu canto profundo.
> Ambos formamos, compañera,
> la extrema izquierda de este mundo.

Despite implicit approval of activities to undermine the State, and the indication that the poet belongs to the extreme left, there is a profound ambiguity in the poem. None of the cicada's attributes qualify it for praise as a radical or fear as an extremist: it merely moves from place to place singing. The poet's intentions are therefore, ultimately, ironical, for he is as docile as the cicada, and there is no question of his actively undermining the State, except through quietly writing the messages of his verse.

A few poems — a handful only — convey Carrera Andrade's hatred for the role played by soldiers on Latin American soil (a country's name is never mentioned in this context). The whole of 'Levantamiento', where the poet's sympathy is clearly with the Indians and their uprising, is devoted to the tragic results of a military intervention leading to a massacre. In part I of the poem the advent of soldiers breaks up the natural order and leaves a trail of blood:

> Con su carrera de sangre los soldados
> despertaron las verdes quietudes del campo.   (OPC 174)

The soldiers have an aura of stealth, fearsomeness, and menace, visualised in the way they move through the darkness, and in the sharpness of their teeth:

> Avanzaban comidos de sombra,
> y un estribillo de dientes afilados
> mordía sus hebillas luminosas.   (ibid.)

Attention is drawn to their rifles. In part II the soldiers lose their human identity and become characterised by the rifles they carry; they are unthinking machines, drilled to kill:

> Soldados, Soldados.
> Ejercicios de puntería.   (OPC 175)

and:

> Compañeros:
> los fusiles nos miran con sus ojos de muerto.   (ibid.)

This attitude, which we have illustrated with lines written during the poet's days of active socialism in Quito before 1928, is closely echoed thirty years later in cantos XVII and XVIII of 'Hombre planetario' (OPC 448-9). Despite the universal level of topics in this poem, the context of these two cantos makes it clear that Carrera Andrade is thinking of Ecuador: the dark-skinned peasant and his family who sought freedom and met death, had their granaries burned and their land stolen. Horror at the growth of soldiers' power is expressed in XVII through the idea that things made by man ('los soldados/de plomo de los cuentos infantiles') have become larger than life. No constructive role is found for the military forces; they are shown to be aggressive, destructive, bringing death even to the worker of the fields, the innocent, simple man close to the land and to natural life. They are, in fact, contrary to the natural order of things.

'Crónica de las Indias' (OPC 465-80) is an extended poem dedicated to the condemnation of tyranny. In the first two sections Carrera Andrade describes the triumphant arrival of the bearer of justice, Pedro de La Gasca, appointed by the Spanish Crown to remove from power and execute Gonzalo Pizarro, who had made himself the first dictator of the New World by assuming control over the land from Quito to the Northern borders of Chile. It is the third section, however, that best reflects the poet's attitude: he opens with a direct address to Pizarro, applying to him the terms 'Monarca de mentira' (OPC 477), 'Vano caudillo' (OPC 477), 'fingido emperador' (OPC 478), and 'Traidor' (OPC 479). Pizarro had betrayed people, and founded an empire on brute force ('ríos de sangre', OPC 478). He had sought things of false value, and his imminent death made a mockery of his acquisition of wealth and power. All these points, though not lacking a certain vindictiveness, serve clearly to establish a warning note that enables the poem's message to transcend the specific

context and to comment on equivalent actions in any age. [27]
In his essay 'Decade of my poetry' Carrera Andrade has
admitted that this poem was partly inspired by recent politics
in Latin America: 'The centuries had not passed. Everything
was at the mercy of tyrants as in other days. . . . It seemed to
me that my country still lived in the days of Gonzalo Pizarro,
defender of the encomenderos. Only the name of the dictator
had changed and the encomenderos were not called by that
title but rather "the oligarchy" ' (SAP 61-2).

It has been shown, then, that Ecuador does indeed receive
some socio-political criticism in Carrera Andrade's poetry. A
few poems denounce the treatment of the Indian population,
others express disapproval of the role played by soldiers,
while one or two reveal a dislike of dictatorships. In total,
however, such verse amounts to comparatively little, even
— as will be seen later — when universal social protest is
involved. Critics have therefore been puzzled, and reticent
about the explanation for this phenomenon. [28]

Carrera Andrade's position is best understood when compared with that of other Ecuadorian poets writing since 1920.
Benjamín Carrión, one of Ecuador's most reputable writers,
critics and scholars of the twentieth century, provides the
clearest picture, writing close to the events concerned, in his
Índice de la poesía ecuatoriana contemporánea [29] which
contains a prologue plus an anthology of poetry published
in the years 1910-1935. According to his assessment, after
the great economic impact of the 1914-18 war, with the
ensuing poverty in Ecuador, and following hard on the heels
of social revolutions in Mexico and Russia, literature began
to develop an increasing social awareness. This trend, which
came first in the novel, soon impregnated lyric poetry. Of
the vital group of poets arising after *modernismo* (especially
Gonzalo Escudero, Miguel Ángel León, Augusto Arias, and

---

[27] 'Crónica de las Indias' is analysed at greater length in Section v of this
chapter.
[28] See for example Ojeda, *J.C.A.: Introducción* ......, p. 87 ; and Hernán Rodríguez Castelo, *Gangotena, Escudero y Carrera Andrade. Tres cumbres de nuestro
postmodernismo*, Clásicos Ariel, Guayaquil/Quito, 1972 (p. 44 of ms.).
[29] Benjamín Carrión, *Índice de la poesía ecuatoriana contemporánea*, Ediciones
Ercilla, Santiago de Chile, 1937.

Carrera Andrade) only Carrera Andrade and Aurora Estrada y Ayala [30] had produced what Carrión calls 'poesía de trasunto social y revolucionario'. [31] But before long there was a more general tendency for issues of destruction and construction, and of collective feeling, to subordinate the more purely subjective themes. [32] In the 1930s the new poets, belonging to the generation after Carrera Andrade, 'tienen todos, en mayor o menor intensidad radical, un solo denominador: la aspiración a ser poetas revolucionarios'. [33] In their contemplation of the Indian's plight, they wrote of his hunger, poor clothing, stolen land, and ill-treatment at the hands of priests, police and local political despots. Making an important critical judgment, Carrión finds the content of these poems accurate enough in their essential representation of the facts, but 'casi siempre exagerado por el propagandismo tendencioso'. [34] What he notes in the previous generation, and particularly in Carrera Andrade himself, is a tendency at this time toward 'contra-rectificaciones'. Without the advantage of a perspective given by time, which we have today, but clearly perceiving that Carrera Andrade's non-political, non-revolutionary poetry was discordant with the key note of the contemporary moment, Carrión proclaimed: 'Carrera Andrade acaba de lanzar, como justificación de su libro *Rol de la manzana*, el grito anunciador: "¡Salvemos a la poesía!" ' [35]

In a far more recent book, *Panorama de la literatura ecuatoriana*, [36] Augusto Arias has been able to place the social, revolutionary poetry in perspective from the year 1971, and in doing so he indicates that its boom period was, in fact, of only limited extent: 'El poema de intención social cumplió con su destino; pero también varios de los críticos afiliados a las propias tendencias no dejaron de reparar en ciertos extremos del poema cartelista que estaba en trance de convertirse en sólo un manifiesto para dejar de ser poesía. El verso nuevo siguió en el Ecuador, por lo regular, las rutas

---

[30] Aurora Estrada y Ayala, born in 1901, had published *Como el incienso*, Guayaquil, 1925.
[31] Op. cit., p. XX.
[32] Ibid., p. XIX.
[33] Ibid., p. XX.
[34] Ibid., p. XXI.
[35] Ibid., p. XXV.
[36] Augusto Arias, *Panorama de la literatura ecuatoriana*, Casa de la Cultura Ecuatoriana, Quito, 1971.

universales, pero manteniendo las peculiaridades del ambiente'. [37] Carrera Andrade therefore seems to have anticipated the trends, first towards social protest poetry and later away from it and back to universal themes.

The truth is, however, that he was never a full exponent of the tendency to social poetry, never a writer of revolutionary poetry. It is clear that though disturbed by the plight of Ecuador's Indians — deeply disturbed, indeed, as his correspondence reveals — he found his poetic inspiration working along general rather than specific lines. He has given the explanation himself. Part of it may be found in a poem written in 1924, when he was editor of the socialist magazine *La Antorcha* and not long after his imprisonment for subversive activities with the leftish paper *Humanidad*: 'Edad de sombra' (OPC 61). This poem makes a categorical statement on his view of poetry's role in a world of turmoil and strife:

EDAD DE SOMBRA

Los guardianes del Orden invocan: ¡Dictadura!
El hombre de la fábrica vocifera: ¡Anarquía!
No hay lugar para el Arte sobre la tierra dura.
La luz no se vislumbra en esta Edad Sombría.

Tú, solo Tú, Belleza, puedes salvar el mundo.
Imprimes sobre el orbe la huella de tu planta
y la vida descubre su sentido profundo.
A la luz de tus ojos el universo canta.

Mujer, encarnación de la Belleza eterna,
eleva entre los hombres la hostia de tu frente,
haz a todas las cosas brillar con tu luz tierna
mientras la vida entorne los ojos dulcemente.

Eres todo un concierto de campanas pascuales,
vaso de amor, estrella de la remota altura.
A tus plantas encienden mis manos fraternales
un fuego precursor de la aurora futura.

Both dictatorship and anarchy are forms of violence and evil from which the world needs salvation, and only Beauty can

---

[37] Op. cit., p. 352.

provide that salvation. Though in the second half of the poem
Carrera Andrade sees Woman as the incarnation of Beauty,
his first thoughts (stanza 1) are of Art as its expression and
manifestation. The poet, therefore, can help to save the world
by producing beauty in his art. His poems, consequently,
have as their primary aim that of being beautiful. They seek
to be, not propaganda, but art.

Carrera Andrade is well aware that other poets have found
it possible to place their verse at the service of politics.
Conscious of the fact that a poet such as Neruda (in collections since *España en el corazón*) was greatly concerned with
themes related to social and political issues, he has defended
his own position and thus indicated one of the major differences between himself and the Chilean. He argues that
there exists a 'tono social' in his own poetry, but warns: 'Tono
social que no debe confundirse con la afiliación política;
porque yo no creo que el poeta deba limitarse a levantar
una sola bandera cuando él tiene en sus manos todos los
pabellones del mundo'. [38] The poet has, therefore, a responsibility to humanity in general, not merely to people of one
particular creed or party. Even more categorically, and
speaking now with Neruda in mind, he denies the political
function of poetry, if it is to be at its best, and stresses that
it cannot be subjugated to any political cause. [39]

In his article 'Poesía y sociedad en Hispanoamérica',
arguing that Spanish American poetry has always been involved in contemporary affairs, Carrera Andrade reveals his
loose, free interpretation of what it means to be a committed
poet. Whether a poet participates in the vicissitudes of his
society or takes up a position against it, he is involved,
compromised, committed. [40] In a key example, he argues that
the *modernistas* did not shun social reality in an ivory tower
but sought to perform a social function by the aesthetic
educating of the people. [41] When asked by Rubén Bareiro
Saguier, in an interview published in the Paraguayan maga-

---

[38] Ojeda, 'Entrevista ......', p. 93.
[39] Ibid., p. 95.
[40] Jorge Carrera Andrade, 'Poesía y sociedad en Hispanoamérica', *Revista Iberoamericana* 78, 1972, pp. 31 and 39.
[41] Ibid., pp. 39-40.

zine *Alcor,* whether he believed in a function for poetry
in society — and in particular in Latin American society —
he replied in a manner completely consistent with this: 'Ab-
solutamente creo en esa función social. El poeta debe ser
solidario de los destinos colectivos. Debe intentar ser el portavoz de su pueblo. En nuestras sociedades incipientes, el
poeta debe servir a la construcción de la cultura, debe aportar
sus conocimientos para ayudar a redimir a su pueblo de la
ignorancia. Desde Dante hasta Valéry la poesía ha servido a
la ascensión humana, a la formación de la conciencia'. [42] In
his own article, mentioned above, Carrera Andrade points
out that there are four types of social poetry: the historical,
the national, the political, and the humanitarian. [43] Clearly,
then, if his poetry is humanitarian it is also committed. To
his mind the poet of Spanish America aims at guiding his
people, at educating them, through books. [44] What is often
understood to be committed poetry, or 'poesía comprometida'
he calls propaganda poetry, or 'poesía de cartel'.

These views, then, complement the attitude of the poem
'Edad de Sombra', written over forty years earlier. The reason
for there being only a restricted number of poems with comment on Ecuador's social conditions and political structure
has remained consistent: it has not been his function as a poet
to make such comment. Indeed these topics have sometimes
been handled fairly crudely, with a simplification of the issues
and a strong emotional appeal (e.g. 'Levantamiento' and
sections XVII and XVIII of 'Hombre planetario'). Only when
the problems are more obliquely treated does one find the
poetry more successful in aesthetic terms (e.g. 'Crónica de las
Indias').

V.   NATIONAL THEMES

Some of Carrera Andrade's early poetry, as we have seen,
reveals a degree of discontent with Ecuador. A few poems
belonging to the period before 1928 are blatantly critical of
social conditions in his country. Without producing a com-

---

[42] *Alcor* No. 36, May/June 1965, p. 4.
[43] '*Poesía y sociedad* ......', p. 40.
[44] Ibid., p. 43.

plete alteration of his attitudes, the first departure for Europe undoubtedly constituted a turning point in his poetic treatment of Ecuador. The discontent has made no reappearance, and social criticism has been confined to occasional innuendos. As soon as he set sail his innate affection and admiration for his homeland clearly suppressed the earlier reservations. 'Exilio fecundo para el corazón', he has admitted, 'que se nutre de nostalgia y ofrece flor y fruta en el poema'. [45]

In the course of his career he has written a number of poems based on esteem for his own country, including some where the praise is quite explicit: 'Tiempo de golondrinas' (OPC 133-40), 'Promesa del Río Guayas' (OPC 160-1), 'Lugar de origen' (OPC 309), 'Canto al puente de Oakland' (OPC 293-7), 'Familia de la noche' (OPC 359-64), 'El río de la ciudad natal' (OPC 154-5), and 'Alabanza del Ecuador' (OPC 413-16). Several lines of verse proudly proclaim his sense of belonging to or possessing Ecuador, such as the following: 'Yo vengo de la tierra donde...' ('Lugar de origen', OPC 309), 'Machángara de menta: eres mi río' ('El río de la ciudad natal', OPC 154), and 'Ecuador, mi país...' ('Alabanza del Ecuador', OPC 415). Occasionally, too, his nostalgia is explicitly voiced: 'No puedo vivir más sin el topacio/del día ecuatorial' ('Familia de la noche', OPC 363).

One level at which Carrera Andrade's allegiance to Ecuador manifests itself in his poetry is that of selecting national topics, referring to local places, representing local scenes, and incorporating features of local landscape, flora, and fauna. Events and epochs of his country's history, therefore, sometimes provide the pretext for a poem. Of such cases the most substantial is the extended poem 'Crónica de las Indias' (OPC 465-80), whose exact basis on historical fact is clarified by the poet in his preliminary words (in prose), under the heading 'Argumento del poema'. The historical event is Gonzalo Pizarro's rebellion against the Ordenanzas y Leyes de Indias and his assumption of dictatorial powers over most of the territory now known as Ecuador and Perú (1545), with the subsequent appointment by the Spanish

---

[45] 'El testigo de su tiempo', IH 64. His words refer specifically to the exile in Paris of the 1950s.

Crown of Pedro de La Gasca as head of a force to restore
subservience to Spain and to remove the usurper (who was
tried and executed in Lima in 1548). The poem has a narrative structure: Part I, 'La expedición naval', concerns La
Gasca's voyage southwards down the coast of Ecuador; II,
'La marcha heroica', traces the continuation of the journey
to the Peruvian coast at Tumbes, where the forces disembark;
they march inland, climb the slopes of the Andes, winter in
Jauja, and advance across the difficult terrain; III, 'El capa-
cete de oro', covers La Gasca's victory over Pizarro's men
at Jaquijaguana and the ultimate downfall of Pizarro. Out of
this chapter in Colonial history Carrera Andrade derives
inspiration for a theme both epic and lyrical. In that he exalts
and ennobles a heroic feature of Ecuador's history, showing
the triumph of justice and the defeat of ill-used power, the
poem may be said to possess an epic quality. The deliberately
bombastic language elevates the theme and heightens the
emotion. The heroism of the men is emphasised. But the poem
falls short of epic stature. Moreover, despite its structure it
is not, fundamentally, a narrative composition. Overriding
the importance of tracing La Gasca's progress is that of creating an atmosphere of triumph for the forces of justice and
of impending doom for the dictator. The whole poem thus
serves the purpose of the third part, where the issue, though
of eternal human importance, is of especial concern to Carrera Andrade. With death imminent, Pizarro's wealth and
power are without significance, and he is as lonely and
helpless as any man — indeed, more lonely than most, since
he has become a kind of outcast, sentenced by the justice of
the Spanish Throne, and also banished from the memory of
mankind into eternal solitude:

> ... Nadie, nadie
> perpetuará tu nombre.
> Proscrito de la tierra y de los cielos,
> Tirano solitario,
> tu vestimenta regia es tu mortaja,
> y eres, con tus inútiles tesoros,
> un humano despojo lamentable,
> fatídico ornamento del cadalso. (OPC 478)

The occasionally vindictive tone, the choice of violently emotive terms ('despojo', 'lamentable'), enable the poem to stand as a warning to tyrants of all countries and all times. It ultimately becomes a symbolic illustration and warning of the perishable, transitory nature of power and riches, an attack against false values, and an exaltation of the force of justice, whose final act of judgment is performed, inexorably, at the time of a man's death.

In 1532 Gonzalo Pizarro's half-brother, Francisco, had advanced from Tumbes with an invading force, founded San Miguel in the valley of Tangarala, and penetrated inland, up the slopes of the Andes. Here they encountered, not military resistance from the Incas, but friendly messengers from their leader, Atahualpa. Halting in Cajamarca, Francisco Pizarro invited the Inca ruler to an interview. Atahualpa ingenuously accepted the invitation, and was treacherously captured; masses of Indians were slain by Pizarro's troops, who used fearsome new weapons: the horse and the harquebus. [46] On this crucial episode in Ecuador's history, Carrera Andrade has based 'Ocaso de Atahualpa' (OPC 459-60), a poem about the opposing outlooks of peace and humility on the one hand, and war and aggressiveness on the other. Without distorting the historical facts, the poet has simplified them in order to make stronger the contrast between the two philosophies. Emphasis is given to the helpless position of the Indian people so that the reader's sympathy might be won for the values they represent. In the final stanza Carrera Andrade makes it perfectly clear that the poem has a symbolic meaning. It is one which may be understood on a personal and a national level. The poet, as a descendant of both men, has within him the natures of both Atahualpa and Pizarro, which reenact the historical confrontation. By the assertion of his will he can bring about a different outcome, in which the blood that is shed is washed by the rain of centuries and Pizarro, instead of seizing Atahualpa, kneels in humility. The poem therefore asserts the need for peace and humility to proceed from the dialogue between the two opposed forces

---

[46] See Oscar Efren Reyes, *Breve historia general del Ecuador*, Editorial "Fray Jodoco Ricke", Quito, Quinta edición, 1955, Tomo I, pp. 122-5.

within him. It is not normal, however, for Carrera Andrade
to write poetry in which an *inner* struggle of this kind forms
his theme, since the forces or characteristics represented by
Pizarro have no hold over him: his own outlook is invariably
that symbolised by Atahualpa. It is likely, then, that this
poem has a primary meaning transcending the private world
of the poet. The events of Ecuador's history have caused
internal conflict; but history may, in a sense, redeem itself by
resolving the conflict in a different way now (perhaps through
a solution to the social injustice still suffered by the Indian
people). [47] By creating the possibility of such a change, with
his poetic imagination, Carrera Andrade becomes not only a
mediator but also a kind of medium.

One of the inferences to be made from this poem is that
the Inca era witnessed a way of life superior to that of the
centuries since the Spanish conquest. In 'Los antepasados'
(OPC 462-3) it is to the pre-Inca civilisations that Carrera
Andrade turns. He pays homage to the legendary founders
of Ecuadorian and Peruvian civilisation, Tumbe — king of
Indian people who arrived by sea and settled in the Quito
region —, Quitumbe — his son —, and Guayanay — son of
Quitumbe [48]—, and appeals to them for sustenance for his
people: for the eternal corn by which they lived. This is
therefore another example of Ecuador's history (or, in this
case, strictly speaking, legend) serving as the basis for a poetic
theme and providing a form of guidance for the benefit of
the present era.

It is evident that the reasons for this choice of an historical
basis for some of his poems are numerous. He was involved
for several years in research into the details of Ecuador's
past, while preparing his prose studies on the theme; [49] inevitably some influence of this investigation has impinged on
the verse. One may also see this as his response to a form of
national awareness, for these poems help readers to appre-
ciate the character of Ecuador and to understand its prob-

---

[47] This national interpretation is substantiated by the evidence elsewhere (such
as that assessed in the previous section of this chapter) that Carrera Andrade is
concerned with the conflicts in Ecuador's society.
[48] See CS 19-26.
[49] i.e. TSV and CS.

lems. [50] The main point to be understood from this approach
to Ecuador's character through its history is that the pre-
Columbian era is seen in idyllic terms as the model of pure,
authentic living, while the entrance of the Spaniards on the
scene marks the intrusion of a discordant note and the violent
destruction of the old order. As will be seen shortly, the
great virtue of Tumbe, Quitumbe, Guayanay, and Atahualpa
is that they all lived close to nature. In addition to this
educational function, the poems serve simply to increase
knowledge of Carrera Andrade's country wherever they are
read, and therefore, like the prose works discussed in a previous chapter, promote its interests or exalt its prestige. But
granted the veracity of such reasons, it must be remembered
that in his poetry Carrera Andrade always transcends the
point of merely illustrating or advertising the realities of
Ecuador. The underlying function of these poems is to enable
him to work out his own preoccupations.

Visual aspects of contemporary Ecuador also provide the
theme or setting for a poem or act as images or symbols (as
in the early poems). Of the topographical features of the
country, rivers inspire the whole of two poems: Quito's River
Machángara in 'El río de la ciudad natal' (OPC 154-5), and
Guayaquil's River Guayas in 'Promesa del Río Guayas' (OPC
160-1). Both rivers inspire thoughts on the Ecuador of past
and present ages; both carry, in their current, memories of
the country's history (and of its recent past) which imply a
message for the present period. But chiefly they serve to
arouse thoughts on the passing of time, the transitory nature
of a man's life, and the loss of childhood.

Mountains and volcanos figure prominently in one or two
poems (e.g. 'Alabanza del Ecuador', OPC 415-6, and 'Crónica
de las Indias', OPC 465-80); occasional poems introduce reference to tropical vegetation and animal life (e.g. 'Expedición
al país de la canela', OPC 119, with its mention of the jungle,
orchids, parrots, and snakes); and many contain mention of
flora and fauna that Carrera Andrade takes as representative

---

[50] The presence of an 'Argumento' summarising the historical context of 'Crónica de las Indias' indicates Carrera Andrade's concern that the factual basis be
known; for the poem derives much of its strength from its historical truth.

of Ecuador, such as the cicada, the parrot, and the humming-bird. This seems to correspond not only to a desire and need to draw inspiration from his native land, but also to a wish that his verse should bear a national seal.

One interesting result of his separation from Ecuador has been the occasional adoption of a foreigner's standpoint. There are, consequently, a few poems in which the local ingredients seem to have largely a curiosity or decorative value, serving to introduce details of Ecuadorian realities for information or identification. It is as though Carrera Andrade were able to perceive what, for the European, are the exotic qualities of his country. One of the best examples is 'Lugar de origen' (OPC 309). In the course of this poem Carrera Andrade refers to a considerable number of plants and creatures, many of which are especially typical of Ecuador. He writes of the custard apple (chirimoya), avocado pear (aguacate), Andean cherry tree (capuli), quail (codorniz), armadillo, palm leaf (penca), and eucalyptus. Moreover, as if to give even greater emphasis to special features which differentiate between the characteristics of Europe and the features of Ecuador, he introduces reference to plants with mysterious powers over human beings, capable of bringing death, love, dream, or joyfulness. What is important, however, is his purpose: deliberately to stress his exotic origin in order to suggest his advantages over people of other lands. Proudly, he represents Ecuador as a land of Nature, from which he comes with a message communicated by the elements ('vientos') and creatures ('pájaros'). Man's allies are found here. It is not, strictly, the exotic or picturesque aspects of Ecuador that concern him in these poems, but the attempt to understand and to express the underlying meaning symbolised by those details.

VI.   INFLUENCES OF ECUADOR ON CARRERA ANDRADE

Carrera Andrade's poems create the impression that Ecuador's distinguishing features have produced a profound effect on him that not even constant absence can eradicate. Being an Ecuadorian becomes not merely a statement of

nationality, or an indication of belonging, but implies inborn
characteristics with far-reaching effects in his daily living.

For a clear exposition of this point it is helpful to turn to
'Alabanza del Ecuador' (OPC 415-6). After eulogising Ecuador's role of consecrating man's alliance with the earth (in
stanza I) he adopts a new approach to indicate what Ecuador, through those same basic qualities, has taught him:

> Me enseñaste las ciencias naturales
> del árbol dadivoso y el árbol curandero,
> de las aves que parlan, más pintadas que frutos,
> la nueva zoología de un mundo fabuloso . . .

The whole of Ecuador's natural life has messages which it
communicates to man. There are provisions and healing
powers in the trees, and the birds' song is an intelligible
language. His country has helped him to be sensitive to such
things. But the fabulous zoological land is one side of the
picture: another is the human society, in which Carrera Andrade singles out for attention the continuing misfortune and
longing, which ceremonies and festivities do not completely
efface:

> y la historia de un pueblo
> que gime hasta en la danza
> disparando su anhelo hacia las nubes
> en cohetes de fiesta,
> fuego que se deshace en lágrimas azules.

What may be inferred from this is that those impulses within
Carrera Andrade that have found expression in his humanitarian and socialist ideals and activities derive from his
experience in Ecuador. In the section above on the plight of
the Indian we suggested that it is, in fact, particularly the
Indian people of Ecuador to whom he is alluding here; but
the ultimate effect has been for Ecuador to instil in him a
love embracing all mankind:

> Tú me enseñaste a amar el universo . . .

In a way not clearly evinced in this poem, Ecuador has
enabled Carrera Andrade to accept a life of moving from

country to country, helping him towards a vision of the whole
planet as his home:

> ...y aceptar mi destino de habitante
> planetario...

Also, Ecuador made him a man close to nature, uneasy in
the dispassionate and insensitive cities:

> ...pastor de vicuñas fantasmas
> por ciudades extrañas donde nadie
> corre en auxilio de una estrella herida
> que se ahoga en un charco.

In the third stanza we are taken a step further:

> Ecuador, tú me hiciste vegetal y telúrico...

This now transcends the idea that Ecuador has given him a
special awareness of, and sensitivity to, nature. It is a question of more than a bond: an identity. The telluric and
vegetable qualities of his country had made him so close to
nature that he is inherently natural as opposed to social, void
of influence from human beings and built on the influences
of the natural world.

Ecuador has also made him:

> humilde cual vasija llena de sombra fértil.

A vessel partly because of the idea of his being made of the
very substance of the land, and in addition because a vessel
serves a useful purpose. In the remaining lines of the stanza,
inner characteristics of the poet — his innate tendencies, his
moods, his outlook on life, his temperament — all are attributed to the influence of his native land by the method of
drawing ingenious parallels with features of the topography:

> Soy desolado, abrupto como la cordillera,
> profundo como cueva de tesoros incaicos.
> En mi interior dormita un lago sobre un cráter.
> Mi frente es un paisaje de páramo con lluvia,
> mi corazón un cacto situbundo
> que pide una limosna de rocío.

We deduce that through his Ecuadorian origins Carrera Andrade has a superficial calmness covering a profound ex-
plosiveness, that his outlook is bleak, grim, and that he feels
barren, needful of something refreshing.

One major influence of Ecuador upon Carrera Andrade
remains to be expounded. It is implied in the following lines
from 'Canto al puente de Oakland' (OPC 293-7):

> Nada se oculta a mis abiertos ojos
> de hombre de una tierra sin vocación de nube,
> donde la luz exacta
> ninguna forma olvida,
> y enseña el peso justo y el sitio de las cosas
> la línea ecuatorial
> que es un fiel de balanza de trópicos y soles
> o el siempre verde, exacto cinturón del planeta.   (OPC 296)

In this poem, which interprets the symbolic presence of the
bridge, the poet's facility for reading the signs offered by the
bridge is derived from his Ecuadorian origin. Two separate
yet interrelated ideas are contained here. One is the effect
of the country's overhead sun, casting an intense light from
a clear sky. [51] In this light things are seen more exactly and
distinctly than anwhere else on earth, which enables precise
perception and judgment to be made. Secondly, Ecuador
holds a geographically central position from which an
unbiased weighing of issues is possible. These are crucial
concepts to which it will be necessary to return. For the
present, suffice to demonstrate that from Ecuador derives
Carrera Andrade's privileged faculty of understanding and
judging things. A good deal of his poetry concerns his condemnation of features of modern society — an issue that will
be studied at length in the following chapter and in Part II.
It transpires that such criticism is made from the vantage
point of his Ecuadorian provenance and with the enlightenment that this affords. Similarly, another major theme of his,
the sense of a universal human brotherhood, arises from his

---

[51] It will be observed that Carrera Andrade is able to allude to Ecuador as
cloudy or cloudless as circumstances require. In his early phase, there is a tendency
for rain and cloud to figure prominently (see Sections I and II of the present
chapter).

origin in a country holding a central position, belonging to neither side of the scales.

VII.   ECUADOR AS THE VIRGINAL LAND

Poems expressing Carrera Andrade's early impressions of Ecuador's countryside (i.e. prior to 1928) already manifest the importance to him of contact with nature and also make it obvious that in rural Ecuador he readily found such contact. Travel abroad not only confirmed but also strengthened his conviction that his native land is fortunate in maintaining its rural qualities. In his poetry he suggests Ecuador's greatest virtue to be that it is one of the few remaining natural lands in the world.

We return to 'Alabanza del Ecuador' as the poem that most clearly expresses his admiration for his native country. With a careful development of ideas he exposes the external characteristics of the land (stanza 1), what it has taught him (stanza 2), what it has made of him (stanza 3), and finally what it can provide for him (stanzas 4 and 5). Significantly, the starting-point of the poem, and indeed the framework which makes possible all other functions of Ecuador, is the question of its rural quality:

> Ecuador, mi país, esmeralda del mundo
> incrustada en el aro equinoccial,
> tú consagras la alianza del hombre con la tierra,
> las telúricas bodas con la novia profunda
> de volcánicos senos y cuerpo de cereales,
> novia vestida siempre de domingo
> por el sol labrador, padre de las semillas.
> Quiero besar todo tu cuerpo verde,
> tus cabellos de selva,
> tu vientre de maíz y de caña de azúcar
> y reposar mi sien en tu pecho de flores.   (OPC 415)

The key to the poem lies in the third line: in Ecuador there exists such a profound alliance between man and the earth on which he lives, the soil which he works, and in which he sows his seeds, that it may be expressed in terms of a marriage, even in terms of the physical bond consecrating the marriage. Images of physical beauty and fertility connect with this central idea.

In 'Ocaso de Atahualpa' (OPC 459-60) what is especially admirable in pre-Columbian civilisation is the proximity of man to the elements: they are 'padres cariñosos del surco y la semilla', 'amadores de la tierra y los astros', companions of animals, and by trade potters and weavers. Similarly, in 'Los antepasados' (OPC 462-3) the legendary kings are imagined learning from the stars, paying homage to the sun, friendly with creatures and protected by them, and above all possessors of something essential to life, symbolised by the corn that they grow, and suggestive of something lost in the contemporary world. If there is a suspicion in such poems that the idyllic state of complete communion between man and nature belonged to an Ecuador of the past — in this case the pre-Columbian era — then in certain other poems the hint is far stronger. In 'Biografía para uso de los pájaros' (OPC 251-2) the last remnants of a civilisation in which man is surrounded by plants and animals are already threatened in the years of Carrera Andrade's childhood:

> Nací en el siglo de la defunción de la rosa
> cuando el motor ya había ahuyentado a los ángeles.
> Quito veía andar la última diligencia . . .

And they have vanished by the time the poem is composed:

> Todo ha pasado ya, en sucesivo oleaje . . .

As will be argued below, the link between the dream-like, idyllic state of the countryside and the years of Carrera Andrade's childhood is a fundamental aspect of the theme.

'Tiempo de golondrinas' (OPC 137-40) also relates present to past. Most of the poem evokes impressions of an Ecuador of past ages still seen today as his ancestors saw it: a land of rural harmony. An ominous note is struck in the last tercet, however. As a swallow, sweeping low, warns of approaching rain, so the poet perceives in contemporary Ecuador threatening signs — signs of changes that, like the rain, '. . . borra el país verde de mis antepasados', making Ecuador unrecognisable. The precise nature of this change is not specified, but beyond the general theme of Time's effect on things it is not difficult to see Carrera Andrade's anxiety that his country may lose qualities passed down from pre-Colonial times (man living close to nature, etc.) and suffer the influence of advancing urban civilisations.

This anxiety that Ecuador may change does not find expression, however, as frequently as his pride in an Ecuador which still retains its essentially rural characteristics. Through living abroad, Carrera Andrade has tended to think of Ecuador not only in terms of its present in relation to its past, but in terms of comparison with other countries of the world. Relatively speaking, Ecuador continues to possess an innocence and a natural character. This is a central poetic theme. It was soon used by Carrera Andrade during his first visit to Europe, in 'Saludo de los puertos' (OPC 190-1), written in 1928 or 1929. Men of Ecuador are seen here as people of the fields, the open air, and the rivers, and are characterised by occupations which keep them close to nature: they are muleteers, farmers, herdsmen, fruit-sellers, rubber-growers, travellers by canoe on the Amazon. By contrast, Europe is a place of 'países manufacturados'.

In chapter II it was observed that Carrera Andrade's essays tend to treat the Latin American countries as a cultural bloc. The poetry adopts a similar attitude. Countries of Europe may be grouped together, in simplified terms, on the grounds that they share common characteristics ('países manufacturados') which contrast them with Ecuador. Similarly, the various republics of Latin America may be considered as possessing certain common features. A natural development of Carrera Andrade's concept of Ecuador, therefore, is to attribute its own essential qualities to the whole of Latin America. In several poems Ecuador itself is not named; Carrera Andrade belongs to Latin America (which he denominates by the term 'América'), and the main contrast is between this bloc and the whole of the mechanised, industrially-advanced world.

The inspiration for 'Viaje de regreso' (OPC 348-50) appears to be a return home after a long absence. [52] In poetic

---

[52] The poem was published in *El visitante de niebla* in 1947. Since his first departure from Ecuador in 1928 Carrera Andrade's life had been spent

terms the poet's life of travel is expressed as a form of dreaming: towns, rivers, islands, faces seen on his journeys, and people he has loved and those who have loved him, all seem now to be of doubtful veracity, as though they were part of a dream. The quality or character of life itself in other lands is thus found wanting. But Latin America awakes him, as the opening stanza announces:

> Mi vida fue una geografía
> que repasé una y otra vez,
> libro de mapas o de sueños.
> En América desperté.

After detailing his life (dream) during time spent abroad, Carrera Andrade returns, at the end of the poem, to the theme of Latin America's effect of awaking him, as though his return were a deliberate measure, in response to his confidence in what Latin America would do for him:

> Vine a América a despertar. [53]

The idea of 'awaking' thus seems to mean a revival of the senses, a revitalising process, which in turn leads to a longing for greater fullness of experience: 'sed de vivir, sed de morir'. Latin America (not specifically Ecuador, it will be noted) is 'tierra del maíz', the land close to nature, capable of providing an antidote to the poison in the atmosphere of other climes.

It is to the inhabitants of such other countries that Carrera Andrade addresses himself in another poem, 'Hombre de cualquier tierra' (OPC 400-1). [54] In a gesture of companionship and assistance, Carrera Andrade offers precisely the kind of natural phenomena that he finds admirable in Ecuador. But in this poem he prefers to see the process in terms

---

mainly in Europe, Japan, and the U.S.A. until 1944, when he was appointed Chargé d'Affaires of Ecuador in Caracas. It is clear from his autobiography that Venezuela pleased him greatly. This return to Latin America may, therefore, be the one alluded to in the poem. Alternatively, of course, he may be thinking of no specific return, but simply of the general idea.

[53] One critic unconvincingly finds ambiguity in the meaning of 'despertar' here, wondering whether Carrera Andrade means 'to waken people' or 'to be awoken' (Isaac J. Barrera, *Historia de la literatura ecuatoriana*, Casa de la Cultura Ecuatoriana, Quito, 1960, p. 1141).

[54] Entitled 'Epílogo' in MVP and PU.

of a Latin American contribution to the world. The sun is therefore 'sol americano' in both the first and last stanzas, the broader concept thus embracing the whole poem, which refers to condor, puma, forest, mountain, ambrosia, pepper, bull, volcano, and rose — i.e. the natural world in its wildness and beauty, which instils a will to create continental solidarity and a sense of love for one's fellow men. This concept of Latin America's contrast with and capacity to assist other lands is a major theme in its own right. [55]

VIII.   ECUADOR AS CHILDHOOD, MOTHER, SELF

It is of great significance that Carrera Andrade did not leave the country during the first twenty-five years of his life, and that he has never since made it his permanent home, for it means that Ecuador is always remembered as the home of his childhood and youth. Rather than literal memories of that period of his life, vague associations with childhood spring to his mind when he recalls Ecuador from the distance of a remote epoch in his life and a remote continent. Precisely when he left his homeland he began to regret the passing of his youth and to sense the transitory nature of human life. Ecuador is consequently associated with a nostalgia for his own past, and particularly with the notion of a lost childhood.

'Biografía para uso de los pájaros' (1937) is the earliest poem to deal clearly with this topic. In a previous section we concentrated on one aspect of the poem's theme: the notion of a pure countryside belonging — regrettably — to an Ecuador of the past which is vanishing with the advance of mechanisation. [56] It is now possible to link this with the other half of the main theme. The Quito remembered as idyllic is the city of his birth; the things whose passing the poet regrets — the rose, the diligence, the trees, fields, and quietly grazing cattle — are all associated with his childhood. In this poem Carrera Andrade's prime intention is not to state his antipathy for modern civilisation and his fondness

---

[55] It is discussed in Chapter IV, IV.
[56] See Section IV of the present chapter.

for the civilisation represented by an Ecuador of past ages (which is his usual emphasis), but nostalgically to evoke childhood scenes: his mother and her guitar, moods of the countryside, men working in the fields, views of haciendas, sugar-cane crops, cacao, and bananas, all building up toward the feelings expressed in the last stanza: wistfulness, a deep regret that all is past, and a sensitive reaction to the fleeting nature of things. His childhood can never be recaptured, only evoked in beautiful, delicate images, surrounded by symbols of threat and death.

A poem that links Ecuador with Carrera Andrade's childhood in more explicit terms and with a different conclusion is 'El río de la ciudad natal' (OPC 154-5). As the River Machángara inspires associations from the poet's youth he externalises them in the form of the river itself. Youth, love, novels, the first experience of pain and solitude, the first anguished questioning about metaphysical issues — these are the notions aroused by contemplation (or recollection) of Quito's river. There is the wistful note found in 'Biografía para uso de los pájaros', but Carrera Andrade transcends this stage to find hope for his future in the river that evokes impressions from his past. The river has its origins above, in the sky, and therefore reminds the poet of the need to take into account eternal issues during his temporary dwelling on earth. With its message, the river thus refreshes the poet's soul.

In the final stanza of 'Alabanza del Ecuador' Carrera Andrade's homeland is addressed in the following terms:

¡oh madre coronada de hielo y colibríes!   (OPC 416)

There are various reasons why Ecuador should be treated as mother. One obvious connection was already indicated in 'Biografía para uso de los pájaros': the country is associated with the poet's childhood. It was observed that the mother, with her guitar, creates a sense of tranquility and harmony. A more detailed treatment of the idea will be found in 'Familia de la noche' (OPC 359-64). In the opening two stanzas of section I Carrera Andrade seems to imagine himself outside a house which he inhabited as a child. The

thought of opening the door and the sight of a nearby tree
conjure associations of a face and a voice from the past,
the memory of a person named here as 'Dueña de las Golondrinas'. It is clear by the end of section II that this is the
poet's mother. In the remainder of section I the presence of
the landscape inspires stanzas preoccupied with the passing
of time: his own childhood in relation to the present moment,
and also more general thoughts concerning the passing of
the ages (the Ancient World, the Middle Ages, the Discovery
and Conquest of the New World). Section II returns to ideas
more immediately connected with the building contemplated
by Carrera Andrade. It begins with an explicit statement of
Ecuador's poetic role as an image of his childhood:

> Tu geografía, infancia, es la meseta
> de los Andes, ...   (OPC 362)

Following the idea of children leaving home, as birds fly
from their nest, comes an evocation of the mother remaining,
sending messages (swallows) and longing for news (from the
clouds). Then the poet emits an intense cry:

> ¡Madre de la alegría de la tierra,
> nodriza de palomas,
> inventora del sueño que consuela!   (OPC 363)

His mother was a bringer of joy, one who cared for the sick,
and one who provided a means of consolation. It should be
noted how this role of hers is inherently connected with the
land, with nature, as is further clarified in the following
stanza: she was a model for nature to imitate, a provider;
she had a message and answer for the needy. Through these
qualities she is intrinsically linked with Ecuador. At the
same time as he appeals to *her* for assistance, Carrera Andrade longs for Ecuador itself:

> ¡Devuélveme el mensaje de los tordos!
> No puedo vivir más sin el topacio
> del día ecuatorial.   (ibid.)

In section III of 'Familia de la noche' Carrera Andrade turns
to the memory of his father, and associations of order, care,

and constructiveness. Childhood is thus recalled as a period
in his life when everything had its meaning, place, and
purpose. But after these thoughts the poem's underlying
theme returns to the surface: all this has disappeared, all the
family has departed, and the poet is left in darkness. In this
poem, whose theme is sometimes reminiscent of the César
Vallejo of *Los heraldos negros* and *Trilce*, Carrera Andrade
implies that his present life, by contrast with his childhood,
is characterised by a lack of meaning and the experience of
anguish. [57] The basis and development of the theme are
different from those in Vallejo, however. For Carrera Andrade, all the virtues of childhood spring from the inextri-
cable mixture of Ecuador (especially Quito), the countryside,
the poet's mother (and father) and joy.

   In a handful of poems Carrera Andrade treats Ecuador
as his own *being*. When dealing with the homeland's influences on the poet we examined ways in which he expresses a
sense of having a bond with his country, of belonging to it,
and even of possessing a telluric quality with features comparable to and derived from Ecuador's topography. [58] It is
but a short step from this point to a complete merging of
identities: he and Ecuador become one. Thus in 'El río de
la ciudad natal' (OPC 154-5) the River Machángara, though
literally crossing the fields on the outskirts of Quito, in poetic
terms traverses Carrera Andrade's very self: his breast ('Atra-
viesas mi pecho y no los prados', in the second line of the
poem) and his soul ('recorres mi alma', in the last stanza).
Moreover, his soul, as it is expressed in the final stanza, is
itself a country, a native land ('—país estéril, patria de la
espina—'). This is therefore a means of establishing his
identification with Ecuador through its topography. Another
poem, 'La llave del fuego' (OPC 353-5) makes the same point
through historical topics. In the opening stanzas he writes of
himself as though he represented the original inhabitants

---

[57] César Vallejo (Perú, 1892-1938): *Los heraldos negros*, 1918; *Trilce*, 1922.
On this topic James Higgins writes: 'The principal theme of the volume (i.e.
Trilce) is perhaps the destruction of the happiness of the past'. Of *Trilce* LXI
he adds: 'For Vallejo the home and the family represent the supreme value, and
this abandoned house is the symbol of the emptiness and desolation of his adult
life.' (Introduction to *C.V. An Anthology of his Poetry*, Pergamon, Oxford, 1970,
pp. 17-18.)
[58] See Section VI of the present chapter.

of America ('Yo soy el hombre de los papagayos'), and as
though he inspired the Independence movements ('acompañé
a Bolívar') and the founding of the Republic ('Yo fundé una
república'). He does not identify himself with the conquistadores and the Colonial period because he does not regard
these as manifestations of Ecuador's essential spirit. But
the indigenous, noble features of Ecuador's past have contributed to his own constitution; Ecuador's past is his past.
Since the land produced him, the banana tree may seem
father-like ('Te miro, bananero, como a un padre'). It is worth
noticing how his themes are interlinked: in the pages above
we discovered a different path to the conclusion that the
poet's own past (his childhood, in that case) is associated
with Ecuador.

IX.   ECUADOR AS LIGHT AND KEY

In 'Canto al puente de Oakland' Carrera Andrade suggests that he possesses the ability to interpret and assess
things with a privileged accuracy and insight because of his
Ecuadorian origins. Ecuador thus provides him with a
starting-point for the discovery of solutions to the various
problems of existence. [59] This is one of several respects in
which his homeland guides him, fulfils his need, and acts
as the key to problems of the world at large. As we observed above, his special faculties of perception and judgment, as he accounts for it in 'Canto al puente de Oakland',
derive from two things: Ecuador's central position, and
light. It is this connection between Ecuador and light that
requires closer examination now. Several poems in fact associate Carrera Andrade's country with things suggesting
brilliance, clarity, and sunshine. Ecuador is an emerald ('Alabanza del Ecuador', OPC 415) not only because of its precious value but because it also has the green brilliance of a
jewel; its sky is as clear and bright as topaz ('Familia de la
noche', OPC 363); in the grey of foreign cities Carrera An-

---

[59] In this section we anticipate some of the argument in chapter VI, I and II,
where a fuller treatment of the metaphysical issues is given. For the present, the
intention is to evince the fundamental role of Ecuador, whereas later the more
general roles of nature and light are analysed.

drade is able, because of his land of origin, to share out portions of sunshine ('Moneda del forastero', OPC 389, and 'Hombre de cualquier tierra', OPC 401); Quito was built, he explains in a prose work, on the equator, which was known by his Indian ancestors as the 'Camino del Sol'. [60] In 'Las armas de la luz' (OPC 372-8) Carrera Andrade's sense of the fullness of the present moment is enhanced by the light falling on creatures and objects of Ecuador. This poem will be discussed fully in a later chapter, [61] but it is worth devoting some attention to it now.

Carrera Andrade begins by creating an impression of brilliant, reverberating sunlight. Without delay he makes it clear that this light has a basic, primeval, heavenly function. It communicates eternal messages, gives birth to all forms, instils a spirit of love, and proves and explains a man's existence (the whole of I and the first line of II). Having established these crucial ideas, Carrera Andrade proceeds to evoke impressions of things in the world around him that reflect light. It is a world of nature teeming with life. Although he singles out for special mention the wasp and the hummingbird, he believes all creatures and objects to have a common root, to be joined in a universal fraternity by an 'esencial correspondencia más allá de sus muertes' (V). What particularly binds them together is the light which feeds each alike, 'en la escala que sube del guijarro / a la escama' (V). There is no doubt that, although the country at issue is never named, the poet is thinking essentially of Ecuador. We know that he regards Ecuador as the land of abundant nature; the idea of the overhead sun is reiterated in mentions of 'mediodía' and 'meridiano'; Ecuador's symbol, the hummingbird, is chosen as an image of light in the animal world ('Sólo es luz emplumada el colibrí, IV); [62] parrots (V) and mountains (II) are referred to; the term 'topacios' (VII) is used in a way reminiscent of the word's use in 'Familia de la noche', where it indubitably alludes to Ecuador; and to clinch it all, mention is made of a central position from which a balanced

---

[60] See CS, p. 36.
[61] Chapter VI, II.
[62] In 'La llave del fuego' Ecuador is denominated 'patria del colibrí' (OPC 353).

assessment may be made ('servidor simétrico del mundo',
and 'tengo . . . / un punto cardinal en cada mano', VI). Light
is twice expressed, moreover, in terms of a fusion with the
notion of mother: it is 'madre del universo' (I), while the
common originator of all things is named as 'la luz madre'
(II) — examples which once again remind us of those other
symbolic functions of mother connected with Ecuador. That
Carrera Andrade should not name the country in this poem
is indicative of the fact that his purpose is not, on this
occasion, to eulogise Ecuador; it is not a poem about his
homeland but about light, and the importance of light in
understanding the world and the eternal problems of human
existence. Ecuador is a means to this end, for it is the country
of light. This, then, is one means by which Ecuador assists
Carrera Andrade in tackling metaphysical issues, one sense
in which it is a key.

Another line of approach taken in order to arrive, ultimately, at this same point of Ecuador as a key to the world
is through the very things that, in 'Las armas de la luz',
reflect the light: the creatures and the natural phenomena
of Ecuador. 'Alabanza del Ecuador' builds up towards this
in the last two stanzas, after Carrera Andrade has already
rendered tribute to his country for establishing the alliance
between man and the land, for teaching him that nature
provides and cures, and for making him vegetable and telluric. In the penultimate stanza this recognition of the innate
merits of Ecuador as the virginal land embraces the idea of
ancient civilisations, pre-Columbian times, when the Indian
tribes — as has been observed in poems such as 'Ocaso
de Atahualpa' and 'Los antepasados' — lived in harmony
with nature and the elements. Through the revival of this
Ecuador of old a message may be obtained. He introduces,
therefore, a note of reverence. The image of Carrera Andrade's participation in an act of ceremonial dancing successful-
ly evokes an attitude of worship, while clarifying the poet's
intention that there should be a revival of the ancient values.
When the gods of old are summoned they will communicate
their message:

Ecuador, vuelvo a ti con vestido de prioste
para danzar sobre tu suelo verde,
danzar hasta morir,
oyendo como late
tu corazón antiguo de pimiento y adobe.
Golpeo con la mano en el arpa de siglos,
despertando a la música en su ataúd de polvo
y al viejo dios del trueno.   (OPC 416)

Similar to this in effect, though less subtle and imaginative, is that moment at the end of 'Los antepasados' when the poet addresses his ancestors:

... ¡oh padres!:
señaladme el camino
de la floresta antigua,
donde el Gran Guacamayo divulga su secreto
en una lengua extraña
olvidada hace siglos.   (OPC 463)

There is no room here for misunderstanding his intention: it is to indicate that guidance for him now may be transmitted from his forefathers of ancient Ecuador. By implication, their influence persists, and it is a question of tuning in to it. Or, expressed in different terms, they are themselves dead, but upon entering the soil of Ecuador in burial they made the land fertile, they were seeds from which new life has formed. This is precisely how Carrera Andrade expresses it in the last stanza of 'La llave del fuego':

Oh, tierra equinoccial de mis antepasados,
cementerio fecundo,
albergue de semillas y cadáveres.   (OPC 355)

The key that Ecuador provides, then, through its Indian heritage, is a form of guidance.

This heritage is but one aspect of the great wealth of aid Ecuador holds for the man who discovers access to it. In 'El río de la ciudad natal' (OPC 154-5) Carrera Andrade expresses his own spiritual condition in physical terms of barrenness ('hombre sediento que interroga', and 'mi corazón, yerma colina'). Then, in the final stanza of 'Alabanza del Ecuador', he formulates the answer to such requirements

as something refreshing, like the dew, green growth, and ice
— all of which are provided by Ecuador. Images of welcome
and of embraces, and the paramount image of mother serve
to enhance his sense of relief and security:

> Dame tu bienvenida de rocío,
> tu gran abrazo verde,
> ¡oh madre coronada de hielo y colibríes!   (OPC 416)

While guidance is an aid towards reaching a desired goal it
is not, of course, in itself that goal; but here Carrera Andrade seems to imply that Ecuador not only provides assistance
in the search for a refreshing truth but that in some part
it actually embodies that truth. Lost from view and memory
in modern civilisation, as though buried like treasure or
precious metals in a mine beneath Ecuador's soil, are the
basic elements, and from these Carrera Andrade seeks to
learn:

> Señálame el camino de la mina perdida
> que guarda los profundos metales del origen.   (ibid.)

And finally, Ecuador possesses special powers of curing and
protecting, powers invested, as though by magic, in nature
and the elements. Invoking a revival of simple attitudes, he
ends the poem:

> Dame tus plantas mágicas, tus prodigiosos bálsamos,
> y el talismán de piedra memorable
> donde el sol ha marcado
> sus signos protectores.   (ibid.)

In this poem what has concerned him principally in his
search for refreshment, guidance, protection, and healing
have been the needs of his own soul. 'La llave del fuego'
(OPC 353-5) has a broader scope. It deals both with the
poet's own problems and those of the world at large,
ultimately showing a way in which Ecuador may be seen
to hold a key available to the whole world. In the first half
of this poem Carrera Andrade shows his identification with
Ecuador, and his communication with its creatures, plants,
and rivers. He then finds inherent in the character of Ecua-

dor extremes of both basic human nature and the elements: a humble people and a proud people, light and dark, violence and tranquility, destructiveness and fruitfulness. From this idea emerges the concept which gives the poem its title:

En ti existe el recuerdo del fuego elemental... (OPC 355)

What concerns us now is the sense in which this fire may be considered a key. As the following lines imply, in Ecuador's plant, insect and animal life, and in its minerals, there persists some quality evocative of the period of the earth's origins:

...en cada fruto, en cada insecto, en cada pluma,
en el cacto que muestra sus heridas o flores,
en el toro lustroso de candelas y noche,
el mineral insomne bebedor de la luz
y en el caballo rojo que galopa desnudo.
La sequedad arruga los rostros y los muros
y en la extensión de trigo va alumbrando el incendio
su combate de gallos de oro y sangre. (ibid.)

The stanza evokes an impression of an Ecuador in which great elemental passions rage, enormous hardship is suffered, deep longing is felt, violent conflict explodes. It is through the image of fire that the concept is expressed. At the same time the stanza also reveals Ecuador as a land with peace as well as violence, humility as well as pride, a land of beauty and of abundant corn. And this aspect, too, is expressed through the image of fire, but fire in a less literal sense, an elemental fire, belonging to the age of the Earth's origins, a purging, purifying fire. It is not only destructive and consuming, but also productive. It brought great changes in ancient civilisations who discovered how to create and exploit it, including the Indian tribes who not only worshipped the sun but also made sacrifices to receive fire from their gods. In this poem, fire is therefore a paradoxical image since it not only causes and expresses a need but also provides an answer or key to a need. It is consistent, however, with Carrera Andrade's attitude to Ecuador in the poem: his country both reflects elemental problems (in this stanza only) and supplies the poet with a message which constitutes a solution to problems.

One is inevitably reminded of the Heraclytian concept of fire. In the Greek philosopher's doctrine that all things in the universe are in a state of constant becoming, not being, fire has this dual function of both generating and destroying. As such, it is conceived of by Heraclitus as the chief of the four elements (fire, air, water, and earth) and as the true principle of cosmic harmony, since unity and harmony result from the concordance of opposites, and each element lives by the death of another. [63] Although it is not essential to pay too close attention to the details of this Heraclitian fire in interpreting Carrera Andrade's poem, it seems certain that an indirect influence has operated loosely in some of the basic ideas. Thus, it helps in understanding the connection between the complete opposites of Ecuador mentioned in this stanza and the supreme truth (including the idea of harmony) that emerges out of them. And it helps in appreciating that fire is, for Carrera Andrade, both an image of thirst, passion and need, and one of key to the needs of the world.

The next stanza opens, therefore, with a triumphant claim, as though his discovery arose out of the complex examination of Ecuador in the preceding stanzas:

> Yo soy el poseedor de la llave del fuego
> del fuego natural llave pacífica
> que abre las invisibles cerraduras del mundo,
> la llave del amor y la amapola,
> del rubí primordial y de la rosa.
> Dulce llave solar que calienta mi mano
> extendida a los hombres, sin fronteras ...   (ibid.)

The key has attributes of the same elemental, primordial kind as the elemental fire. [64] Clearly, the idea of fire has helped to determine some of the specific images: the colour

---

[63] *Enciclopedia Universal Ilustrada Europeo-Americana*, Hijos de J. Espasa, Editores, Barcelona, 1925, vol. XXVII, pp. 1098-1100.

[64] Hernán Rodríguez Castelo suggests that the key alluded to here is, in fact, poetry (*Tres cumbres......*, p. 52 of manuscript). There seems insufficient evidence within the context of the poem to support his view, but he makes a more convincing case (later) when proposing that the key is also light (p. 55 of manuscript).

of fire influences the choice of poppy, ruby, pomegranate, pepper, and rose, while the heat is carried over into the use of the sun. In its turn, the notion of a key naturally gives rise to that of the opening of locks which represent the world's barriers. Apart from these points, however, the main concepts arise independently and coincide with ideas Carrera Andrade has expressed in other poems. Peace is an answer to problems; a peaceful approach means that doors will be opened, permitting harmonious co-existence in which love (fellowship, human solidarity) will reign. [65] With love comes an appreciation of simple, natural beauty and value, things that provide extra quality. The sun of Ecuador, which gives life to all these elemental things, produces a warmth that is equivalent to peace and love since it encourages fellowship with men of all lands and all types, whether (as the next four lines imply) warlike, commercial, welcoming, or soul-searching. Ecuador has provided Carrera Andrade with the key of love, fellowship and peace, and this he offers to the world at large.

It is hoped that these pages will have demonstrated the great importance of Ecuador as a poetic theme — an importance not fully reflected, we must acknowledge, in the number of poems dedicated to the theme. If we compare Ecuador's treatment in the poetry with that in the prose we are struck by the fact that, although there is basically the same combination of attitudes in both, a far greater proportion of the prose is devoted specifically to Ecuador (slightly more than fifty per cent). The reason is not difficult to find: the prose springs more directly from his career of journalism and diplomatic service. It is even at times a clear extension of his diplomatic role. The poetry, on the other hand, is treated as though its function were distinct from that of prose. Ecuador, the world, cities are in the poetry often abstracted and internalised, becoming part of a united poetic world which includes — on precisely the same level

---

[65] The idea of fire as love inevitably draws from or is connected with Christian doctrine: God manifested Himself to Moses in the burning bush; and more particularly, the Holy Ghost — God's Spirit on Earth — bestowed Its powers to spread truth, peace, and love by means of tongues of fire descending on the disciples.

— the emotions, life's experiences, and ontological enquiry. In other words, as these last sections have sought to show, Ecuador is often a symbol through which Carrera Andrade expresses more general problems, some of them metaphysical.

IV

FOREIGN LANDS

D E S P I T E his impatience with Ecuador, his sense of tedium, and his interest in literary and political events overseas, Carrera Andrade wrote few poems about foreign lands before his departure in 1928. There are just occasional signs that distant countries beckoned to him, offering rich promises as in 'El camarada parte de la tierra natal' (OPC 101), the chief allurement being a mixture of novelty, excitement, and an awakening of the senses. So great was his interest in foreign lands, however, and so carefully had he gleaned information about them from his reading that he already seemed to be acquainted with them. It meant that when, eventually, he visited Paris and other distant places it was like returning to familiar ground:

> Las calles de París nos son conocidas
> aunque no las hayamos visto nunca.
>
> ('Tercera Clase', OPC 224)

In 'Boletín de viaje' (OPC 183-4) Carrera Andrade's first allusions are to the idea of leaving behind an Ecuador which engenders sleepiness in him and causes him pain, both by its restricting effect and by its innate problems. The next stage of the poem's development corresponds to the moment of embarcation, when the poet turns to contemplate the meaning of his journey. Struck by the enormity of it all, he expresses a sense of wonder that a man from Ecuador should be crossing to a distant part of the world:

> embarqué mi baúl de papagayos
> hacia otro extremo de la tierra.

That the stars should seem to communicate to him as though
by means of a language ('el alfabeto de las constelaciones')
again evokes a sense of the transcendental importance of this
occasion for him. The journey becomes an exploration for
the meaning of existence. With the prospect of such a voyage
the poet is filled with optimism, so that he imagines scenes
of swift movement, full of gaiety and youthfulness:

> Giraban gozosos los puertos niños
> en el carrousel del horizonte.

When he thinks of the ship's arrival at its destination his
impatience causes the sea and the distance to appear a barrier. The whole experience is to be the fulfilment of a dream:

> Se amotinaron los mares
> y los cuatro vientos
> contra mi sueño de almirante.

But with the final stage of the poem's development — which
deals with the poet's actual arrival in Europe — comes a
significant change. In a series of impressions, what he singles
out for mention are glimpses of cloud and machinery, and
hints of his concern for the living conditions of the proletariat. The poem in its entirety reflects, therefore, a complex
frame of mind in which the attractions of foreign lands,
while not fading totally into disillusionment, seem over-
whelmed by the first encounter with what are later to become
two of Carrera Andrade's major topics: the plight of the
working class in modern society, and the drawbacks of urban,
mechanised civilisation.

Travel itself is an underlying theme of many poems written during the years of his first departure from Ecuador and
residence in Europe. In this verse the question of drawing
conclusions about the countries concerned does not arise.
What inspires Carrera Andrade in these poems is a sense
of novelty, promise, curiosity, and adventure. Ports are therefore suitable topics, affording new scenes for observation.
A few poems to which these comments may be applied
form part of the collection headed 'Mujeres y puertos' in

Rol de la manzana.[1] 'Campanas del Havre' (ROL 75-6; OPC 209), for example, creates an impression of the sounds and sights of the French port: bells and accordions, ships, sailors, and girls. 'Puerto a las ocho' (ROL 69-70; OPC 206)[2] expresses a sense of the sleepiness of a small port during the hours of darkness, and a certain mysterious quality, glimpsed in the lights moving about on the water. Turning to poems outside that group we find that in 'Canción del continente negro' (OPC 133) Carrera Andrade makes use of travel imagery in order to express a kind of temporal concept: the evening's fading into the darkness of night is translated into terms of a ship's arrival on the shores of the African continent, which gives rise to associated notions of adventure into the unknown. In the final stanza of one of the more important poems of this period, 'Saludo de los puertos', the topic is Carrera Andrade's awareness of his fascination for travel, his role as observer and recorder of new sights in new countries, and his privilege to learn from these experiences. Connected with the prospect of travel are the ideas of good health and spirits, and youthful zest:

> Mi salud canta oyendo los aviones
> de la primavera internacional
> aserrar la madera preciosa del cielo.
> Estoy en la línea de trenes del Oeste
> empleado en el Registro del Mundo,
> anotando en mi ventanilla
> nacimientos y defunciones de horizontes,
> encendiendo en mi pipa las fronteras
> ante la biblioteca de tejados de los pueblos
> y amaestrando el circo de mi sangre
> con el pulso cordial del universo.   (OPC 191)

Feeling as though it were his official function to survey and report, Carrera Andrade seems to derive a sense of delight from the constant changes of the horizon, and contentment from the whole experience (it will be observed that his pipe accompanies him as he acquires knowledge from new places). It is clear that such a convivial impression of the world is

---

[1] This heading does not appear in OPC.
[2] Entitled 'Puerto en la noche' in OPC.

based on an optimistic outlook. In the course of this poem he has made rapid pen-sketches of European places, sending them, like post-cards, to his fellow-countrymen in Ecuador. His intention is to illustrate the point (made in the first stanza) that these sights are both remote from Ecuador and different in their essentially urban character — 'países manu-facturados', he calls them. What he selects as poetic material are, from the point of view of an Ecuadorian of the twenties and thirties, exotic characteristics: Amsterdam with its neat, garden-like appearance, Hamburg bristling with shipyards, Marseille's colourful boats and African contacts, and the great tourist attractions of a Paris of which he had heard and dreamed in Ecuador (the Seine, the Luxembourg Gardens, and the Eiffel Tower). A similar predisposition towards the exotic is revealed in the poem 'Niña de Panamá' (OPC 201), where it is a non-Hispanic aspect of the Central-American city that draws his attention: the negro quarter.

The aura of romance which is closely associated with these attractions of foreign lands sometimes acts, in its own right, as the poet's stimulus. There are, for instance, a few poems about women. Although a name is used once (the poem en-titled 'Klare von Reuter', OPC 208) the woman is usually un-named and seems to be partly, or wholly, imaginary. Woman and love are treated in these poems as though they have in common with travel and foreign lands some idyllic, dreamlike quality, evocative of adventure, novelty, mystery, and joy. They are created as the antithesis of routine and the familiar. Nowhere is this more simply expressed than in the poem 'La Coruña':

> Una novia en La Coruña
> y una casa junto al mar:
> ¿Existe mayor fortuna? (OPC 217)

It will be noticed that the word 'novia' is used in preference to one such as 'esposa', perhaps to suggest a less permanent relationship; and the house is well placed for a quick depar-ture. Another poem, 'Escala' (OPC 204), more emphatically reveals the kind of relationship the poet has in mind. He writes, not of a permanent abode, a haven, or a goal, but of something transient, as is immediately implied by the title. In the first line of the poem a note of romance and adventure is introduced by the use of the epithet 'corsario' applied to the wind. But the main intention of the poet in the ensuing lines is to handle obliquely and delicately the theme of carnal love, which remains as the memory of a night spent close to the Azores. Once more, 'Destino' (OPC 207) illustrates this theme of transitory relationships with women, as though it were part of the general theme of travel. Admittedly there is expressed, in this case, a sweet melancholy at the inevitability of departure (a departure suggested by the constant background of ships' masts) and the end of a period of fertility and domestic life. [3] What is significant, however, is that romance and travel should repeatedly be interrelated in the poetry of these years. [4] New ports, fresh countries, different women — it all amounts to a kind of evasion of monotony and routine. But besides acting as a substitute for fantasy, it is a great exploration and forms part of Carrera Andrade's search for a meaning to his existence. [5]

II.   IMPRESSIONIST SCENES

Although allurement was certainly an important factor, it could not be said that this was by any means the sole aspect of Carrera Andrade's interest in foreign lands expressed in his poetry of the period 1928-1935. It was an extreme manifestation of something more general. He was engaged in 'el Registro del Mundo' — to quote his own words from 'Saludo de los puertos'. Following up his use of the expression in this poem, he made of it the title of a volume which collects most of his verse from the years 1922-1939. He clearly regarded

---

[3] The poem brings to mind Carrera Andrade's affair in Hamburg with the girl he calls 'Marión' and 'la desconocida del Alster' in his autobiography (VC 59-60).

[4] And, in turn, this reflects the poet's growing awareness of the fleeting nature of all experience, later to become a major theme. (See Chapter V, iii.)

[5] Some aspects of the complex interplay of these motives have been recognised by Carrera Andrade himself and admitted in his essays. Thus, he recalls that on one level 'What I longed for above all was "to reconnoitre" the planet I had glimpsed in my reading' ('Poetry of Reality and Utopia', SAP 71), and 'My voyage of discovery of countries and civilizations was a great feast of knowledge' (ibid., SAP 72), while on another level, he reminds us, the poems 'contain ontological perspectives and metaphysical wonder at the marvels of the world' ('Decade of my Poetry', SAP 59).

it, therefore, as an apt summary of his approach to poetry. [6]
What he means to imply by the words is, essentially, that his
poetry explores and takes notes from the whole world of
nature and objects. Since this idea is crucial to an understanding of Carrera Andrade's treatment of foreign lands, it
is worth pursuing by the elucidation of a poem usually taken
to be a major expression of his poetic credo: 'El objeto y su
sombra'. [7] The text of the poem is as follows:

> Arquitectura fiel del mundo.
> Realidad, más cabal que el sueño.
> La abstracción muere en un segundo:
> sólo basta un fruncir de ceño.
>
> Las cosas. O sea la vida.
> Todo el universo es presencia.
> La sombra al objeto prendida
> ¿modifica acaso su esencia?
>
> Limpiad el mundo —ésta es la clave—
> de fantasmas del pensamiento.
> Que el ojo apareje su nave
> para un nuevo descubrimiento.   (OPC 179)

A great deal is made of the supremacy of reality over
dream, of things over shadows, of tangible objects over
abstractions. The reality that may be observed — especially
the physical reality of objects — is not deceptive, not the
shadowy representation of a superior world, not merely a
world of appearances (following the platonic concept), but
may be fully trusted as exact and authentic, as the very
substance of life itself. Let the poet therefore deal with that
reality; let him start from objects (from an empirical basis)
and not from vague concepts and philosophical meditations.
Although it appears *prima facie* that Carrera Andrade is
demanding that objects (reality) should be allowed to stand
bare of abstractions and thoughts, this is not his prime intention and certainly not his practice. Poetry must start with

---

[6] Pedro Salinas entitled his essay 'Registro de J.C.A.' in *Revista Iberoamericana*, vol. V, 1942, pp. 285-94, and René L.-F. Durand studies aspects of the
poet's attitude to the physical world under the sub-heading 'Inventaire du monde'
in his introduction to *Jorge Carrera Andrade*, Editions Seghers, 1966, pp. 30-70.
[7] It is placed at the beginning of PE, and printed in italics, as though it
had such a function.

the observed reality, which is why the poet must travel, observe, and discover new things, but Carrera Andrade takes an object as only a point of departure, a skeleton which he clothes with his thought. Sometimes the observed reality is transformed by metaphors, as was remarked in the last chapter. His poetry is not, therefore, the mere representation of reality, but an utterly personal interpretation of it. In these earlier poems inspired by foreign countries the places, inhabitants, and physical characteristics are regarded as new discoveries of reality, which the poet allows to impinge on his private sensibility. The places observed are not reflected in the poems in their unadorned reality but as Carrera Andrade's own impressions. It is a kind of impressionism. In its application to literature the term does not usually retain the specific features of impressionism in painting. What is meant here is the conveying to the reader of the poet's own impressions of a scene rather than an exact description from which the reader may derive his own impressions. It often happens, however, that Carrera Andrade's scenes capture fleeting moments and omit details, as is generally the case with impressionist painting.

In the sense that the observed world has always prompted poetic responses in Carrera Andrade it may be said that he has written impressionist verse at all periods of his life. But it is more appropriate to confine the use of the term to refer to poetry up to 1935 (*El tiempo manual*). Until this moment the location or scene which inspires the impression is not only the starting-point but remains the focus throughout the poem. With *Biografía para uso de los pájaros* (1937) comes a shift of emphasis, the eternal thoughts, prompted by the reality, now assuming prime importance and dominating the poem. It is, of course, a difference only of degree, and this is why it is argued that Carrera Andrade's interest in foreign lands has always formed part of his preoccupation with a kind of discovery more metaphysical than purely empirical.

A result of this emphasis, in the period up to 1935, on the scene or geographical location itself is that impressions of foreign countries often have a picturesque quality. 'Color de La Habana' (from *El Tiempo manual*, OPC 225-6), longer than most poems of this type, emphatically illustrates the technique. The present tense of the verb is used throughout, as is usual in such poems, since they are not related to a sequence of events, nor do they introduce an awareness of past and future, but allow the reality to be presented as though in a picture before the reader's eyes. We have the sense of things reproduced in their immediacy. It comprises a series of fleeting impressions of various parts of the city. A considerable number of places are actually named and there is abundant mention of local inhabitants and plant-life. The place names and objects evoke responses, conjure ideas, create visual effect, and above all characterise Havana. Never is the place or object simply named: it is always accompanied by an impression or thought. We read, for example, not simply 'Mar', but 'Mar en continuo parpadeo de fosforescencias', and not 'Mujeres', but 'Mujeres de piel de tabaco y de canela'. [8] The objects usually afford Carrera Andrade a pretext for producing imaginative verbal expressions — the metaphors discussed in the preceding chapter — which at best sensitively and succinctly extract the essence from the scene. It is important to note, however, that occasionally a metaphor becomes an end in its own right — ingenious, surprising, even impressive in the way it juxtaposes two contrasting phenomena, but not serving primarily to promote thought. The final lines of the poem illustrate the point:

> Y la luna menguante cuelga como un plátano
> del bananero del cielo.

It would be possible to argue that ideas such as height, darkness, density, and even productivity are insinuated. But it is doubtful whether we are justified in looking this far. The image is created because of the visual similarity between the form of the moon and a banana, and because the banana tree increases the indigenous character of the poem. 'Color de la Habana' operates mainly on this relatively superficial level: the place is the focus of attention; it is evoked in

---

[8] Carrera Andrade's intentions are to introduce associations with the local tobacco crop and to derive a double sense from 'canela': (a) cinnamon, (b) (in Cuba) mulatta — in each case stressing the regional flavour.

picturesque terms; and it affords material from which the poet may construct ingenious metaphors. [9]

Although thoughts on eternal issues exist only in a much diluted form in this poem, there are other poems fundamentally similar in appearance where these ingredients are far more substantial. Three of the group 'Ciudades de la línea' (ROL 117-125) [10] (in which Paita, Havana, Nassau, Saint-Georges, Vigo, La Coruña, Santander, La Pallice, and Guayaquil receive Carrera Andrade's impressionist treatment) derive much of their impact from profound thought. 'La Coruña' ponders over the relation of woman and home to life, travel, and search. 'La Pallice' is about the relativity of each individual place to the world as a whole, every place being at the same time unique and part of a united world. [11] 'La Habana' provides the most intriguing case in view of its comparison and contrast with 'Color de La Habana':

> La Habana cuenta sus frutas
> y planta sus chimeneas,
> inmensas cañas de azúcar.
>
> Emigran los cocoteros.
> Se van el ron y la rumba
> y crecen los rascacielos.   (OPC 216)

In the poem discussed earlier there was but a faint taste of what becomes the central theme here. The sight of proliferating chimneys and sky-scrapers, and the diminishing number of natural elements in the environment, reminds the poet of the changes that are taking place. In face of the impersonal society that is taking over, human gaiety is disappearing. Meanwhile, commercial interests are profiting from the natural products (fruit, sugar). It is a forerunner of the many poems which, subsequently, deal with the incursion of an impersonal, commercialised urban life in the natural order of things, though at this stage, it is worth emphasising,

---

[9] Cf. the discussion on impressions of the countryside in Chapter III, II, and on metaphors in III, III.

[10] Most of these poems are grouped under the heading 'Dibujos de ciudades' in OPC (pp. 213-18).

[11] It is worth noticing how this idea foreshadows Carrera Andrade's later concept of the oneness of the world, such as it is discussed in Chapter VI, III.

the ideas are closely attached to the reality which has inspired them: the basis of this poem is still Havana itself, rather than the abstraction of the theme.

In poems of this period (1928-1935) [12] Carrera Andrade does not show an exclusive interest in any one country or in any one area of the world: Curaçao, Amsterdam, Trinidad, Marseilles, Panama, Paris, the Azores, Barcelona, Paita, an unnamed port in Holland, Havana, Le Havre, Nassau, Vigo, Saint-Georges, La Coruña, New York, Santander, La Pallice, Berlin, Cologne, and the Basque country. Well over half these places are, of course, ports. Travel is a major aspect of the role played by foreign lands, as are new sights, adventure and romance. Foreign countries provide raw material with which the artist may work in the construction of ingenious metaphors, and at the same time they give rise to neat and often penetrating personal impressions, and inspire thoughts on eternal issues.

III.   SOLIDARITY WITH THE EUROPEAN PROLETARIAT

During the years 1928-1933, while he was still writing impressionist poems, Carrera Andrade was profoundly concerned with the plight of the European proletariat. His social awareness and political involvement had already been awakened in Ecuador, and stimulus was added by the experiences he underwent in Europe. He found life hard, particularly at first, when he shared the feelings of the unemployed, sought casual labour, and took a variety of jobs in the desperate need to earn his bread. [13] Rubbing shoulders with Europe's working class, he also underwent the influence of the socialist intellectual environment. These were years of world depression, and of notable political developments when capitalism, communism, fascism and socialism were constantly discussed. The pages of *Latitudes* are full of these issues. Although it could not be said that the pages of Carrera Andrade's verse are also full of them, there are some poems on the subject,

---

[12] *Boletines de mar y tierra* (1930), *Rol de la manzana* (1935), and *El tiempo manual* (1935).
[13] See VC 63 ff.

especially in *El tiempo manual* (1935), a small book whose title alludes to the epoch of the working class masses. [14]

Before turning to this collection it is worth considering again the poem 'Boletín de viaje' (OPC 183-4). As though these were his first impressions of Europe, and as though he expected them to last, Carrera Andrade declares at the sight of smoking chimneys that human gaiety is evaporating in this industrial society. There are signs, he implies, of the proletariat laying claim to its share of the food, and such urgent issues are being raised in all the cities, with a feeling of cooperation. Through witnessing these phenomena Carrera Andrade has made a discovery relating to his own vocation:

> Descubrí al hombre. Entonces
> comprendí mi mensaje.   (OPC 184)

The words imply a sense of duty to mankind: they also allude to his awareness of the common need. In the course of time it becomes a question of solidarity not only with the working class but with the whole of humanity, but in the context of this poem the emphasis is upon his solidarity with the proletariat, and it is this aspect that we take up now.

An uneasy social climate is expressed in oblique terms through the symbol of weather in 'Boletín del mal tiempo' (OPC 164). There are ominous signs; black clouds are building up on the horizon; there will be no more sun; flowers will be struck down; the first rain squalls arrive; the wind sweeps the streets and sends people running for shelter; fires are lit in the refuge of houses; the good weather is completely overcome. But it is not a case of merely guessing or inferring the symbolism of these terms, for each has its counterpart — explicitly named within the poem — in political, social, economic, or military terms. The main equivalents are as follows: clouds/flags, horizon/barricade, sun/money, flowers/monopoly, rain/bayonets, wind/new social order, passersby/bourgeois, shelter of bars/reactionary retreat, fire-place/cockade, dead leaves/ambulance, end of good weather/capitulation. The change in the weather therefore conveys the

---

[14] It is based on a line from Rimbaud; see MVP 20.

idea of a violent proletariat uprising against the capitalist
social order. The poem does not imply the poet's own attitude
to such a solution of problems; it is a dispassionate impression of a current mood, the dramatisation of an idea.

Turning now to the collection *El tiempo manual,* we
notice that the treatment of these themes is on the whole far
less oblique. 'Historia contemporánea' (OPC 229-30) seems at
first to be an impressionist poem like 'Color de La Habana'.
In this case, however, the impressions are all determined by
a particular social point of view. Carrera Andrade looks at a
European city through the eyes of the unemployed and the
working class. The sights that inspire lines in the poem all
allude to the industrial scene, to the growing plight of the
poor and the penniless, and to the increasing threat constituted
by such features. In the first stanza the series of images
creates a sense of imminent disaster. In the next Carrera
Andrade proceeds to find a symbol in the way typewriters,
anvils, and sewing machines beat out the rhythm of a message
with increasing speed. With the likening of a typewriter to a
machine gun the threat to the established order becomes
quite clear. The typewriter represents the use of propaganda
as a weapon to attack the establishment; but it also represents
the machine age and industrial society, in which Carrera
Andrade finds these social conditions prevalent. In the following lines there are impressions of the unemployed gazing
at the sky as though hoping for food and salvation, and of
beggars and vagrants shivering in the cold. Closing the poem,
Carrera Andrade suggests the solidarity of the working class
people who draw comfort from what food they find amid the
squalor of sewers and rubbish tips. An impression of the
suffering and the solidarity spreading throughout the world
brings to a close this grim picture of a European city during
the years of the world depression, where there is no hint of
solace except in the strength that people draw from each
other. Like 'Boletín del mal tiempo' this poem responds to
portents observed by the poet and becomes a portent itself.
Its structure is contrived to produce an intensification of the
effect: at first signs have to be inferred from scenes that are
ostensibly neutral, but later the scenes clearly express their

own austere message. To reinforce the sense of crescendo, Carrera Andrade introduces three moments into the poem: stanza 1 closes with the image of a stone destined to bring about a car accident; stanza 2 ends with the accelerating rhythm of sewing machines; and the whole poem is rounded off with shadows spreading gradually further over the city, the nearby fields, and finally the whole world.

Even more forthright in expressing Carrera Andrade's reaction to the plight of working class people and to what the future holds is the group of five poems collected under the heading 'Poemas de pasado mañana' (OPC 243-6). With its chronological and almost narrative framework the collection becomes a kind of moral tale — an allegory of the progress of industrial societies up to the period of the world depression, and a vision of the future. Throughout the first poem and half of the second the nascent and developing era of civilization seems full of optimism, which is reflected in the way the sound of machines is denoted 'música industrial' and 'risas sin fin'. But there is a sudden transition to the position of overproduction, the absence of markets, and the closing of factories. Poem III observes the marching strikers and the unemployed, while IV is an imaginary speech by a shop steward or a union leader calling for physical action to restore a just order. Casting an imaginary eye at the future, in poem V, Carrera Andrade implies that workers who rise against the order of society will be put to death (an impression reminiscent of the massacre of rebellious Indians in 'Levantamiento'); in a final development, however, the arrival of the international workers' forces brings the triumph of peace. The series of poems thus illustrates how Europe's capitalist society brings hardship to the working class, rebellion, the violent suppression of the rebellion, and finally peace with the victory of the workers united throughout the world. It is all brought to life by the particularisation of events: the poet writes of one factory; he names two workers; he imagines the last moments of one individual facing the firing squad.

Carrera Andrade himself has guided our reaction to the conclusion of poem V in one of his autocritical essays:

> Los profetas de desastres sabían que mañana —un mañana que du-
> raría varios años— los gendarmes de casco de acero pondrían al
> hombre manual e intelectual contra el muro. Pero, pasado maña-
> na . . . . Había que esperar con fervor mesiánico en un mundo me-
> jor. [15]

Totally unexpected, restricted to a mere four lines of verse,
this conclusion is insubstantial and unconvincing. The vision
is made to seem an extremely remote prospect, if not a
fanciful dream; the brighter future is not a probability but
a necessity, as though Carrera Andrade preferred to super-
impose his idealism upon his realism. [16] It may be safely
deduced, however, that although he does not urge rebellion
(and a similar point was made in chapter III concerning his
social protest poetry in the context of Ecuador) he writes in
solidarity with the proletariat and condemns the way industrial society has developed. It is also clear that the poems
may be considered as a warning to society.

Besides illustrating Carrera Andrade's awareness of the
poverty and hunger of an oppressed working class, the poems
discussed in this section give a foretaste of important aspects
of his attitude to highly industrialised foreign countries. They
reveal his wariness of factories and machines, and his distaste
for the ambience of industrial production and capital gains.
They show that picturesque impressions of foreign lands
were, even in this period of his poetry, only one side of his
vision. In fact, they constitute a rather more extensive and
impressive production than those social poems sympathising
with the South-American Indians' cause. Carrera Andrade's
experiences during those first years of exile proved to be a
turning point in his attitude to foreign countries, preparing
the way for the antipathy he was later to express, repeatedly,
for modern industrial civilisation. Since 1933 — the year of
his first return to Ecuador — his poetry has made far less
direct reference to European or other foreign lands; and the
poet's alignment with the proletariat has given way to a far

---

[15] 'Edades de mi poesía', PE 23; EP XVI.
[16] In Canto XIX of 'Hombre planetario' a brighter future for the whole of
the human race is promised; again, the vision does not seem a logical probability
but a remote ideal based on the poet's need to have faith in the future.

broader vision. But this vision has been irrevocably influenced
by those earlier years. [17]

IV.   CITIES AND MANUFACTURED LANDSCAPES

In one of the first poems he wrote from Europe, 'Saludo
de los puertos' (OPC 190-1), Carrera Andrade sends home
greetings to the men of Ecuador, who live close to the land,
from what he denominates 'estos paisajes manufacturados'.
Although at this stage the term is a partly jocular one, the
underlying thought grows in strength until it dominates all
other attitudes to Europe expressed in his verse. The countries
of Europe are seen, essentially, as forming an antithesis to
Ecuador, in that the countryside is dominated by the town,
the natural order by the man-made. Ultimately not only the
landscapes but the countries themselves are manufactured
— in the sense of artificial — and a number of dangers are
found to be inherent in this condition.

So great was Carrera Andrade's disquiet at the course he
believed European industrial society to be following that
he wrote those premonitory or prophetic poems discussed
above. Closing *El tiempo manual,* as if to sum up the characteristics of the civilisation he foresees, is 'Dibujo del hombre' (REG 133-4; EP 155-6). [18] Significantly, while the rest of
the collection focuses on Europe, this poem broadens its
vision to embrace all countries of the world, for Carrera
Andrade recognised that the civilisation developing in European countries was not peculiar to them alone, and that it
would inevitably spread. This poem therefore presents an
impression of man in modern society, partly imaginative in
its predictions of the future, but mainly based on observable

---

[17] Although no poem on the subject of the Spanish Civil War is included in
any of Carrera Andrade's collected verse, he wrote one entitled 'Carta al General
Miaja' which affirms that Phalangist troops would never be allowed by the
Spanish people to enter Madrid (see VC 114). The poem was published in *Nuestra
España. Homenaje de los poetas y artistas ecuatorianos,* Talleres Gráficos Romero,
Editorial "Atahualpa", Quito, 1938 (Enrique Ojeda, *J.C.A.: Introducción...* 'Bi-
bliografía', p. 391). The poet's comparative reticence on this topic — notable when
compared with the verse written by other Spanish Americans such as Vallejo,
Neruda and Nicolás Guillén — is probably explained by two things in particular:
he had begun his diplomatic career in France, political comment thus becoming
difficult; and his proletariat vision was giving way to a broader preoccupation
with the materialistic technological world.

[18] It appears under the heading 'Poemas de pasado mañana' in OPC (pages
247-8).

fact. One outstanding feature of the poem is the environment of modern man: he lives surrounded by stone, picking his way among towers, chimneys, and telegraph poles, returning each day to a sky-scraper. The way in which telegraph poles are obliquely referred to as 'una vegetación eléctrica de avisos' subtly discloses the poet's attitude, for the implication is that they take the place of true vegetation. This poem is the natural development of impressions dating back to Carrera Andrade's first sight of the coast of Europe in 1928: in 'Boletín de viaje' (OPC 183-4), as he records the immediate impact of the scene when the anchor is dropped, he singles out the sight of towers, mechanical cranes, mechanical ploughs, and chimneys. His fundamental impressions of the urban environment have remained unchanged, for what was a partly visionary picture of the 1930s has now become a fact. What has changed — as will be argued later — is his vision of the future. [19]

In surroundings where man-made objects dominate, Carrera Andrade, the admirer of rural environments, naturally longs for escape to the fields. This desire prompts some lines of a poem written more than thirty years after 'Dibujo del hombre': 'Les Halles' (OPC 507-8). Lorries bearing produce from the fields to Paris's central market bring symbols of the countryside and stimulate a yearning for the freshness of 'un mundo enjoyado de rocío'. In the final stanza, moreover, there is a close relation between the poet's vision of the countryside beyond the city boundary and that of the paradise of life after death. The city imprisons as the body imprisons, and, like the body, is transitory, perishable. It is comparable even to death itself.

The imprisoning effect of a city is often likened to that of a cage. By extension, the image of a cage frequently serves to characterise modern civilisation as Carrera Andrade has found it in Europe and the U.S.A. The enclosing of trees and grass within railings is in itself a sight that repels the poet, since it is contrary to the natural order. But it is also symbolic to him of the enclosing of man's natural spirit. In 'Se prohibe

---

[19] See Chapter VI, iii.

andar sobre el césped' the poet accusingly addresses Europe
(which he names), complaining of precisely this imprisoning
effect in images of encircled parks and caged birds:

> Yo conozco tu mundo de parques encarcelados,
> de pajareros que venden
> toda la música del bosque en una jaula   (OPC 433).

Cities are both the product and the expression of this
civilisation, epitomising its more general tendencies. On a
more universal level, when in canto VIII of 'Hombre planetario' Carrera Andrade creates an impression of Woman of
the twentieth century, he includes among her characteristics
those which imprison her self-expression, restrict her spirit,
and treat her emotions as though they were but precious
ornaments. And again the image of a cage appears:

> Cuida su corazón en una jaula
> con flores, hijos, pájaros   (OPC 443).

The crux of the matter is that this society is suppressing
nature, negating the natural order of the universe. In parks
trees are often arranged in rows, and this artificial organisation is reflected in human behaviour: in the way children
are lined up, for instance, in 'Se prohibe andar sobre el césped'. Carrera Andrade dislikes the excessive neatness of
Europe's parkland scenery — as indeed he dislikes the landscape of Japan [20] — because it reflects the imposition of man's
will on the natural order. In particular he is averse to the
way it sometimes impinges on human activity; when it entails
the repression of an instinctive need. A sign that prohibits
encroachment on the grass in parks is an affront to mankind
since it prevents his contact with nature and symbolises the
negation of his inherent inclination. Also, as 'Se prohibe andar
sobre el césped' implies, such a sign discourages men from
paying attention to spiritual things. It is, the poem suggests,
a kind of intrusion that threatens to penetrate to the very
working of the mind, for the prohibition of walking on the
grass prevents contemplation of the stars and meditation on

---

[20] See 'Poetry of Reality and Utopia', SAP 73.

the mysteries of the universe. [21] In this condition civilisation is denying itself the essential requirements for life, and in consequence it is decaying. Europe is compared in this poem to a withering tree:

> Castaño europeo: tiéndeme tu mano amarillenta
> que se desprende y vuela para morir.   (OPC 433)

The predominance of an order imposed by man over the natural order is reflected in the machinery found in all facets of daily life in European countries and, of course, also in others (such as the U.S.A.) with an equally advanced development. The presence of machinery everywhere is another illustration of the idea that the countries themselves may be considered essentially manufactured. According to the impression of modern (or future) man in 'Dibujo del hombre' (1935) machines have a similar function to chimneys and skyscrapers in constructing an artificial environment. He is 'amaestrador de máquinas', travels in trains and aeroplanes, and lives in cities that are surrounded by railway lines (OPC 247-8). Twenty-five years later, while exposing in 'Hombre planetario' his opinion of the ailments and evils of the modern age, Carrera Andrade again draws attention to the omnipresence of machines. Whereas the Eve of the Garden of Eden walked naked, Woman of the twentieth century wears the hide of a serpent (converted into a garment by a machine), and 'acude al paraíso en automóvil' (PU 90). Her home is occupied by a telephone, washing machine, television, and refrigerator. In order to stress the fundamentally artificial condition of life surrounded by such man-made objects, Carrera Andrade here constructs each image on oxymoron, contrasting a machine with an aspect of nature in each case:

> ... paraíso privado con teléfono,
> máquina de lavar hojas de parra,
> televisión azul como la luna
> y refrigeradora con manzanas.   (OPC 443-4)

---

[21] Thoughts akin to these, but directly inspired by a setting in the U.S.A., are found in 'Señas del Parque Sutro' (OPC 338-9). The final stanza focuses on the restricting effect of notices and rules for behaviour in San Francisco's park. A deep paradox is suggested; the place is a prison, yet men should be allowed to walk there freely; the signs forbidding the throwing of peel or the climbing of trees prohibit free expression and contact with nature.

Mechanised forms of transport have not always aroused antipathy in him. In 'Saludo de los puertos' (1930, OPC 190-1) the sound of aeroplanes, associated with ideas of adventure, novelty, exploration, and the discovery of new countries, inspires in him a sense of vigour and well-being: 'Mi salud canta', he can write. And he is quite content to sit in a train observing the changing scenes from his window, as is clear from 'III clase' (OPC 223-4). But a lifetime of travel and a deepened preoccupation with man's loss of his natural ways has completely changed this outlook, so that in 'El pasajero del avión' (1966, OPC 521-2) modern forms of transport are found to be so rapid that they prevent contact with the fields, the trees, and the men who work on the land. Aeroplanes bear man constantly from city to city until his mind is set in a whirl. Such mechanised transport does not, moreover, afford the opportunity for using one's initiative; there is no sense of exploration, since all is organised.

Despite the predominant sense of impending disaster in the poems of *El tiempo manual*, there are occasional expressions of hope. 'Evasión del lunes' (OPC 227-8) indicates the positive aspects of life in the countries of Europe, aspects that men should heed and develop. This message is achieved by the method of contrasting apparently necessary evils with the underlying potential of good, of contrasting the world that fills the pages of newspapers such as *A.B.C., Le Journal, Nachtausgabe,* and *The Times* with the world of nature. The society observed by the poet seems steeped in words, and authentic life is submerged in a sea of methods, systems, and doctrines, all of which constitute another expression of the tendency for such a society to impose an artificial order on things, comparable with the way the city parks imprison nature. Carrera Andrade therefore urges contemporary man to look beyond and to see the pleasures of natural beauty, the delights of satisfying natural appetites, the satisfaction derived from the intense experiences of the senses. At the expense of a world shrouded in propaganda he asserts the value of the elemental world:

> Hay algo más que métodos, sistemas y doctrinas:
> el aire libre, la luz libre, el agua libre,

el perfil de la voz calculado por el eco,
el alzamiento de los vegetales contra la Economía Política.

(OPC 228)

In this poem hope appears almost within men's grasp, for Carrera Andrade complains that they receive a false impression of the world; the true impression is full of promise. Even cities are in reality places with pleasure and natural beauty, where there is an opportunity for the delight of the senses: 'la verdadera fisonomía de las ciudades / llenas de cines, frutas y mujeres' (OPC 227). The problem is to perceive all this. Later, however, the hope becomes far more remote, for the poet's concept of what is a true and what is a false impression changes. In fact, the false picture outlined in this poem becomes the true image of modern civilisation. Nowhere is this more powerfully expressed than in cantos IX, X, and XII of 'Hombre planetario'. Men live in an artificial, indoor environment, indulging in petty activities, and suffering from an ill-disguised sense of tedium derived from a loss of natural values and full experience. Plants have become mere decorations; a rubber plant breathes in cigarette smoke, and, amid their total indifference, a dove is run over by a car. The beauty of a sunset is unnoticed. The change in the environment of men from natural to artificial has its counterpart in human behaviour, where truth has been conquered by falsehood. Lying and deceit are commonplace. The senses are dulled, for the use of vitamins (and perhaps, by implication, the taking of drugs) has grown out of hand. Wealth having taken over as one of the supreme ambitions of life, every commodity has its commercial value. The height of distortion is to apply a price to things of the natural world. In 'Se prohibe andar sobre el césped' (OPC 433) we find the idea of having to pay for the delights of natural beauty expressed through the image of buying a caged bird. In 'Museo universal' (OPC 391-3) an entrance fee is required before one may see artistic representations of eternal themes of life and death (i.e. paintings) on display in the Louvre; it means that the floor, the chairs, the very air have been attributed a commercial value: flowers, fish, music, and the dew all have to be bought. And returning to 'Hombre planetario', we read in canto X of the avarice and deceit of men being so great that human emotion, relationships between people, and even spiritual things — 'la amistad, el amor, el cielo mismo' — are used for bargaining in the acquisition of wealth (OPC 444-5).

In several of the poems that express these views on modern civilisation Carrera Andrade actually names Europe, or a European country, city, or institution. There is no doubt, moreover, that in many other poems Europe is the place implied, or the source of Carrera Andrade's thoughts. There is little specific mention of other technologically advanced countries. The Japan known personally to Carrera Andrade was pre-war; its influence on him was of a kind more closely connected with the feeling of solitude and the notion of the transitoriness of earthly things. (And even so, there is virtually no naming of Japan in any poem.) [22] Although it is clear from his correspondence and his prose works that the U.S.A. produced impressions of the kind under discussion in this section it is rare for any mention of the U.S.A. in this light to occur within the poems themselves.

It would be wrong, however, to attribute excessive importance to Carrera Andrade's apparent concentration on the evils of Europe, and his apparent indifference to similar evils elsewhere. Writing empirically, he is bound to base his impressions on the places where he spent the bulk of his life since 1928. In a recent essay, 'Decade of my poetry', he makes it clear that wherever the origins of his impression lay, in the course of time he has recognised the universality of the characteristics: 'Since 1960 I have visited the United States, Chile, Brazil, Venezuela, Nicaragua, France, Belgium, and Holland. Everywhere I came upon the palaces of Babylonian proportions and labyrinths of traffic which characterise our era. They are the same in Paris as in New York, in Santiago and in Brussels, in the Hague and Rio de Janeiro; they proclaim the presence of a civilization based on economic foundations with the object of increasing the physical well-being of the greatest number of men'. [23] What his poetry does — and in this respect its emphasis differs from that of

---

[22] 'Islas niponas' (OPC 501-2) is the exception.
[23] SAP 61.

his prose — is to create a general impression of the civilisation of the economically and technologically advanced countries of the world in order to epitomise the condition of mankind in the twentieth century. The empirical basis of his ideas — which has been formed in specific countries — develops into a process of generalisation.

There is no intimation in his verse of the practical, intimate, and slightly mundane issues of his life, such as the reasons why he should continue to live in countries whose type of civilisation he finds distasteful (his diplomatic career, his preference for a superior cultural environment, the better facilities for writing, the amenities, and the family needs). In his poetic vision such matters become submerged in a general state of ontological disquiet and a process of enquiry. Intent on transcending purely private experience, Carrera Andrade gives sensitive expression to the mood of our present age.

PART II

A QUEST FOR MEANING

V

ONTOLOGICAL PROBLEMS

I. SOLITUDE

T w o fundamental aspects of Carrera Andrade's life have been taken as points of departure for the study of his poetic themes: his complex relationship with Ecuador, and his travel abroad. As we have seen, they are major themes in their own right. But it is now hoped to show that, more significantly, these two topics, closely associated with the poet's private experience, have an inherent connection with his metaphysical thought.

Broadly speaking a distinction may be made between the growth of the poet's anguish and the formulation of solutions to his problems. It is not pretended that there is any neat progress from one to the other; they have always existed side-by-side. On the other hand, it is certainly clear that there have been phases in the poet's life when anguish has outweighed other issues, and others when the solutions have held considerable promise.

Writing in 1942, Pedro Salinas was able to detect in Carrera Andrade's latest books waves of doubt and mystery which threatened his earlier world of observation. [1] Carrera Andrade himself has drawn attention to the way his poetry of the late 1930s became increasingly introspective. [2] For a period of some twenty years there were only glimmers of light in a dark poetic world. Though he posed many questions, he found few answers. It is notable that the general development of his treatment of foreign countries loosely coincides with this process of introspection. In Chapter IV it

---

[1] 'Registro de J.C.A.', *Revista Iberoamericana*, vol. V, No. 10, 1942, p. 293.
[2] 'Edades de mi poesía', PE 25; EP XIX; see also MVP 23.

was observed how, on his first departure from his homeland, foreign countries lured him and offered him opportunities to discover new things. Travel was initially one expression of his search for meaning, holding the promise of possible answers. Then came a growing sense of alienation in the great cities of those countries, and his dislike of their artificial way of life; and this was accompanied by a steadily intensifying solitude and awareness of the transitory nature of all things. Not only has the search for meaning run parallel to his life of exile, but it has actually been intensified by that exile. Failing to produce the answers it had promised, travel helped to strengthen the existing ontological problems.

William F. Heald, in his article 'Soledad in the poetry of Jorge Carrera Andrade' sees the poet's preoccupation with solitude and isolation as being characterised by 'a curiously mild regret at the human predicament, and, at the same time, a calm, resigned optimism'. [3] It is difficult to agree with the emphasis of such an assessment. Far from provoking a mild or optimistic reaction, solitude is a fundamental aspect of the poet's ontological anguish. Of the various factors contributing to this feeling of solitude one of the most significant has been the influence of life in the large industrial cities of Europe and the U.S.A. The poet himself has recognised this: 'En Berlín, París, Londres y Nueva York se fue acentuando mi convencimiento de ... la victoria irremediable de la soledad'. [4]

'Soledad' is a generic term by which Carrera Andrade denotes various shades of experience. On the level of private feeling it may refer to regret at the absence of company and the need for somebody or something to fill a void (an ex-

---

[3] William F. Heald, 'Soledad in the poetry of J.C.A.', P.M.L.A., LXXVI, 1961, p. 608. He admits that Carrera Andrade's later poetry 'shares with other literary efforts of our time the anguished conviction that solitude is the ultimate reality of man's existence'; he perceives that solitude derives from the poet's awareness of man's alienation from nature, his purposelessness, and his isolation from other men; but he believes that the poet's discovery of partial solutions attenuates the anguish; the solitude is, therefore, 'not dominated...... by a sense of despair and frustration' (ibid.).

[4] MVP 19-20. Carrera Andrade knew Berlin in 1928 and Paris in 1929; he visited New York in 1938; his first recorded sight of London was in 1947. It is evident from this lapse of twenty years that he is implying a gradual cumulative effect rather than a sudden impression.

perience which in English is known as 'loneliness'). [5] In 'El extranjero' he writes:

> Entre rostros cambiantes y edificios que
> crecen busco la salvadora compañía.   (OPC 266)

The very fact of living in foreign countries, constantly on the move, unknown by the local people, ignorant of local customs, and, above all, speaking a different language induces this loneliness in Carrera Andrade. As a foreigner and a stranger he encounters acutely that basic problem of the individual's lack of contact and communication with other people and consequent isolation: '... su sentido pierden los terrestres idiomas', 'Ni un gesto de amistad...', '... vadeando soledades como ríos, / la muda geografía del planeta atravieso' (ibid.). The hostility he senses around him is seen as a characteristic of his physical surroundings; these, it will be noticed, are essentially urban: 'Extensiones de plantas y ciudades', 'edificios que crecen' (ibid.) and the threat that they hold is implicit in the fact that they are spreading.

His personal loneliness finds echoes in the other people he observes. Thus, in 'Soledad de las ciudades' images of loneliness are a bricklayer on a scaffold, remote, singing as though to compensate for his isolation; a traveller whose newspaper is a substitute for a companion; and a waiter who, separated from people dear to him, keeps their photograph in his inside pocket, close to his heart (OPC 221).

The term 'soledad' in Carrera Andrade's poetry tends to extend its sense beyond that of mere loneliness to embrace the idea of isolation from all other matter, and ultimately to include those of abandonment and orphanhood. ('Solitude' becomes a more apt expression in English.) There is a tendency to see other people not as individuals but as faceless crowds. The environment becomes dehumanised, consisting of inanimate things such as walls, streets, buildings, and machines: the perpetual environment of the city dweller. In this way it even seems as though the very substance of the

---

[5] The *Diccionario de la lengua española*, Decimoctava edición, Espasa Calpe, Madrid 1956, offers the following among its definitions: 1. 'Carencia voluntaria o involuntaria de compañía.... 3. Pesar y melancolía que se sienten por la ausencia, muerte o pérdida de alguna persona o cosa." (p. 1211).

surroundings has a solitary character. Carrera Andrade's solitude is therefore composed of the things that constantly surround him and form part of the daily routine, as in these lines of 'Soledad de las ciudades':

> Esta soledad es nutrida de libros,
> de paseos, de pianos y pedazos de muchedumbres,
> de ciudades y cielos conquistados por la máquina.
>
> (REG 109; OPC 222)

Everywhere he turns he sees, not things themselves, but representations of solitude — 'la soledad multiplicada'. Amid these isolating features of the city, the countryside offers a vision of solace. There, he imagines, lies at least part of the answer, for there man may commune with nature; peasants are less lonely than city dwellers since they are at one with and a part of the earth ('forman una misma cosa con la tierra'). It transpires that, as his experience in large industrial cities increases, the appeal of his own basically rural homeland becomes stronger, with the repercussions that were examined in Chapter III.

One of the reasons why cities make solitude more acute is that they have a dominating, imprisoning effect. For Carrera Andrade solitude is often associated with concepts, not of vast expanses (except in the context of the sea, as will be observed below), but of confined spaces between walls. He finds himself 'cercado de murallas y de límites' in 'Soledad de las ciudades', and captured in the city's 'red de piedra' in the first canto of 'Hombre planetario' (OPC 439). This latter poem illustrates well the way a city becomes a kind of maze in which the poet gropes vainly for a means of escape:

> Camino, mas no avanzo.
> Mispasos me conducen a la nada ...   (Canto II, OPC 440)

Bewildered and perplexed, he not only feels lost, but loses his grasp of a sense of order: 'No hay norte ni sur, este ni oeste' ('Soledad de las ciudades' — OPC 221). He vainly seeks to find his own place in the order of things. As though his name no longer represented an explanation of his identity, and in order to de-personalise himself, he introduces the idea of being a mere number by giving a new use to an idiomatic expression: 'Sin conocer mi número' (ibid.). He sees himself from outside his body, featureless and anonymous: 'el personaje adusto / con un gabán de viento que atraviesa / el teatro de la calle' ('Hombre planetario', I — OPC 439). In the opening of 'Hombre planetario' he can get no nearer to discovering his identity than perceiving himself as a figure in a city street, going through life as though he were acting in a play. Only when he introduces notions of the natural life as it is found in the countryside is he able to discover his identity. Solitude as it is experienced in the city therefore includes, together with the sense of isolation from other people, a metaphysical notion, an anguish arising from an acute awareness of his loss of identity, and of his separation from the natural order of things.

Although his solitude has its direct origin in the influence of cities and in the sense of being a foreigner, many of his poems make no allusion to these sources. In 'Soledad y gaviota' (OPC 277), for example, the idea of isolation is strongly conveyed through the image of the sea. Even here, however, it will be noticed that his exile in foreign lands, remote from the comforting influence of Ecuador, is indirectly associated with the image. The vast expanse conjures a sense of separation (from an unnamed aspiration) by great distance; at the same time it introduces the suggestion of travel that seems possible yet is denied. Although the seagull presents a solitary figure against the background of the surrounding sea, it can at least fly into the free spaces. This pictorial representation of the poet's solitude, stark in its features, forcefully and clearly communicates its idea; an emotional ingredient, added in the last four lines, closes the poem on a note of pathos, besides indicating that for Carrera Andrade this solitude is not merely an intellectual concept but also an emotional experience, dampening the spirit and inflicting pain as though it were a weapon used against him:

> y mirando y oyendo
> sólo la lluvia armada
> la soledad batiendo
> con su líquida espada. (OPC 277)

Ultimately the poems transcend the specific context of Carrera Andrade's private life to give voice to the view that solitude is an inherent feature of the human condition, the common denominator of human experience. One of the earliest expressions of this idea occurs in 'III clase' (OPC 223-4). After evoking impressions of fleeting scenes observed from a railway carriage — predominantly proletariat and city scenes, it is important to notice — Carrera Andrade comes to the conclusion that people everywhere share 'la misma soledad hospedada en los huesos'. [6] The poem 'Soledad habitada' (OPC 286) contrives to demonstrate that not only human beings but all the creatures of the planet are solitary, from the inhabitants of the sea and sky to those of the land. Man therefore follows the pattern of all nature. In the line 'soledad despoblada, soledad habitada' lies the crux of the problem, which is given emphasis by the use of the antitheton: solitude is like a country — 'única patria humana' — with inhabitants, yet without people; that is, inhabitants who live in isolation as though the land were unpopulated. It is manifested in the things around, it penetrates to every place, and, like a trap or net, allows nobody to escape it. Solitude is the essence of life on earth; in fact, it is the earth itself, for the earth confines its inhabitants, isolates them, reduces them to vain attempts to escape their terrestrial state. [7] Man, as though he were gnawing at a net that holds him fast, aspires to reach the state of spirit, to attain an eternal quality:

> En tu red prisioneros para siempre
> roemos el azul de la infinita malla.   (OPC 286)

The earthly state of solitude is, however, inescapable, for it is an adjunct of man's confinement within a body. Man has a vegetable quality: like plants he must grow and wither within a physical form. Apart from death itself there is no

---

[6] At this stage of his development — that of *El tiempo manual* (1935) — people are also found to share 'la misma afirmación proletaria', though this is an aspect which diminishes in importance in the later poetry, while the sense of common solitude and the idea of universal fellowship increase.

[7] Compare Carrera Andrade's own words: 'La soledad es ciertamente la desembocadura final de nuestro planeta. Es igualmente la materia prima de que están hechas todas las cosas. Es madre de los elementos y de las formas efímeras. El río es una soledad de agua. El viento, una soledad errante en el espacio. Todo es una afirmación de la gran soledad de la tierra' ('Edades de mi poesía, PE 26).

end to his solitude. Hence, in 'Dolor vegetal' Carrera Andrade writes:

> En mi bosque sentía andar las nubes,
> los senderos buscaban compañía
> cerca de un manantial inconsolable
> llorando soledad, agua infinita.   (OPC 498)

Since solitude is all men's condition, all are doomed to suffer melancholy. In 'De nada sirve la isla' (OPC 346-7) a day of recreation, joyful though it may be, is merely a temporary repression of the basic state which inevitably returns, thus removing all meaning and purpose from the gaiety. Men are therefore 'hombres grises, / uniformados de soledad'. The day is an island surrounded by a sea of solitude, an image that serves to remind us that the concept has its origins in Carrera Andrade's personal experiences of travel in foreign lands.

In several of his youthful poems, written before he first left his homeland, Carrera Andrade is able to contemplate solitude in far less anguished terms than those discussed in these pages. Solitude, whether chosen or enforced, is capable of exerting a constructive as well as a destructive influence, and there is evidence that solitary walks in the countryside and hours spent alone in his room have been capable of inducing a mood of meditation and of providing actual inspiration for his verse. Thus, Ecuador, with its provincial character, is the place 'donde halla el solitario su estrella más florida' ('Provincia' — OPC 31); in the countryside,

> ... los sauces me convencen
> en el solitario paseo
> de que hay un placer dulce y fino
> en dar el corazón al viento.
>
>   ('Los amigos del paseo' — OPC 45)

While, indoors, the 'objetos amigos' communicate to the poet with their 'canto solitario' ('El canto diminuto' — REG 13; EP 7).[8] It is beyond question that his persistent sense of

---

[8] The findings of William F. Heald, in his article 'Soledad ......', loc. cit., are certainly applicable to this phase. This poem is omitted from OPC.

solitude has been an important factor throughout his life not only in the production of his poetry but in the discovery of solutions to his ontological enquiry. This fact does not find expression, however, within the verse itself. Except in some of his early verse, solitude as a poetic theme represents a negative force against which man pits himself: a painful sense of loneliness, abandonment, and imprisonment, inducing a mood of profound melancholy. [9]

II. THE ANGUISH OF MODERN MAN

It was remarked previously that Carrera Andrade associates his mother with childhood, home, Ecuador, and a state of proximity to nature. [10] Her loss is therefore the loss of an age of innocence. In place of that age the poet finds one of machines and distortion, in which he experiences the conditions common to all men in advanced technological civilisations. The idea of Carrera Andrade's own progress from childhood to adulthood serves as a model for his concept of the course taken in the history of mankind. Man too has lost his innocence, and suffers in consequence.

'Juan sin Cielo' (OPC 329-30) deals clearly with this theme, a note of poignancy being struck by the device of permitting modern man himself to speak, as though he were an individual. The choice of the name Juan — 'Juan Todos', 'Juan Cordero' — indicates his humble identity, his representation of common man. Juan recalls a time when he lived in peace, in contact with nature, and in spiritual harmony (stanzas 3-5). Now this state of original innocence, this life of paradise, has been destroyed by evil forces (hunters of angels, executioners of swans), and in its place has emerged a system of money-seeking, of falsehood, 'humo, nada ...'. Juan, now feeling a prisoner, whereas before he was free, laments the loss of the

---

[9] In her book *La soledad y la poesía española contemporánea*, Ed. Insula, Madrid, 1962, Birute Ciplijauskaite argues that the Romantic poets regarded their solitude as a privilege (pp. 12-13), that Kirkegaard looked for solitude since it was the only way in which man could come into contact with God (p. 13), and that certain Spanish poets of the twentieth century (particularly Unamuno and Juan Ramón Jiménez) sought solitude, at least during part of their career, as a means toward solving their ontological problems (pp. 72 and 105). Little of this kind of attitude is expressed in the verse of the mature Carrera Andrade.
[10] See chapter III, VIII.

past. Modern man is dispossessed of his previous spiritual treasures and, an insignificant creature, is abandoned in a hostile universe: 'perdí la altura', '¡un tesoro de siglos he perdido!', 'Juan es mi nombre, Juan Desposeído', 'Soy Juan y nada más, el desolado / herido universal, soy Juan sin Cielo' (OPC 330).

The connection between Carrera Andrade's vision of man in the twentieth century and his view of highly developed, industrialised countries, particularly of Europe, is even more patent in 'Los terrícolas' (OPC 385-6). Tuning in to the terminology of the Space Age, he contemplates the planet Earth and its civilisation from the imaginary point of view of an extra-terrestrial being. As in 'Dibujo del hombre' (OPC 247-8) and other poems discussed in Chapter IV, money, machines, and cities predominate. The inhabitants of the planet are no longer recognisable as simply men: they are denominated 'terrícolas'. One of the devices from which the poem derives strongest effect is the deliberate omission of any redeeming feature in this civilisation; in fact, rather than evoke an impression of what there actually *is*, Carrera Andrade concentrates on building up an impressive list of what is lacking: springs of water, sunlight, appreciation of flowers, the open sky, music, swans, [11] etc. In this cataclysmic vision mankind exists with his thirst unquenched, and in darkness.

Both 'Juan sin Cielo' and 'Los terrícolas' contain the idea of man's loftier aspirations having succumbed to his baser instincts. They both express the point by contrasting two types of being: in the first poem the peaceful, humble man of the fields is conquered by an aggressive army; similarly, in the second poem true human beings are being overrun by dehumanised creatures:

> El planeta contempla la agonía
> de los últimos hombres
> acosados sin fin por los terrícolas ... (OPC 386)

---

[11] It is possible that in his allusion to 'el mundial degüello de los cisnes' he is deliberately putting to a new use the old *modernista* image of the swan and recalling the metaphorical expression 'Tuércele el cuello al cisne de engañoso plumaje' with which Enrique González Martínez helped to mark the end of the *modernista* epoch.

In one of Carrera Andrade's neatest poems, 'El condenado' (OPC 434), the point is expressed with greater subtlety, with the result that the complexity of the conflicting forces inside each man is more vividly shown. The 'yo' of this poem is assumed to be the condemned man referred to in the title who, as he is led to face a firing squad, pleads his innocence of any offence and begs for mercy. In the first eight lines of the poem it is inferred that the charges made against him concern the instigation of acts of violence and destruction against natural beauty and the natural sources of daily living. It is as though such deeds had given rise to a bloody revolution. The condemned man pleads that he has been an upholder of the very things he is accused of destroying (natural life, love, etc.). But one thing that prevents the poem from concerning simply a miscarriage of justice is the anonymous firing squad. The reader is at pains to decide who they represent. At first, it appears that they are defenders of beauty and natural life; but later, if the condemned man is what he claims to be, the executioners must be seen as forces of violence and injustice. More significant still is the deliberate ambiguity over the condemned man's identity, a complexity most powerfully introduced by the line: 'Yo no soy yo'. What the words mean is that to disclaim responsibility for the acts referred to in the first eight lines is to deny his own identity. As a human being he shares the guilt of all men. His executioners are therefore acting quite in order ('verdugos inocentes'). All men, however, also partake of his ideals ('soy la parte más noble de vosotros'); his executioners are thus putting to death a part of themselves, and in this sense they too are victims ('al mismo tiempo víctimas'). The condemned man is both innocent and guilty, a giver and a destroyer of life; he is both himself and a part of the other men. Similarly, the executioners themselves are both evil and just, both castigators and victims. From this impression of the inner turmoil of modern man emerges a dominant idea: his baser nature is suppressing his nobler character. The probable allusion to Christian precepts should not be ignored. The protagonist of this poem takes on the guilt of the world, seeks only to bring life to men, and is executed by the men he wishes to save, men who thereby destroy a part of themselves.

One result of modern man's loss of innocence and destruction of the natural order of the world is his inability to comprehend the meaning of his existence. Carrera Andrade expresses this notion both as a result of his personal anguish and in order to act as a spokesman for his age. In 'De nada sirve la isla' no purpose is found for any aspect of human life. Things that are beautiful and give pleasure, whether organic nature (like the rose) or the mineral world (like precious stones) or abstract things (like music or merriment) are of no avail ('de nada sirven') in face of an overwhelming absurdity, an absence of explanation for ontological problems:

> porque el cielo guarda un obstinado silencio.   (OPC 346)

Incomprehension of the workings of the universe also underlies the first half of 'Nada nos pertenece', giving rise to the bewilderment in the lines:

> Nadie sabe por qué existen los pájaros
> ni tu tonel de vino, luna llena,
> ni la amapola que se quema viva,
> ni la mujer del arpa, dichosa prisionera.   (OPC 284)

Carrera Andrade emphasises the paradox of the situation: all those things that he names here are suggestive of fullness and richness. Such things might be expected to contain an explanation for human life, but, like the beautiful objects named in 'De nada sirve la isla', they fail to overcome the ultimate lack of meaning for existence on this earth. Only at night is some sign available to the poet. But even now, despite the hopeful note struck by the line 'Entonces hablas, Cielo', he does not receive the answer that will justify the act of living:

> Tu alta ciudad nocturna se ilumina.
> Tu muchedumbre con antorchas pasa
> y en silencio nos mira.   (OPC 285)

There is a deliberate contrast between 'hablas' and 'en silencio', between the expectation and the actual message. This

advent of the night, with its visual suggestion of the vastness
of the cosmos, and of eyes that look down on man from the
mysterious and menacing darkness, provokes thoughts of
death. Man's inexorable death is the only answer given, an
answer that merely serves to reinforce the poet's earlier lack
of understanding. He now recognises death as a fundamental
law of human existence, but his search for meaning remains
unanswered.

Man is therefore denied that which he most needs: an
explanatory message. 'No hay' expresses this negation through
a series of repeated images based on the notion that meaning
is normally to be discovered in words either printed in books
or spoken from the lips. But by use of auxesis Carrera Andrade categorically denies the existence of any communication of this kind:

> En las librerías no hay libros,
> en los libros no hay palabras,
> en las palabras no hay esencia:
> hay sólo cáscaras.   (OPC 500)

And as for the hope for a spoken message:

> En las bocas hay sólo humo.   (ibid.)

The world, deprived of this meaning, is a wasteland from
which nothing frees man. It is important to notice the use
here of the images 'Sahara' and 'desierto': exile too is represented by such images, for, as will be shown later, exile is
a condition which underlines the poet's lack of meaning. [12]

In the confused state of mind arising out of a loss of all
that gave meaning and order to his existence, Carrera Andrade sometimes reaches the point of no longer recognising
in himself the man he once assumed he was. He loses confidence in signs that once may have indicated his identity.
Something of this grappling with conflicting notions of
identity is glimpsed in 'El condenado'. But the problem is
dealt with more explicitly and at far greater length in 'Hombre planetario', for this poem takes as its point of departure

---

[12] See chapter VII.

that loss of identity of Carrera Andrade (and modern man). Repeatedly, in cantos I, II and IV the poet is prompted, as though by the sight of his reflection in the river under a bridge and in the shop windows, to question the connection between himself and what he sees: '¿Soy ese hombre...?' (OPC 439); '¿Soy esa sombra sola...?' (OPC 440) (with the alliteration effectively hissing out his distaste). He is detached from the image of himself, surprised and dismayed that it does not immediately convey something meaningful. All he sees are the external appearances, the anonymous shape and impersonal clothes:

> ... el personaje adusto
> con un gabán de viento... (OPC 439)

Having weighed up his life, in canto II, and found no progress, no goal, no achievements, no gain of any kind, he is reduced to wondering, in canto IV, whether his condition as a human being is nothing more than the sum of his external features, epitomised as face, name, and body — merely a being with the same level of existence as a vegetable:

> ¿Soy sólo un rostro, un nombre
> un mecanismo oscuro y misterioso
> que responde a la planta y al lucero? (OPC 441)

In the course of 'Hombre planetario' an answer is discovered to such questions as this; but many poems express only the problem. 'Imagen entera' (OPC 528), for example, reveals Carrera Andrade again in the process of self-assessment, and again concluding that he has been living more as a body than as a mind, living as though he were an object or a plant, controlled by external forces. The impression with which the poem ends, movingly, is of a man imprisoned within his bodily condition, doomed to solitude, and led to even greater anguish by the awareness of his condition.

If escape from this position were possible Carrera Andrade would have discovered the solution to his problems. In the next chapter it will be suggested that among the solutions tried by the poet is that of escape — escape, that is, from an urban environment, from the technological world, and even

from his corporal condition. [13] Although there is no doubt
that some of his posited solutions are successful, at least
occasionally, in comforting him, the idea of evasion and flight
amounts to a half-measure. However profoundly cherished,
the idea seems ultimately improbable to him, as several
poems suggest. 'Presagios', for example, neatly and emphatically sums up the contradiction of the idyllic dream by
the ominous signs. Through the four stanzas Carrera Andrade
seeks to affirm that the future will consist of a perfect existence in the midst of nature: house, cornfield, river, gardens
of flowers and vegetables — all of which may be interpreted
as both a yearning for withdrawal from urban life and the
need to believe in eternal life. In either case, however, the
vision is negated: the second half of each stanza contains,
within brackets (as though the message were intruding in a
whisper) warnings of disaster, reaching a climax in the total
hopelessness of the last lines of the poem:

> En la tierra de minas de esmeraldas
> tendremos una huerta de legumbres.
> (Ni casa ni sembrado, nada, nada:
> está escrito en la forma de las nubes)   (OPC 427)

It is worth noticing, finally, how Ecuador is connected with
the idyllic vision in this poem (the characteristics of the
topography and vegetation). In the poems discussed above
the ontological problems of solitude and anguish tend to be
associated with urban life and modern civilisation, which he
finds in foreign lands.

III.   TRANSITORY LIFE

For Carrera Andrade life is characterized, therefore, by a
sense of solitude, an incomprehension, an anguished sense
of lost spiritual well-being, and a loss of identity. One of his
supreme problems, however, is the knowledge that life itself
does not last. This awareness of the transitory nature of
human existence, and indeed of all things on this earth, has
been a major theme for him since the 1930s. Whenever

---

[13] See chapter VI, I.

writing about the first years of exile in Europe and the later
period in Japan, in his own surveys of his poetry, he consistently recalls these preoccupations: 'la certidumbre de la
muerte, la fragilidad de la morada humana, el sentimiento
de que todo pasa y seguirá pasando eternamente'; [14] 'el sentimiento de la fragilidad de las cosas' and 'la fragilidad de
las obras humanas'; [15] 'I thought about how rapidly the world
was changing and that very soon nothing of the past would
remain except dust'. [16]

The sources of this deeply-felt problem are both the
objects of the world around him and his own body. Ultimately the two will be seen as simply different manifestations
of a universal law; but since Carrera Andrade's emphasis
varies from poem to poem it is proposed now to begin with
an examination of his concern for the external signs and to
work towards his treatment of the theme in relation to the
individual.

Exploring the world and discovering objects, Carrera Andrade was gradually struck by the flimsiness of things he
observed — by the fragile human dwellings at the mercy of
mighty elemental forces in Japan, for example. [17] His verse
reflects a view of the world according to which everything
is crumbling, decaying, ageing, withering, drying up, being
consumed in fire, and turning to dust. Two typical poems,
from the late 1930s and the 1940s, which express this transitoriness of things through the symbol of dust are 'Polvo,
cadáver del tiempo' (OPC 280-1) and 'Tres estrofas al polvo'
(OPC 324). The product of things that have crumbled and
broken up ('emisario de las ruinas' — OPC 324), dust settles
on cupboards, doors, unused hats, and neglected crockery;
it reduces the effectiveness of light; and — a neat touch
stressing the link with time — it stops clocks. Wherever it
settles it is a reminder of the decay from which it originates
and of the passing time during which it has accumulated. It
is not only omnipresent, but since it is so often unnoticed
there is something sinister about it; 'sutil visitante', it is called

---

[14] 'Edades de mi poesía', PE 24.
[15] MVP 22 and 23.
[16] 'Poetry of Reality and Utopia', SAP 72.
[17] MVP 23; 'Poetry of Reality and Utopia', SAP 73.

in 'Polvo . . .' and 'clandestino emisario' in 'Tres estrofas . . .'
This has an important side effect. Since every object carries
the warning that it is transitory, Carrera Andrade is unable
to derive unhampered delight from the sheer perception of
things. He is left constantly grieved by the underlying threat
that all these external signs hold for his own existence. For
dust is death's ally ('aliado innumerable de la muerte' — OPC
324).

It is not only that the world of objects constructed by
man crumbles away, but that all living parts of nature meet
an inevitable death. In 'Lección del árbol, la mujer y el pájaro' (AYE 13-16; OPC 333-5) [18] a once stately pine tree,
whose intense form of existence has previously been represented by the enormous number of its needles, and whose
apparent permanence has been reflected in the way nests
have been built in its branches, stands bare of all signs of
life: with worms eating away at its trunk and threatening to
bear it into complete oblivion, it is even now merely a
memorial — 'Columna en memoria de las hojas', as the title
of section I names it — and therefore, besides being an object
to lament it serves as a warning. Birds and fruit become
symbols in this poem of fleeting delight. Both give rise in
the poet's mind to an abstract notion: beauty of flight, beauty
of taste; but both are perishable. Thus there is nothing
permanent in the experiences since they are dependent on
the limited life-span of the physical forms which produce
them. Nature has a relentless progress. It will be observed
below how Carrera Andrade thinks of this, at times, as a
cyclical movement which, in a sense, evokes an idea of the
eternal. But more frequently his stance is less strategic, less
distant, not permitting him to perceive the overall rhythm
of ending and recommencing and compelling him to concentrate on the constant dying as everything responds to natural
laws. Thus, in 'El reino de las cosas' (OPC 486) clouds
remind him of the ephemeral quality of everything because
of the way they change shape, while dew symbolises the
same quality because it no sooner comes into existence than

---

[18] The arrangement in OPC obscures the poem's structure in four sections.

it inevitably evaporates. Clearly, an association of ideas connects the two images: the evaporation contributes to the endless cycle of nature. But Carrera Andrade has preferred to pass over this aspect of the situation.

A sign of the transience of all life is the death of the mighty and the vanishing of great civilisations. This is the topic of poems such as 'Torre de Londres' (OPC 336-7) and 'Mediterráneo' (OPC 396-7). The physical structure of the Tower of London strikes Carrera Andrade as a symbol of permanence in comparison with human lives. Discarding, for the purpose of this particular poem's imagery, the notion of man-made constructions crumbling to ruin, he obtains great irony in the idea of something built by mankind lasting over the centuries while the designers have long ago perished, and with them successive reigns, each for its space of time mighty and wealthy. Important though it is, this would not seem to be the main theme of the poem, however. It is from the Tower's purpose that the fundamental point is derived: its function as a prison and an antechamber to death. Not only has it outlasted human lives, but it has actually contributed to the death of men; these men, moreover, have perished within its walls. It becomes a symbol of the prison within which all men are condemned to exist: the world, the human condition (not, in this case, the human body):

> Las nubes nos vigilan, condenados
> prisionero y guardián a igual sentencia
> en la terrestre cárcel encerrados.   (OPC 337)

In the later poem, a tour of the Mediterranean sites of Ancient Greek civilisation reminds Carrera Andrade of the nobility and splendour that once existed during the days when new buildings stood where now there are ruins and grazing sheep. The idea of impermanence gains greater dimensions in terms such as these, for he contemplates not merely the relic of one man's brief existence but the remnants of civilisations that spanned many life-times. Ultimately, he recognises, there is no difference: in the vast order of the universe, in the great dimensions of eternity, one man's life is essentially the same as the existence of a civilisation, one day is no more insignificant than a century (OPC 397).

A deep poignancy accompanies such thoughts. It is clear that, however much Carrera Andrade may be perplexed by the transience of objects and epochs, his underlying concern is with his own impermanence. In 'Vida del rocío' (OPC 526) the image of the dew-drop serves as a good link between the external world and the inner problems of the individual. The aspects of a dew-drop that concern the poet here are its freshness (an answer to thirst), its brightness (a negation of dark meaninglessness), its ability to act as a prism which reflects wide views of the countryside (an antidote to the cities), and, ultimately and most significantly, its fragility, delicacy and brief existence, the characteristics which remove any question of its becoming a recipient of trust or hope, or a token of transcendental value. Amid the various images introduced in the opening stanza, that of a tear serves to anticipate the poem's development. It suggests, of course, a sadness, the melancholy induced by the thoughts of fleeting life. But it also helps to draw attention to the dew's similarity to the human condition. Besides being likened to a human tear it is attributed a throbbing heart:

> Late, vive un momento,
> ínfimo corazón
> de pura transparencia.

There is a great number of poems in which an awareness of the transitory nature of human life is expressed through such symbols drawn from the world observed by the poet. Also numerous, however, are those in which Carrera Andrade directly establishes the personal basis of the issue by the use of the first person. In 'Morada terrestre' (OPC 270) he sees nothing but progressive ruin in the things around him; these structures ('un edificio de naipes, / una casa de arena, un castillo en el aire') constitute the very world in which he is compelled to live, and indeed the very substance of which his life is composed. His own death will coincide with that of everything else: fish, stars, birds, all will become 'polvo sin memoria'. Since the external world is represented as dying with the poet, his own death is seen to be the supreme factor in all existence, as though the structures and creatures of his dwelling place were dependent for their existence upon his perception. By suggesting that all life ends with his own, and the very framework of life too, he aptly evokes a powerful sense of the magnitude and completeness represented by his death.

It is not, of course, a question of Carrera Andrade's adherence to the idealist philosophy of Berkeley, but of his use of a poetic image. Far more characteristic of his thought is a sense of the individual man's insignificance in relation to the permanence of the universe. It is sometimes the case, therefore, that instead of noticing signs of constant decay and impermanence in the creatures and plants of nature, as in poems such as 'El reino de las cosas', 'Lección del árbol, la mujer y el pájaro', and 'Vida del rocío' (discussed above), he finds a reminder of the reproductive cycle which endows nature with a kind of eternal life. This is the case, for example, in canto V of 'Hombre planetario'. In his search for the meaning of his existence he casts his eye around for some indication that eternity might come within his grasp. But all the signs indicate that he alone will fail to attain that state. Everywhere there is evidence of eternity: in the immutable hardness of stone, withstanding the passage of centuries; in rivers, whose flow is ceaseless; and in the rhythmic cycles of trees that wither and spring up again and of days that have both dusk and dawn. The effect, therefore, is to isolate mankind, and in particular the poet himself, as being the sole transient inhabitant of the earth:

> Eternidad, tus signos me rodean,
> mas yo soy transitorio:
> un simple pasajero del planeta. (OPC 442)

One of the most acute aspects of this preoccupation, one of the features of the human condition that causes Carrera Andrade the most profound anguish, is his awareness of living within a frame that will inevitably perish. The intellect seeks for itself — or for the soul — a permanence and thus a meaningfulness, denied it by the body. There is some evidence that a religious answer to the problem has at times been taken into consideration by the poet, as will be suggested below, but he never reaches the point of discovering eternal life of this kind. [19] He is therefore led to meditate, in canto IV of 'Hombre planetario', with bewilderment, almost with disbelief, on the paradox of believing that he has control over his body yet discovering that its fate inevitably determines his temporary existence. In the absence of any escape for his mind (or soul) he is no more than his body, no more than a clothed shell, a form in the constant process of chemical change leading to its disappearance, as though it were eaten by quicklime. One may see how Carrera Andrade's repugnance at his corporal form is reflected in the use of a disparaging term, 'armatoste'. Not only is his body thus transformed into something impersonal — an object — it is also considered coarse and inefficient:

> Yo sé que este armatoste de cal viva
> con ropaje de polvo
> que marca mi presencia entre los hombres
> me acompaña de paso ....   (OPC 441)

In 'Hombre planetario' this preoccupation constitutes only one of many problems posed by his existence, fundamental though it is. In an earlier poem, 'La alquimia vital' (OPC 263), written while Carrera Andrade was in his early thirties, his whole attention is consumed by the way his body is already on the way towards death. He can think of himself as — outwardly — an essentially youthful figure. But the visible signs of deterioration in the quality of his flesh serve as a reminder that death is an inevitable outcome. He reacts with repulsion, writing of decomposition and of the sound of liquids in his body carrying out the chemical deterioration while he sleeps. Far from calm resignation to this fate he feels indignation, as though it were all an act of antagonism against him. Hence, responsibility may be attributed to a symbolic old man working within his body. Just as dust is a sinister agent of destruction in the external world, conspiring against objects ('Polvo, cadáver del tiempo' and 'Tres estrofas al polvo'), so this old man works in a sinister fashion

---

[19] See chapter VI, II.

within Carrera Andrade's body ('conspira en lo más hondo'). Death works against man and deceives him into believing life itself to be a permanent and meaningful state. But Carrera Andrade has been able to perceive the signs of death, and this has led him to a deep mistrust of his existence.

Inherent in the theme of the transience of life is a preoccupation with time. Recognising time to be one of the oppressive factors contributing to his ontological anguish, he has recently complained, in 'Libro del destierro XI':

> Lo fugaz, la extensión, el tiempo, el número:
> Son los cuatro barrotes de mi cárcel
> metafísica . . . .   (OPC 546)

And in the following canto of this poem he refutes the conventional concept of time as a steady flow whose movement may be perceived by man. On the contrary, it is man who is transitory, whereas time is the eternal background, the constant against which his own limited existence may be measured:

> El tiempo no transcurre, nosotros transcurrimos
> al igual que las cosas
> ... ...
> El tiempo inmóvil mira nacer, crecer, morir
> y permanece entero sin gastarse, infinito.   (OPC 546-7)

But Carrera Andrade rarely devotes his poems to the actual analysis of time in the abstract; he expresses an inner torment at the effect of time on all things connected with his own life. Thus, in canto III of 'Hombre planetario' he runs chronologically through the names of the days of the week, referring, as he does so, to the humdrum activities of everyday life. One effect is to evoke an impression of incessant and rapid progress toward no meaningful end; another is to imply that routine removes importance and substance from human occupations. All his existence is felt to be in a state of constant flux: no day is complete in itself, since it is part of a flow from the preceding to the succeeding day:

> Lunes, puntual obrero, me visitas
> con tu faz de domingo ya difunto,
> pero en verdad más martes que otro día.   (OPC 440)

In the routine that characterises his life he is swept along remorselessly in a predetermined direction with no opportunity to look around or to choose his route; his life is a series of vaguely perceived experiences in a whirl of movement and in a mood of sadness. In the middle of the week, therefore, Wednesday and Thursday are

> perdidos en el fondo de ese túnel
> con un rumor de ruedas y vajilla,
> con pasos y con lluvia. . . .   (ibid.)

It will be noticed that a constituent factor of this view of life is a sense of monotony and insipidity. It is a mood in which Carrera Andrade is far from responding to communication from the natural world, far from pausing to observe the realities around him, and far from discerning any value in the many moments that compose each day and each week. [20] Although 'Hombre planetario' itself evolves toward a solution to these problems, it is worth stressing that much of Carrera Andrade's thought — particularly from the mid-thirties to the late fifties — has this negative characteristic, reflecting an attitude to existence typical among his contemporary poets: man's daily life lacks interest, is part of an inevitable rush toward death, and has no purpose. [21]

Time's passing brings about the loss of youth; this is Carrera Andrade's emphasis in 'El visitante de niebla' (OPC 289-90). A physical existence is attributed to time, as though it were the substance in which his youth has been consumed (the earth in which his youthful corpse has been buried). In another respect, time has imposed a misty barrier between his present person and the young man he used to be. The image is extended, it will be noticed, by the additional sense of distance between his present abode (in exile) and the land of his youth (Ecuador). Written in 1939, this poem belongs to that stage in his life when Carrera Andrade showed concern for the transition from youth to middle age, with his

---

[20] The solutions to his ontological disquiet which are offered to him, but at this stage of the poem (and in this frame of mind) are unknown or unheeded, are examined at length in chapter VI, I and II.

[21] Only since 'Hombre planetario' has any consistent shift of emphasis been perceptible.

focus on the dim memory of his younger self. He was contemplating his life mid-term, analysing his reactions to its swift journey. Having approached the end of the voyage, he has recently focussed attention on old age itself.

As might be expected from a poet who has tended to express the course of his life through the image of a journey, many poems written during recent years have expressed the idea of agedness as a stage where the end of that voyage is within sight. In canto II of 'Hombre planetario', as he realises that the moment of reckoning is at hand, he acknowledges, with a touch of irony, that he does not need to produce proof of having spent a valuable, meaningful life in order to die since:

> se pasa sin pagar al fin del viaje
> la invisible frontera. (OPC 440)

In 'Estación penúltima' he writes of his 'Inútil viaje' (OPC 495) as though he were in a position to assess it in its completeness; in 'Agua germinal' he seeks future refreshment after 'tantos años de viaje / a través del desierto' (OPC 512); and in 'Libro del destierro' XV he pictures himself as 'Capitán de mi nave anclada en el ocaso' (OPC 548) as he obeys the call to sail to a final destiny. It will be clear from some of these examples that old age is sometimes treated as a time of hope. [22] On the other hand, although he never despairs, Carrera Andrade often finds in agedness further cause for anguish. 'Paraíso de los ancianos' neatly captures the essential mood, negating the ideas of beauty, contentment, and joy. The failing powers of Carrera Andrade himself are externalised: in the world of the aged nature lacks its normal attributes, and behaves in an unaccustomed way:

> En el paraíso de los ancianos crecen flores de escarcha.
> Los pájaros son mudos y vuelan a escondidas.
> Las hojas llevan a rastras su carga de suspiros.
> Los árboles mojan sus arrugas con lágrimas de lluvia. (OPC 560)

---

[22] The senses in which Carrera Andrade comes to terms with death are examined in chapter VI, II.

It is a place of mist, darkness, menacing clocks, artificial fruit, and dreams of 'viajes nunca realizados'.

Agedness is represented primarily by the image of autumn: the penultimate stage of an inexorable development ('Estación penúltima' is the title of a section of poems in the collection *El alba llama a la puerta*). Old age is already barren, like a tree with dry leaves ('Taller del tiempo' — OPC 419-20; and 'El alba llama a la puerta' [23] — PU 195-6), or a desert:

> .... En otro tiempo
> habitaba una alondra
> dentro de mi pecho,
> hoy gran tumba de arena.
>
> ('El desierto interior' — OPC 429)

One feature which makes agedness particularly difficult to accept is the lack of things to which the poet had once been accustomed, things associated with youth, the spring, freshness, vigour, greenery and moisture. Another, however, is the fact that the riches gathered in old age — whether a wealth of years, of experience, of knowledge, or financial wealth — are all false. Like golden leaves, they are bound to fall, as in the poem which likens his present life to an apple tree in autumn, 'El alba llama a la puerta':

> Mercader amarillo,
> tus objetos de oro
> son falsos ....   (OPC 523)

Such an awareness of the lack of value in everything that he has accumulated throughout his life gives rise to the sense that, in retrospect, the whole course of his life has been void of ultimate value. Thus, in canto II of 'Hombre planetario' the total of achievements, acts, experiences, and gains seem to have been wasted: '¿Malbaraté el caudal de mi existencia? / ¿Dilapidé mi oro?' (OPC 440). Death in any case reduces everything to the same worthlessness, requiring no payment. In the mood of bitterness occasionally induced by

---

[23] In OPC this poem appears with no title under the new section-heading 'IV: Estrofas del alba', pp. 523-4.

these thoughts, he is even led to reject the companion who
has consoled him during numerous years of solitude — nature — and to accuse it of providing false hope, of deceptively
claiming to be of value. Thus, in 'Taller del tiempo' he turns
on nature in the following vitriolic terms:

> Yo te grité mi amor, Naturaleza impávida,
> ciega de ojos azules, sorda de nube y rocas.
> Nada me diste; sólo la deseada manzana:
> un mes de paraíso, cien años de serpiente.   (OPC 419)

From the perspective of his old age he finds that nature has
been insensitive to his needs, unresponsive to his tender advances. The delight experienced in the countryside, though
it once seemed to be of absolute value, has proved as transient as everything else. [24] In nature, moreover, Carrera Andrade found signs with which to interpret his existence. He
acquired knowledge, and with that awareness of his human
condition has come the destruction of paradise and an
enduring sense of anguish. It is true that this poem contains
a willingness to adapt, to accept the inevitable; but it is a
bitter, angry appeal, for the poet who must now force himself
to come to terms with disillusionment has the same heart as
the younger man of his memories. Changes have reduced his
body to a state of ruin and barrenness, but no corresponding
adaptation has taken place within his heart. He does not
simply admit that time must have its way, therefore, but
also requests that it make its work complete by forging a
new heart, softening it in order that it might be moulded
according to the form imposed on it by old age:

> Ablanda, forjador otoñal, en el yunque
> mi corazón forrado del metal del olvido.
> Dale una oscura forma de escarcela de lágrimas.
> A cada golpe tiembla un nido de paloma.   (OPC 420)

In this poem we see one example of Carrera Andrade's
inability to be fully resigned to the end of life. Something

---

[24] It must be emphasised that this attitude to nature, even in his latest verse,
is exceptional. Normally nature continues to afford solace and to permit an
understanding of the mystery of existence (see chapter VI, 1).

within him, uninfluenced by the withering of his corporal frame, refuses to yield and retains its vigour, but because of its limitations causes severe longing and renders all the more arduous impending death. Here this inner dynamo is called his heart; what he means by the term, however, is not literally the mechanism but rather the source of his emotions. Another way of conceiving the idea is as that part of man which yearns for immortality. Thus, in 'El alba llama a la puerta' it is expressed first through the symbol of a bird, intensely-living but imprisoned in a cage:

> El pájaro escarlata,
> en la jaula del pecho,
> quiere escapar al bosque
> de aire libre y eterno.   (PU 195; OPC 524)

It becomes clear that what Carrera Andrade is on the brink of naming is his soul. It is a belief for which he longs, according to the verse of his old age at least, since it would provide the solution to his ontological problems. In this particular poem, for example, it would still his anxieties concerning the destiny of his 'pájaro escarlata' after the cage of his body has perished. As will be shown in the following chapter, however, he has never been able to express in his poetry a confident belief in eternal life and a God who is the creator and saviour of mankind. What he has is a thirst, a need, an appetite for the fulfilment of religious experience. Life itself being no longer something to which he can cling, he expresses the intention of applying patience while he awaits the dawn of something new:

> Con los años yo perdí
> el frenesí de vivir.
> Hoy vivo pacientemente,
> asceta junto a la fuente.
>
> El alba llama a la puerta
> y cada día despierta
> mi sed de cielo y de sol
> y mi apetito de Dios.   (ibid.)

Precisely what the dawn will bring, in this poem and in the whole collection of the same title, is deliberately left obscure.

In commentaries on the meaning of the image in relation to the collection as a whole, Carrera Andrade has encouraged a plurality of interpretations: it may be the emergence of a new social order, the arrival of religious revelation, or the advent of death at the end of a nocturnal life. [25] Most relevant to the use of the image in the individual poem, however, is that sense to which he draws particular attention: 'My first intention in choosing dawn as a symbol was to express indirectly the awakening of consciousness and the exaltation of light, or rather of metaphysical clarity' (SAP 64). Despite the impression of optimism encouraged by the idea of dawn, the promise it holds is, clearly, of a kind of enlightenment which does not necessarily bring a religious solution. [26] There is some reason for hope, but attainment of the aspired goal remains incomplete, with the result that the poet's ontological disquiet is not stilled. Although there are many poems in his later books which express various degrees and kinds of hope for a discovery of the meaning of life, there are many too which continue to voice his metaphysical anguish. Thus, in 'Fantasma de las granjas', a poem belonging to the same book as 'El alba llama a la puerta', he writes:

La angustia cósmica de las ranas me atraviesa.
Las ranas metafísicas dialogan con los atros.   (OPC 493)

The problems discussed in this chapter — solitude, incomprehension of the meaning of existence, man's loss of innocence in the modern age, the transitoriness of human experience, old age, and death — are so fundamental and so universal that it is not appropriate to speak of literary influences. Besides, for Carrera Andrade these are not literary themes but genuine problems. It would be fruitless, of course, to argue that they have been caused only by his

---

[25] 'Decade of my poetry', SAP 63-4, and 'Poetry of Reality and Utopia' SAP 79.
[26] In fact, his metaphysical solutions tend to turn back into life on this earth, as the next chapter will attempt to demonstrate.

exile; indeed, there is evidence of an incipient anguish before 1928. In his autobiography he recalls that during his late adolescence: 'A tientas iba yo por el laberinto oscuro, en pos de las verdades eternas: el amor humano, la fragilidad del ser, la angustia como expresión existencial, la omnipresencia de la muerte' (VC 27-8). There are one or two signs of these themes in the early poetry. In 'Tribulación de agosto' (OPC 40), [27] for example, he deals with the confrontation between death and burgeoning life: a man has shot himself in a hunting accident, and his body lies prostrate in the midst of the countryside, the contrastive effect being intended to express bewilderment at the finality of a human being's death, and to suggest the growing realisation that all forms of life are ultimately transient. As it is suggested in chapter I, Carrera Andrade's first departure from the homeland is partially a subconscious attempt to resolve dissatisfactions related to latent ontological problems. On the other hand it is beyond question that residence abroad, in alien environments and in isolation from Ecuador produced the stimulus that brought these latent problems to the surface and made them acute. The imagery through which his poetry expresses these themes has, therefore, a direct source in his experience. When the Russian philosopher, Nicolas Berdyaev, in *Solitude and Society*, describes the psychological effects of solitude he uses images closely resembling those of Carrera Andrade:

> An extreme sense of solitude tends to make everything else appear alien and heterogeneous. Man feels himself to be a stranger, an alien without a spiritual home. [28]

He calls it a 'feeling of spiritual *exile*' and later a *prison*. [29] It is useful to notice that solitude, alienation, exile and imprisonment may be thought of as psychologically analogous experiences. Carrera Andrade's use of the image of imprisonment is certainly a subconscious reaction to one or more

---

[27] Entitled 'Episodio' in ROL (p. 37).
[28] Nicolas Berdyaev, *Solitude and Society*. Translated by George Reavey. Geoffrey Bles: The Centenary Press, London, 1938, p. 92.
[29] The italics are mine.

of these experiences. But in the case of alienation and exile it is not a question of the subconscious, nor, ultimately, of imagery, for these are of literal significance in the poet's life. His solitude is all the greater precisely because it coincides with those associated experiences.

Carrera Andrade's manner of treating these ontological themes bears an unmistakable hallmark. Solitude, anguish, awareness of the transitory nature of things, death — these preoccupations are fused with his reactions as an Ecuadorian to the urban, technological lands. His own exile in an inauthentic world constitutes a pivot between the two kinds of theme. The homeland, as will be seen in the following chapter, consequently offers the prospect of solutions to those problems.

VI

SOLUTIONS

I T has been widely recognised that Carrera Andrade's poetry does not present an impression of unmitigated despair in face of his ontological problems. René L.F. Durand, for example, sees Carrera Andrade as 'un poète de notre angoisse, mais aussi de notre espoir'.[1] H.R. Hays finds him 'too vital a person to abandon hope for the world which has nurtured him for more than half a century'.[2] Francisco Lucio argues that his sombre vision is 'lejos de sumir al poeta en un pesimismo negativo'.[3] And Vicente Moreno Mora even believes that his 'visión sonriente del mundo se encuentra en todas las etapas de su poesía'.[4]

Two critics have assessed this hopeful side of Carrera Andrade in direct relation to his sombre vision. In the last three pages of his article, 'Cosmovisión de Jorge Carrera Andrade', William J. Straub elucidates three ways in which the poet seeks to save himself, or 'superar la vida sórdida en que vivimos': communion with elemental beings, love, and 'la presentación de lo que él concibe como el mundo perfecto'.[5] William F. Heald, on the other hand, sees things in terms of answers to the poet's solitude: 'He does, however, find alleviation for the pain of *soledad* in several ways. First, the fact that man's reason and knowledge are extremely limited opens up the possibility that there may be a purpose in the universe and a significance to human life that presently

---

[1] René L. F. Durand, *J.C.A.*, Editions Pierre Seghers, Paris, 1966, p. 88.
[2] H. R. Hays, *Selected Poems of J.C.A.*, State University of New York Press, Albany, 1972, p. xxiv.
[3] Francisco Lucio, 'J.C.A. y el "Hombre planetario"', *Cuadernos Hispanoamericanos*, 1969, 235, p. 210.
[4] Vicente Moreno Mora, *La evolución de la literatura americana*, Casa de la Cultura Ecuatoriana, Cuenca, 1948, p. 256.
[5] William J. Straub, 'Cosmovisión de J.C.A.', *Cuadernos Americanos*, CLXXXI, 1972, p. 186.

escapes us. Then he shows us that if we adopt an objective point of view, placing man on the same level as other "things" in the world, men's problems lose some of their power to hurt. Finally, he takes a hedonistic pleasure in just being alive'. [6] In his book on the poet, Enrique Ojeda rightly observes the chronological significance of Carrera Andrade's more resigned, contented, or hopeful standpoint in *El alba llama a la puerta* (1966): 'La exaltación de las cosas que Carrera Andrade había iniciado cincuenta años atrás en sus primeros poemas alcanza en esta última obra radiante plenitud. La vida y la muerte, antes contradictorias, forman ahora una unidad cielo-tierra que florece eternamente. La desasosegada búsqueda de una existencia inmortal que penetró la obra del poeta encuentra en esa conciencia de la continuidad de la vida, más allá de toda muerte individual, satisfacción plenaria'. [7]

Although in some measure the idea that Carrera Andrade has found solutions to his problems has been demonstrated by the critics, the issue has been handled, on the whole, briefly and inadequately. In particular, the question of animism, the poet's attitude to religion, and the poet's universal identity have been ignored or misunderstood. Some critics have been led to reach what — to the present writer — seem excessively optimistic assessments of the poet's solutions; that, for example, his verse is 'un mensaje optimista y cordial' [8] and that his latest phase suggests a 'satisfacción plenaria'. [9] It is proposed in this chapter to attempt a full treatment of the subject, revealing in the process that the various types of solution discovered or at least contemplated by Carrera Andrade are inexorably linked with Ecuador, as the ontological problems tend to be associated with life in foreign lands.

---

[6] William F. Heald, 'Soledad in the Poetry of J.C.A.', P.M.L.A., LXXVI, 1961, p. 610.
[7] Enrique Ojeda, J.C.A. Introducción al estudio de su vida y de su obra, Eliseo Torres & Sons, New York, 1971, p. 380.
[8] William J. Straub, 'Cosmovisión ...', p. 188.
[9] Enrique Ojeda, loc. cit.

I. THE ROLE OF NATURE

The Elemental Life Force

¡Afuera preocupaciones!
Dejemos la cama tibia.
Esta lluvia le ha lavado
como a una col, a la vida.   (OPC 126)

In these lines from the early poem 'Noticias de la noche', [10]
Carrera Andrade expresses an attitude to nature and to life
which has fully matured in recent years. He was not without
perplexities, of course, even in those days of his youth, but
his poetry rarely took them as a central theme. This poem
helps us to see why. The night has been a time of inactivity
for the body's senses, making the bed — which reminds the
poet of the period during which life paused — an un-
welcome place. At the same time violence has afflicted the
countryside, an impression of destruction and melancholy
that suggests the poet's mental turmoil. Morning brings a
new start, announced by messengers from nature: the birds.
More than this, the rain has washed clean and refreshed
the countryside, and the poet's inner preoccupations have
cleared themselves up. The world of nature now beckons,
in fullness and freshness, appeals to the poet's senses, and
instils in him an urgency, a sense of vitality. With this vitality
he is able to thrust aside the perplexities. In effect, therefore,
nature, which instils the zest for life, enables him to perceive
that he should waste no time in anxiety over the problems
of existence, but take hold of it, live it.

In the numerous poems about the countryside — strictly
speaking, Ecuador's countryside [11] — written during that
early period, Carrera Andrade affirms his belief in the
positive value of nature. The sensual experiences of life itself
are reflected in it. Nature is, in fact, the elemental life force.
Later, his perplexities force their way to the surface. His
sense of solitude, his awareness of the transitory nature of
existence, his incomprehension of life's meaning, his repulsion

---

[10] Entitled 'Ha llovido por la noche' in ROL (p. 22).
[11] See chapter III, II.

for the state of modern civilisation, his tenderness for Ecuador — all his social concern and his ontological problems become dominant themes. Though nature is still always present, always forming part of the content of his verse, it lacks the power it originally had. Whereas, before, it was an attainable reality, now, it becomes an ideal, an aspiration. There are two paramount reasons for this change. Carrera Andrade's youth has departed, and with it the momentum, the inherent vitality, and the intrinsic validity of living. Simultaneously, he has ceased to live in his homeland; moreover, he has left the rural environment for that of the great cities.

Recently Carrera Andrade has been returning toward the point of departure, developing a renewed faith in the elemental power of nature. It is important to note, however, a subtle difference in this new position. In his earliest attitude, nature offered him the means of reducing his perplexities by affirming its own supreme value. That is, the basic, disturbing preoccupations were, in a sense, suppressed by the enticement to turn his attention to nature. The fundamental questions about existence, in a nascent state, were but vaguely posed, or gently answered by the countryside. He turned to nature intuitively. But now, in his latest poetry, he turns to nature after a vast metaphysical exploration. Nature thus emerges out of his problems, supplying a clear, precise answer to them.

It will help to elucidate this attitude if a recent poem is taken for illustration. One of Carrera Andrade's latest collections, *Misterios naturales,* [12] offers numerous instances; the ideas are succintly expressed in the poem 'Apetito de realidad', the text of which is as follows:

> El silbo de un pájaro despierta las semillas
> envueltas en la miel del mediodía.
> La mente es una cerca donde salta un pájaro
> que picotea en el tramo de la percepción
> con apetito de realidad,
> afirmación solemne de la vida fecunda.   (OPC 536)

---

[12] Published as a collection of nine poems in *Cuadernos Americanos,* CLXXXI, 1972, pp. 167-71; these nine poems were also included as one section of a book with the same title, consisting of 34 poems, published by the Centre de Recherches de l'Institut d'Etudes Hispaniques, Paris, 1972. In OPC pp. 533-96 'Misterios naturales' is combined with 'Vocación terrestre', also of 1972.

The main idea concerns the sharpening of one's perception of reality. The poet gives a brief description of a scene that he witnesses or imagines, followed by his interpretation of the message conveyed by that scene. A bird's song breaks into a static, tranquil setting, as though urging the seeds to develop their potential fertility. Similarly, nature itself, in the form of a bird, intrudes in the poet's range of awareness and urges him to develop his own form of potential, to make his life fertile. It seems to draw his attention to the sights and sounds around, superimposing physical sensation over mental processes. Thus the bird's own 'apetito de realidad' is granted. It is important to notice the character and quality of the reality to which the poet's senses are awakened. There is something comparable between growth, production of nourishment, and reproduction in the world of nature on the one hand and human life itself on the other. As opposed to the ontological doubts examined in the last chapter, what Carrera Andrade is expressing here is an affirmation of the value of existence. It is not the discovery of a cause or purpose outside life, but an acknowledgement that intellectual doubts are answered by physical experience itself. The mystery of existence is reflected in nature; indeed, the elemental life forces represented therein are attributed a supreme and almost sacred value.

A World of Signs

Carrera Andrade has been a constant observer of nature. The value of such observation consists in the fact that nature is full of signs: a cricket is therefore comparable to a page in a book ('Vida del grillo' — OPC 125); a bird is equivalent to a newspaper ('Ha llovido por la noche' — OPC 126); trees pronounce syllables, their leaves contain written letters, and together they translate the language of a wood ('Lenguas vivas' — OPC 529). Even when it is not actually imagined as written or spoken words, nature is often called by a term that suggests its ability to communicate messages, such as *symbol* ('El alba llama a la puerta' — PU 195; OPC 523), *master* ('La vida perfecta' — OPC 129); or *image* ('El reino de las cosas' — OPC 486). The world of nature is meaningful because it is life itself. It is not a deceptive world of shadows. As Carrera Andrade expresses it in one of his statements on the poetic art, 'Cada objeto es un mundo':

> La vida no es sólo apariencia.   (OPC 435)

The key to understanding the world lies in nature:

> Las aves —lección del instante—
> nos dan en su escuela volante
> la clave de un mundo cambiante.   (ibid.)

In an outwardly changing world, the poet may keep in touch with the constant values and basic truths by continuous attention to nature. Not only should elemental things be examined and understood, but such is their value, service, or function that they should be treated with veneration:

> Comprende y venera al objeto.   (ibid.)

One should not be misled into believing that this is merely advice for the poet on how to approach his vocation. For the poet is not essentially different from other men (except in his ability to act as their guide). What he regards as his task as a poet is also his task as a man; all men, if they wish to live authentically and find the truth of their existence should seek to interpret the signs in nature — and, more generally, in the whole world of perceptible physical objects. One of the senses in which nature is a key to ontological problems is, therefore, that it acts as a medium, messenger, or model. In this function nature is not in itself the Truth for which men yearn, but the key which opens up the way for that Truth to be discovered. This ambiguous position is well illustrated in the poem 'Lección del árbol, la mujer y el pájaro' (AYE 13-16; OPC 333-5). In sections I, II, and III Carrera Andrade gives examples of things whose fullness and freshness have passed: the tree bare of its leaves, fruit plucked from its tree, a bird no longer flying, a woman whose body is old. In the final section he sums up: all these things tell their story in a 'lenguaje elemental'. [13] It is, quite

---

[13] The title of this section is 'Lenguaje elemental'.

obviously, a message that all forms of life are transitory. But the issue is not as simple as this, for the poem is not only an expression, through symbols, of the fleetingness of human life, but also an attempt to draw attention to the significance and function of nature. The reader is invited to share the poet's observation and his attempts to interpret. It is for this reason that, instead of making plain statements, and instead of allowing the symbols to work totally unexplained (as they do in many other poems of his) he poses the question:

> ¿Qué escribe sobre el polvo ese gusano?
> ¿Qué trata de advertirnos ese grito
> de pájaro que cruza el infinito?   (OPC 335)

The reader recognises that by following the poet's example, and making his own enquiry, he himself may discover the answers. The poet has taught the reader how to look at nature, and how to penetrate the mystery of life. In the last three lines Carrera Andrade strikes a different note from that of the poem hitherto, a more constructive and hopeful note:

> La clave de la vida está en tu mano:
> Goza, aprende el lenguaje que te ofrece
> el mundo elemental, después perece. (ibid.)

Since, as the bulk of the poem has demonstrated, death is inevitable, life should be relished while it lasts; and meanwhile nature should be studied in order that the truths of existence may be discovered.

It will be noticed that in 'Lección del árbol, la mujer y el pájaro' the idea of nature acting as a key is conveyed by the use of the word 'clave'. Nature is the key to a code; it has a function of a linguistic kind. In another poem, 'Prisión humana' (AYE 27-30; OPC 343-5), a different word is used: 'llave'. Nature is thus the key to a lock. [14] Clearly, its role is the same: to help an understanding of the world. The sea horse gives access, by opening a lock, to the mys-

---

[14] Both 'clave' and 'llave' are used metaphorically in common speech; they have, of course, essentially the same etymology. But Carrera Andrade is consciously applying to each term a different primary context.

teries of the sea, to the message of youthful memories, to the awareness that time consumes everything. In both poems the effect is to attribute to nature the supreme power of solving ontological problems. Ultimately it must be recognized that it is, in fact, a partial answer only, for nature itself is still a mystery; the mystery of the universe. The image of a key, it should be noticed, is reminiscent of the poem 'La llave del fuego' (OPC 353-5). In Part I this poem was discussed in order to suggest that Ecuador (and the tropics) may also be regarded as a key. [15] It is a clear example of the tendency to associate nature and his homeland with similar aspects of his metaphysical thought.

Animism

Asked about the fundamental characteristic of his images, Carrera Andrade once replied that it was essentially a question of giving human qualities to things: 'humanización de la imagen'. [16] Insofar as this may be considered a poetic device, the general term 'personification' is applicable. It is indeed a pervasive feature of his verse, as a random glance at poetry from all periods of his career quickly reveals. On the first page of *Registro del mundo*, in a poem dating from 1922, we encounter a line which attributes intelligent human action to one of the body's organs: 'El corazón enciende su lámpara de arcilla' (REG 9; OPC 31). On the second page personification is taken closer to its limits in lines where plant life is endowed with human physical attributes and senses: 'La rosa es una copa llena de olor humilde / que toca el aire tímido con sus dedos sutiles' (REG 10; OPC 33). Turning to the last page of the same collection, to a poem written in 1939, we find that the Oakland bridge is treated as a young man and imagined to be capable of human behaviour in its 'matrimonio dulce con la isla' (REG 180; OPC 297). In the first poem of *Poesía última*, which dates from 1957, the elements act according to human custom: 'Se engalanan las nubes con vestidos de fiesta' (PU 26; OPC

---

[15] See chapter III, IX.
[16] William J. Straub, 'Conversación con J.C.A.', *Revista Iberoamericana*, 79, 1972, p. 313.

390). And finally, on the last page of the collection *Vocación terrena,* which appeared in 1972, plant life once again behaves in human fashion in the lines: 'Las vanas lentejuelas del rocío / esplenden en la danza de las plantas'. [17]

Although personification is a common literary figure whose history may be traced back to the earliest poetry of mankind, it merits particular attention in Carrera Andrade's verse for the significant way in which it emphasises and serves his attitude to the world of nature and objects. Above all, Carrera Andrade's use of personification responds, not to a search for a means of expression, but to the special relationship between himself and the things and creatures of the world. If we look closely at the personification of willows in 'Los amigos del paseo' (OPC 45), for example, we notice that when he refers to the trees as 'buenos amigos' it is because they assume the role of substitutes for human beings in his solitary walk. They seem to feel emotion, to have memories, and to meditate because he senses a kind of intimate confidence between himself and them, and receives from them a lesson about life. The personification is highly effective in establishing the relationship between poet and nature. What makes its use particularly apt here, however, as in many other poems, is that the very theme is that relationship, for the willows teach him that 'hay un placer dulce y fino / en dar el corazón al viento'. The idea of finding satisfaction in taking one's emotions to nature gains strength when nature is seen to come alive and respond in human fashion to one's needs.

To the English reader it might seem appropriate to apply to this type of personification the term 'pathetic fallacy'. [18] Not only does Carrera endow inanimate things with human characteristics and emotions, he also treats nature, to some extent, as a backcloth to the working-out of subjective themes, setting the mood of the scene to suit the human feeling

---

[17] 'Vocación terrena', in *Arbol de fuego* (Caracas), No. 51, 1972, p. 23. Also OPC 539.
[18] The term 'pathetic fallacy', which is derived from an essay by Ruskin (*Modern Painters,* v. 3, Pt. iv), is defined as 'The presentation of the inanimate world as having human feelings', and is said to be applicable when 'Poets ..., dramatists, novelists, have ... set the moods of nature in accord with the events or emotions of their tale' (*Dictionary of World Literary Terms,* Ed. Joseph T. Shipley, George Allen & Unwin, London, 1970, pp. 233-4).

involved. In 'Los amigos del paseo', of course, the trembling, the memories, the pensive mood, and the melancholy (reflected in the willows' quivering movement, slimness, and aroma) all belong to the poet, who translates the abstract state of mind into pictorial form by recourse to this imagery drawn from nature. But it is worth stressing again that for Carrera Andrade this is not merely a poetic device. Besides reflecting his mood, nature plays an active role in influencing it. Thus, the willows help to add a degree of pleasure to the initial melancholy; they are not only a backcloth but also actually take substance and teach him.

It is more accurate, therefore, to speak of an attitude than of a poetic device. In place of an essentially literary or aesthetic term, such as personification or pathetic fallacy, it is preferable to use a philosophical one: animism. [19] In fact, he consciously applies to his poetry the animist cult that was a basis of certain Indian religions in pre-Columbian Ecuador. As was observed in chapter III, Carrera Andrade treats his Indian ancestors as inhabitants of a purer, more authentic civilisation than that of today. He even appeals to them for help and guidance. Clearly, their close, intimate contact with the soil has influenced his own attitude. What is more, however, the Indians used to converse with nature; in his account of that period of Ecuador's history he singles out this cult of animism as a significant aspect of their customs and beliefs:

Los Caras practicaban un culto animista.... Igual cosa sucedía con los Pansaleos. El indio de estas regiones "en cualquier parte donde estuviese, jamás se creía solo; antes, por el contrario, se imaginaba acompañado por todos los objetos que le rodeaban, y entraba en comunicación con todos ellos". Tenía la costumbre de "hablar con las cosas", es decir, solía dirigirles la palabra como a seres dotados de inteligencia. (CS 36-7) [20]

---

[19] The term 'animism' is defined as '1. The doctrine of the *anima mundi* (Stahl 1720); the doctrine that the phenomena of animal life are produced by an immaterial *anima*, or soul, distinct from matter. 2. The attribution of a living soul to inanimate objects and natural phenomena 1866. 3. By extension: Spiritualism; the belief in the existence of soul or spirit apart from matter 1880.' (*The Shorter Oxford English Dictionary*, Clarendon Press, Oxford, 1922, p. 68.) It is chiefly the second of these three definitions that concerns us here.

[20] The passages placed by Carrera Andrade between inverted commas are quoted from Onffroy de Thoron, *Amérique équatoriale*, Paris, 1866.

Referring, in a different work, to his adolescent years as a 'poeta bucólico', he alludes to the similarity between his own practice and that of these Indians:

> Fui un adolescente apasionado por las cosas, con las que solía dialogar como los aborígenes de mi tierra. (IH 107)

His dialogue with nature has never ceased, for this poetic practice is the expression of an innate tendency and the application of an indigenous custom which he recognises for its authenticity. [21] A natural corollary of his personification of objects, and especially of objects in the countryside, is therefore the pronounced tendency to address the words of a poem to them as though they were human beings or divinities capable of hearing him. It has been shown that his contact with nature has enabled him to perceive that it is continuously communicating messages to him; in this aspect the relationship is that of message and interpreter, lesson and student. But ultimately the relationship is a far more intimate one, a kind of communion, in which nature's side of the dialogue is spoken through signs and the poet's expressed through verse.

It is revealing to consider more closely the kind of words that Carrera Andrade addresses to nature. In the first place, he often poses questions which he hopes it will answer. Realising that it is full of messages, groping to understanding the connection between an inner problem and signs that seem to be offering guidance, he often turns to nature as though to ask precisely what it is trying to teach him. Thus, of the tree in 'Lección del árbol, la mujer y el pájaro' he enquires:

> ¿Qué lección insinúas en las rocas
> oh pino de tus hojas desvestido? (OPC 333)

And as he strives to comprehend the significance of the rose, in 'Hombre planetario' XV, he poses a number of questions, including the following:

---

[21] Antonio de Undurraga, in 'La órbita poética de J.C.A.', *Revista Iberoamericana*, vol. IV, no. 8, 1942, p. 298, goes as far as to make the dubious suggestion that a degree of Indian blood in Carrera Andrade may have some connection with the influence of nature on him.

¿Qué vienes a decir con tantos labios?   (OPC 447)

When he discovers the meaning of nature's signs he frequently reacts, not with a question, but with an exclamation of praise or admiration. In 'Aquí yace la espuma', for example, when the various saintly, healing, providing, and fighting qualities of the foam are revealed to him he exclaims:

> ¡Oh Santa revestida con vellones de oveja!
> Les dan una final cura de cielo
> a las rocas heridas tus albísimas vendas.   (OPC 327)

and later:

> ¡Oh monja panadera!

and again:

> ¡Oh monja capitana!

Or else, less emotively, he quietly acknowledges that he has received a message, as in 'La vida perfecta' when he gratefully informs the rabbit:

> Tu vida me ha enseñado la lección del silencio.   (OPC 129)

Much of his poetry is of this last kind, for it is a convenient means of exploring the various properties of an aspect of nature while simultaneously establishing the close bond between himself and the object or creature from nature to which his words are addressed. In 'La vida perfecta' — to continue with a simple instance — he proceeds to trace those features of a rabbit's life that endow it with ideal qualities: its isolation from worldly cares, its acquaintance with the wisdom of the elements, and its innocence. As he informs the rabbit of its characteristics it is as though he were holding a mirror before it. But, clearly, the essential function of the exercise is to inform himself, not the rabbit, in order to enable himself to interpret the signs one by one. The reason for addressing the animal is precisely to make contact with it, to form a relationship with it, and to express his attitude toward it (which in this case is a mixture of admiration and gratitude tinged with mild envy and humour).

In this relationship of intimacy — almost, one might say, of love — with nature there are inevitably moments of disillusionment. He expects such great favours that nature seems, occasionally, to let him down. As in a lovers' quarrel, he knows that the bond will endure this moment but is compelled to pour out recrimination. In 'Taller del tiempo', for example, he complains that years of love on his part have failed to secure a durable response; their relationship has proved as fleeting as everything else:

> Yo te grité mi amor, Naturaleza impávida
> ciega de ojos azules, sorda de nube y rocas.
> Nada me diste; sólo la deseada manzana:
> un mes de paraíso, cien años de serpiente.   (OPC 419)

In similar vein, in 'De nada sirve la isla' he breaks off from his anguished monologue about the uselessness of all things which appear at first to offer refuge from a meaningless existence, and in the central section turns on the very things that he (or other men) has found beautiful and precious (and therefore of value): 'De nada sirves, rosa . . .', 'de nada tú, diamante . . .', 'de nada, frescas borlas o alfileteros del sicomoro . . .', 'De nada sirven, tierra, tus piedrecillas de colores' (OPC 346). The poem acquires a greater power to convey his disappointment by means of this direct accusation.

It is evident that one great advantage for Carrera Andrade in his ability to converse with plants, insects, animals, rivers, mountains, the sea, etc. is that he need never feel completely without company. He is in the position of the Cara or Pansaleo Indian who, in practising his animist cult 'jamás se creía solo' (CS 36). It is, therefore, one respect in which he has learned from his Indian ancestors about an innocent and more authentic type of life. Associated with this is the advantage such perpetual company has for the man who is disenchanted with a world of cities and machines. In his failure to find among human beings, in the city, relief from the solitude that dominates his life, Carrera Andrade is able to resort to the more soothing company of the world

of nature. There he always finds a listener and often receives
comfort.

When turning to nature for guidance, it is notable that
he sometimes assumes an air of humility, as though he were
an insignificant creature invoking a figure of might. One may
even say that, after the manner of his Indian ancestors
— from whom he has learned — Carrera Andrade invokes
nature as though it were a god, or an infinite number of
gods manifested in every creature and in all the elements.

> Te invoco, dios del aire,

we read twice in 'Invocación al aire' (OPC 527). The poet,
replete with crowds of people and thousands of vehicles,
imprisoned within his urban environment, begs the air to
grant him space. In 'Agua germinal' it is water he invokes
— water that is the product of an elemental force: a storm:

> Tormenta inmemorial: lava mi frente ...   (OPC 512)

Time separates him from his former childlike view of the
world, and separates this present world from its earlier innocent state; but storms, which, with their elemental quality,
come to us from antiquity, when life was purer, can remind
the poet of his youth and of that earlier period; he requests,
in addition, the ability to love the world again. Another
poem, 'Teoría del guacamayo', attributes to a bird the power
to help Carrera Andrade in his supplication:

> Ave roja triunfante,
> clarinada del trópico:
> imprime tu figura
> sobre el códice
> de mi pecho aborigen.   (OPC 457) [22]

It is partly a question of asking that he be reminded of the
value of life close to nature, as in the tropics, and as in
the days of Atahualpa. [23] But the important point is that the

---

[22] The poem is printed in PU 114-16, but with many errors. A complete
page is omitted, including the last two lines quoted here.
[23] Carrera Andrade himself has commented that the bird, with its alluring
colours, also represents a 'false paradise' (SAP 77); he seems to imply that it

macaw was worshipped by at least one of Ecuador's pre-Inca tribes, the Cañaris. [24] Indeed, its sacred function is acknowledged in another line from this poem: 'Ave sagrada de las tribus' (OPC 458). We observe once again the conscious attempt by Carrera Andrade to adopt his Indian ancestors' attitude to nature, and indeed to draw closer to those ancestors by invoking their gods.

It will be noticed that this treatment of nature as though it contains numerous gods, or reflects a divine presence, is a form of pantheism. Initially, the term seems a useful one since Carrera Andrade's thought embraces other aspects of that philosophy, in particular the idea that men, animals, plants, inorganic matter, the elements, the cosmos itself (and God) form a single, united substance. [25] But he is disinclined to accept that pantheism is an appropriate term for these topics in his poetry. He believes it more applicable to the ancient cultures of Europe, whereas his attitude belongs to an indigenous Spanish-American heritage. Animism, he insists, is the correct term. [26] Although it would be futile to deny the influence on Spanish-American poetry — his own included — of those European cultures to which he refers, his distinction seems justified in the light of his own deliberate attempt to imitate the essentially indigenous aspects of Ecuador's culture. It is also important to notice that each time he adopts a poetic attitude of veneration toward the natural world it is to supplicate help in his anguish over the loss of childhood and innocence. His invocations to nature are therefore always in order to request some form of return to those lost states. It is a case of making use of nature in accordance with his own ontological preoccupations, rather than adherence to any pantheistic philosophy.

---

deceives man into believing that his earthly existence may acquire attributes of paradise.

[24] See the poet's own history of Ecuador, CS 39.

[25] This other aspect of pantheism is discussed below, in section III of this chapter.

[26] A view expressed during an interview with the author, in Paris, 7 July 1972.

Visions of Utopia

It is tempting to distinguish between those instances where Carrera Andrade treats communion with nature as an answer to his private needs and those where he presents it as the solution to the basic problems of contemporary man. It is clear, for example, that such communion provides a kind of comfort to the poet in his solitude. It is equally evident that resort to nature can act as an antidote to his personal suffering in the venomous environment of modern urban civilisation. In the preliminary note to *Rol de la manzana* (1935) he explains how the discovery of nature's delights had inspired his poetry until the machine destroyed the idyll. The apple, which had always seemed to him like a miniature globe, a miniature Earth, takes on a special symbolism in the midst of machines, factory smoke and social unrest in the industrial cities of Europe. It is, in effect, nature in microcosm: '... cantimplora del cielo en esta vida de ruido y de carbón. Promesa de goce virginal y sin doblez. Signo de la vida sencilla' (ROL 12). There is undoubtedly a touch of escapism in such an attitude. In a poem like 'La vida perfecta' his desire for a life free from worldly cares, quietly attending to mere physical necessities, seems more like a wish to avoid issues than to solve them. Indeed, a longing for escape inspires a good deal of his verse. 'Islario' (OPC 315-6) seems to express the crux of the matter in its suggestion that refuge from the mass of cities and machines might be found in remote places still untouched by advanced civilisation, such as islands, which are protected and isolated by the sea. Places such as the Islas Molucas, Dampier, Cabo Verde, Fernando Po, Galápagos, Hawaii, the Antilles, and the Canaries, where he may pass the time of the day

> aprendiendo la ciencia
> celeste de los pájaros
> y haciendo al sol del trópico
> la ofrenda de mis años.   (OPC 316)

It is remarkable that here the idea of inhabiting an island does not illustrate a sense of solitude but rather one of

freedom, for it is the cities that induce a feeling of solitude. [27]
Another notable feature of the poem is that Carrera Andrade
is clearly aware that the private solution offered by such
escape is an impossibility: the poem is a dream, a longing.
The desire for withdrawal into himself is a part of the dream,
the temptation of a kind of reclusion. A similar yearning
prompts the invocation of the pure air in 'Invocación al
aire'. He requests not only purification and the resuscitation
of his natural life but an escape from the crowds of people
into the air itself: a withdrawal from modern civilisation into
seclusion:

> ... cédeme una parcela de tu reino.
> Dentro de mí la multitud habita
> y ya no tengo sitio para vivir conmigo.   (OPC 527)

On the other hand, his conviction that the simple life
close to nature has a supreme value leads him to present it
not merely as a form of personal escape but as a means
of salvation for mankind as a whole, in poems such as 'Aurosia' (OPC 398-9). This poem introduces an imaginary planet
— the epitome of Carrera Andrade's utopian vision of a
future human society. It is a significant fact that the main
features of life in this ideal world are love between men
(which will be discussed in the third section of this chapter)
and harmony with nature. Aurosia is a planet of gardens,
springs, birds, fruit, and corn, whose inhabitants are 'Amigos
de las aves y los ínfimos seres'. In 'Hombre planetario' XIX,
when he affirms his faith in the future of our own planet,
he returns to precisely these points: 'El mundo será entonces
de las fuentes / y las espigas' (OPC 450). Though one may
be struck by the sheer optimism and ingenuousness of such
a picture, it is important to bear in mind two points. The
first is that this vision of a future way of life on Earth is
based on the same yearning for the unattainable as his
longing for personal escape. That is, however remote the
achievement of the ideal may seem at the present time and

---

[27] As will be seen in chapter VII, the image of an island frequently does
represent the idea of imprisonment, solitude, or exile; it serves to suggest refuge
in several poems besides 'Islario', however.

in the present environment, he affirms the necessity for this change to take place if a solution is to be found for his own and mankind's problems. [28] Secondly, his universal solution comes as a consequence of his profound faith in the powers of nature for himself on a personal level.

Finally, it must be emphasised that Carrera Andrade is not advocating for man the complete rejection of all technological advances. It is not a question simply of returning to the state of innocence attributed by the Romantics to the noble savage, not a rebirth of the era of the pre-Inca chieftains Tumbe, Quitumbe, and Guayanay, or of Atahualpa himself, [29] but a harmonious blending of all the advantages that modern civilisation has brought with all the basic virtues of primitive civilisations. Thus, although he complains in 'Hombre planetario' XIII of man's excessive attention to machines at the expense of his natural instinct (even to the extent of wastefully concentrating his energies on space-travel) (OPC 446) he can see a place for machines in his Utopia, or, rather, in his 'Aurosia':

> Máquinas silenciosas andan, cavan, construyen,
> producen luz, transforman en mil cosas el oro.   (OPC 398)

Clearly, he recognises their constructive, productive functions. It is a question of balance and of priorities. Machines should serve mankind, but unobtrusively ('silenciosas'): and before travelling in machines to other planets man should improve his own: 'Por ahora me basta con la tierra' ('Hombre planetario', XIII — OPC 446).

In the course of this section it has been argued that nature plays a major part in providing solutions to Carrera Andrade's ontological problems. Most of the ideas and attitudes discussed here could hardly be considered completely original. Communion with nature, the use of themes taken from the countryside, the view that nature reflects and influences the poet's mood — these fundamental precepts will

---

[28] 'No puedo abandonar mi fe en el hombre', he admitted to the author in an interview in Paris, 7 July 1972. Evil and destruction were transitory. He was, therefore, 'optimista en cuanto al futuro humano'.
[29] See 'Los antepasados' (OPC 462-3) and 'Ocaso de Atahualpa' (OPC 459-60), and Chapter III, VI, where the poems are discussed.

be found underlying verse throughout the ages. More particularly, they are important aspects of the *modernista* climate in which he grew up and the *postmodernista* period in
which he began writing. The French Symbolists' working
principles that there exist equivalences among the different
senses; that the poet's own senses have corresponding images
in the world at large and *vice versa;* and that the reality
around us constitutes a world of appearances that have a
mystical basis perceptible to the visionary eye of a poet, [30]
clearly pertain to Carrera Andrade's own practice and attitude. Yet it is maintained that with these commonplace
materials he has built a structure that reveals his own peculiar character. The combination and the emphasis are his.

These chief aspects of nature's role in his poetry may be
summarised as follows: It acts as the elemental life force,
instilling vigour in the poet's daily existence, and encouraging attention to the pleasures of the earth. So influential
is nature, and so intimate its relationship with the poet,
that he endows it with a character sometimes human and
sometimes quasi divine. There is a dialogue between him
and nature. It speaks to him through signs, leading him to
believe that he — and all men — should learn about the
world and about existence by studying these signs. In return
he himself addresses nature, posing questions, expressing his
delight or his gratitude, and even invoking its god-like
powers to help in his afflictions. It provides company in his
solitude, and an antidote to the inherent ills of city life. In
all these respects, nature's function is first on a private level;
but the solutions it provides extend to all men, in the same
way as Carrera Andrade's ontological problems were found
to be those typical of modern man.

It will be noticed that some of these functions of nature
were anticipated in chapter III, when the poet's treatment
of Ecuador was under discussion. The reason lies in the
close link between nature in general as a poetic theme and
Ecuador specifically. In the first place, Ecuador is regarded
as the virginal land; like nature in general, it stands in

---

[30] See Marcel Raymond *De Baudelaire au Surréalisme*, José Corti, Paris, 1940,
pp. 23-5.

opposition to the world of cities. Also, the poet's animist treatment of nature has been seen to derive — at least in part — from the culture of his indigenous ancestors. Ecuador is treated as a key to problems: indeed a key to some of those same problems resolved by nature. It offers refuge from a technological world, spiritual comfort, and a means of dreaming about the recovery of lost youth and innocence. And like nature, Ecuador is treated as though it had divine power to answer the poet's supplications. In fact, the two are not merely linked, they form an indissoluble unit.

II. THE ETERNAL PRESENT

The Limits of Religious Experience

After his primary education Carrera Andrade spent a brief period at a school of religious instruction, the Colegio de la Merced. Although he was soon transferred to the secular, Liberal, Instituto Nacional "Mejía", that period, combined with the more substantial Catholic influence of his mother and his aunts, produced a significant influence on him. Within the Colegio de la Merced, he recalls, he received 'la revelación de la paz beatífica' (VC 25). The environment had an overwhelming effect on him: 'Tantas luces, tantos oros, me deslumbraban. Tanto incienso, tanto olor delicado de estolas y casullas me embriagaban hasta el punto de hacerme olvidar las miserias terrenales, en un transporte de mis sentidos' (ibid.). José de la Cuadra, in a section of his *Doce siluetas* dedicated to Carrera Andrade, emphasises perhaps excessively the absence of religious influences on the young man: '... No sintió pesar sobre su infancia, en el hogar paterno, la tristeza religiosa. Su niñez no fue una noche fanática, sino un amanecer pagano'.[31] But he is undoubtedly right in saying that melancholy and fanaticism were absent from any religious influence, and the poet's own recollections of the Colegio suggest an almost pagan sensuality in his reactions to the atmosphere. It is important

---

[31] José de la Cuadra, *Obras completas*, Casa de la Cultura Ecuatoriana, Quito, 1958, p. 829. *Doce siluetas* was first published in 1934.

to establish from the outset that despite his Liberal education, his thirst for knowledge, his temporary lapse into bohemian living (around 1926-8), his constant metaphysical disquiet, and his apparent failure to find an answer for his problems in the Christian religion, the evidence suggests that he has not rebelled violently against the Catholic church; not, at least, with sufficient violence to direct any attacks against it in verse or in prose.

Some of his early poems may indeed be taken as the work of a man inspired by religious sentiment. 'Nueva oración por el ebanista' (OPC 131), for example, is a prayer for a humble man who has died. Carrera Andrade virtually requests that he be granted a place in Heaven. In the collection entitled 'La hora de las ventanas iluminadas' (OPC 103-20) [32] he often evokes, uncritically, an impression of saintliness or of mysticism. The poem on his aunt, 'Isolina', is of this kind, respectfully and admiringly depicting her as pure, innocent, pious, and industrious; above all, she has an ethereal aura: she is 'Envuelta en una limpia claridad de manzana' and she moves about with almost angelic wings:

> Isolina: un revuelo de ropa almidonada
> que aletea turbando el corredor monjil.   (OPC 106)

This unearthly quality is perhaps the most typical feature of the collection.

In these early poems, moreover, Carrera Andrade often uses Christian terminology. At times the intention is to introduce a religious note. But such usage does not necessarily imply acceptance of the doctrines or institutions to which the terms refer. In 'Primavera y Compañía' (OPC 123), for example, the comparison of a blossoming tree to a person dressed for his 'primera comunión' is contrived to introduce associations with youth, innocence, and purity, and to evoke simple visual impressions of colour. In instances of this kind the Roman Catholic religion is used as a framework for poetic imagery, as a result of certain habits of thought and

---

[32] Originally only eight poems in ROL (pp. 43-57).

speech which formed during his religious education and took firm root.

The poems do seem to suggest, however, a certain inclination toward the mystical side of religious experience. The poem 'La hora de las ventanas iluminadas' best illustrates these points:

> Desde mi sillón tatarabuelo
> oigo el dulce llamado de novena.   (ROL 56; OPC 110) [33]

The poet is attracted by the idea of acts of worship; indeed, he gives the impression of being old and infirm, and of needing their warming effect. It is clear that he is thinking of his spiritual health (in the penultimate line he uses the word 'alma'). Yet despite the suggestion that he has a great longing for spiritual comfort, there is also the idea that he is unable actively to look for it, since he seems incapable of moving from his chair. Unable to stir, his soul is an 'alma paralítica'. The call to Novena is like having God within reach, between praying hands. But the key note of the poem seems to be struck when Carrera Andrade exclaims, as though with yearning and regret, that he is unable to respond:

> Ah, no poder calentar esta vida
> cerca de un corazón cual de una estufa.   (ROL 57; OPC 110)

This is a nostalgia for spiritual life grown cold, a desire for religious experience to take the place of inner aridity. At the same time there is a possible hint that this longing is contradicted by his own inertia. [34]

Thirty years later, in 'El alba llama a la puerta', he expresses a feeling essentially similar to this. In the autumn of his life he is needful of the concept of God and of the accompanying experiences. What he has is, not a belief in God, but an 'apetito de Dios' (OPC 524). It is an impression strengthened by a passage from an even more recent

---

[33] The version in OPC gives 'repique' for 'llamado'.
[34] Carrera Andrade's later alteration of 'llamado' supports the argument here. In place of a word which suggests a beckoning, or a call from God, he substitutes one which merely designates the sound of the bells.

poem, 'Estaciones de Stony Brook' (1971). In section III, where the poet contemplates the bleakness of winter, whose snows blank out the signs of nature as though the countryside were a page without words, a part of the scene is as follows:

> La Sagrada Biblia está abierta sobre la mesa
> en el capítulo de los Salmos.   (OPC 588)

There are two significant points here. In the first place, the very presence of the Bible implies that he is far from completely rejecting its message. Secondly, however, the reading of the Psalms would seem to suggest not a search for the truth of the Christian gospel but a search for comfort in those songs where poets lament their tribulations and beseech God for his succour and protection. [35] Carrera Andrade's mood is reflected in that of the psalmists. It is a question of the attraction of God, rather than of the Christian faith or the Catholic church. Clearly, he is tempted by the solution that a faith in God would bring to his ontological problems but he seems unable to make the leap. In the opinion of H. Rodríguez Castelo (the only critic to have given any serious consideration to Carrera Andrade's position with regard to religion) it is a question of the poet's fear of encountering God: 'Pero después de haber dado algunos pasos .... siente vértigo; le acometen, acaso, oscuros e inconscientes temores de dar con Dios, y como quien se ahoga vuelve por aire y luz....'. [36] Whether it is this fear that holds him back or some other factor, such as the inability to renounce his doubt, it is difficult to say with any certainty. What is clear, however, is that his reason produces insuperable obstacles. He is tormented by the absurdity of an existence limited to the duration of the human body. Moreover, God occasionally appears in his poems in an unfavourable light. Thus, in 'Nada nos pertenece' the poet expresses the idea that man lives in unquestioning enjoyment of his experiences until the moment comes for him to be

---

[35] The psalms also sing in praise of God; but it seems unlikely that Carrera Andrade is thinking of this here.

[36] Hernán Rodríguez Castelo, *Gangotena, Escudero y Carrera Andrade. Tres cumbres de nuestro postmodernismo*. Clásicos Ariel, Guayaquil/Quito, 1972, Estudio preliminar, p. 67 of ms.

confronted by the vastness of the universe, his own insignificance, the transitory nature of all earthly things, the inevitability of his own death, and the anguished search for an explanation. God's role is seen as that of a harsh master:

> cuando Dios te espolea te arrodillas
> y sólo la memoria de las cosas
> pone un calor ya inútil en tus manos vacías.   (OPC 285)

His preoccupation with human suffering and with the injustices of life on earth adds to this metaphysical problem. He does not find God to be answering the needy or to be insisting on justice. In 'Hombre planetario' XVIII he expresses the idea of the violent repression and destruction of innocents through the image of an Indian farmer, peace-loving and simple, demanding only his freedom, who is mercilessly crushed by the army, which acts on behalf of the law of the country. In face of such patent injustice, Carrera Andrade is perplexed and even, it would appear, antagonised by the silence of the Church, by the fear among God's servants, or by God's own indifference or inability to prevent such a situation:

> (Dios estaba escondido en una granja
> y contempló en silencio
> el sacrificio de los inocentes
> y su mundo en escombros.)   (OPC 449)

In fact, the role normally attributed to God is sometimes assumed by other things in Carrera Andrade's poetry. 'El libro de la bondad' constitutes the neatest example of the quasi divine power of nature in his system of thought. The poem openly states that the physical world of nature has the ability to instruct him in such a way as to improve his moral behaviour and constitution. He deliberately establishes a comparison between the Church and the countryside; as God's truth is discerned in the Bible, that of nature is decyphered in the view from a window. The last four lines clinch the point:

Bebo el vaso del éxtasis y aprendo a ser más bueno
sentado a la vidriera, el fiel libro del campo,
donde una confesión de monja es el silencio
y el sauce la celeste meditación de un santo.   (OPC 108)

When he seeks spiritual help his verse invokes, not God,
but a variety of phenomena in the natural world, such as
the vine (OPC 396), the Mediterranean (OPC 397), the River
Machángara (OPC 155), Ecuador (OPC 416), autumn (OPC
419), the macaw (OPC 457), the rain (OPC 515), storm water
(OPC 512), and the air (OPC 527). The evidence is not
incontrovertible: it is possible to conceive of nature as reflecting the perfection of God himself in Christian as well
as pagan terms. But in Carrera Andrade's verse the emphasis
is sensual rather than religious. It appears ultimately that
he expects the answers to his questions about existence to
come not from the Christian God, not from outside the world
of his experience, but from the Earth itself.

Coming to Terms with Death

In recent years there are signs that Carrera Andrade has
been able — in some measure — to become reconciled with
death. At the time (1937) of 'La alquimia vital' (OPC 263),
it will be recalled, he was horrified and repelled by death,
whose effects were perceived at work on his own body. Life
itself was considered a process of dying. From this period
he was tormented, and at times, it seemed, obsessed, by
the signs of dying in all the world around him, as in 'Polvo,
cadáver del tiempo' (OPC 280-1). Death was seen as destructive, sinister, antagonistic to man. But in *Poesía última*
and *Misterios naturales* there are several poems which indicate a partial change of attitude. Recognising death's
inevitability, accepting it as a law of nature, he is able to
reduce the degree of torment, horror, fear, and indignation.
Moreover, death no longer always seems unjust.

The new attitude is envisaged as one that it would be
possible for man to hold in a Utopia. 'Hombre planetario'
XIX, where Carrera Andrade gives an impression of his ideal
future world, includes a passing reference to the end of a
life of peace, warmth, cheerfulness, harmonious brotherhood,

and abundance, in which men have been free of any fear
of death catching them unawares ('libres ya de la muerte
solapada'). Under such conditions, men can accept and even
welcome the arrival of death:

> Los ancianos tan sólo, en el domingo
> de su vida apacible,
> esperarán la muerte,
> la muerte natural, fin de jornada,
> paisaje más hermoso que el poniente.   (OPC 450)

It is, therefore, a natural emergence out of a life close to
nature, one of nature's laws. The fact that it is enduring
does not prevent its having a certain beauty. Another version
of Carrera Andrade's Utopia, 'Aurosia', far from excluding
the notion of death, far from making life itself appear a
permanent state, treats death as perfectly acceptable as long
as it is not accompanied by illness, misery, or senility:

> Jóvenes de cien años, vigorosos y lúcidos,
> en los jardines de oro van a esperar la muerte.   (OPC 398)

This process of coming to terms with death, which at first
seems to have been most clearly revealed in poems where
Carrera Andrade is dealing not so much with his own private
experience as with a vision of the ideal condition of mankind,
gradually evolves as an aspect of the poet's preoccupation
with his own destiny. In this aspect it is best illustrated by
the short allegorical poem 'Interior':

> Sombra: me espías detrás de las ventanas.
> No te conozco
> y cierro las cortinas
> para no ver tu rostro.
> Luz de interior bendita.
> Sirven el postre azul del destino en bandejas.
> Todo vuelve a lucir de íntimo gozo.
> Descorro las cortinas:
> Sólo la noche guiña detrás de las ventanas.   (OPC 537)

Ostensibly the poem concerns Carrera Andrade's reaction to
the darkness outside while he is dining in his house. But we
know that every part of nature, every object of the world

is capable of acting as a symbol for him, and that darkness
and night have often served to represent death (as in 'Morada terrestre' — OPC 270). His main theme here is not the
night but death. [37] Windows have always been especially
significant for Carrera Andrade as the opening through which
his eyes might discover the world. Darkness, preventing that
discovery, is suggestive of the negation of life's essential
activity; in other words, it is evocative of death itself. Death
therefore fills the frame of the poet's vision, taking the
place of the world of objects (visible during the daylight
hours). It is threatening in its appearance: not only is it
actually seen, as though it were an object, but it appears
to be peering in at the poet. The use of the verb 'espías'
suggests the idea that Carrera Andrade feels himself to be
singled out, as though he sensed that death had its attention
riveted on him. But more than this: death is apparently
acting with stealth. All these factors combine to express a
sense of being menaced. The fear is intensified by the fact
that darkness, denying perception, denies knowledge and
understanding, and thus creates mystery. At this stage in
the poem Carrera Andrade's attitude toward death is ap-
proximately that discussed in the chapter on his ontological
problems: he is afraid of both its menacing power and its
unknown quality. His reaction is to shut out any awareness
of its lurking proximity. With the curtains drawn, however,
the light inside the room restores his confidence in an ability
to see things, to discover messages, to live, despite the presence of death; the food serves to instil a feeling of inner
delight. Now he is able to accept his destiny, as if it were
something that could be served to him in the same way as
a dessert is brought (near the *end* of a meal, it will be
noticed). He can confront death without fear, without a
sense of menace or of incomprehension. It is not the mysterious unknown ('sombra') but the known phenomenon to
which a name is attributable ('noche'). Thus, the experience
of life itself — its delights — brings an acceptance of death.

---

[37] The word 'destino' in the sixth line is a precise indication of the poet's
allegorical intentions.

In this most recent phase of his thought, Carrera Andrade is able, at times, to transcend the mere acceptance of death's inevitability, and to find even a positive value offered by it. Several of the 'Quipos' of *Misterios naturales* express the various facets of this attitude. [38] In III he suggests that death may be a kind of birth, a beginning, something that gives man the identity and meaningfulness that he has lacked during his life-time:

> Somos nadie
> hasta que nos da a luz
> la muerte-madre.   (OPC 578)

In IV the idea is suggested that death could be seen as the key to life's secret:

> guardiana del secreto
> del mundo verde.   (OPC 579)

An analogous idea is that death may be an eternal spiritual experience (or an eternal day of rest), as in IX:

> Es el domingo
> sin fin
> de los héroes sepultados.   (OPC 580)

Further discussion of this topic is reserved for the following chapter where, in the course of an analysis of 'Libro del destierro', it will be shown precisely how this new outlook on death relates to the poet's other major themes. Enough has been said to establish the point that death has sometimes emerged as not so much an instigator of Carrera Andrade's ontological problems as a possible solution to them. It should always be remembered, however, that his anguish has by no means been completely dispelled in recent years (as was indicated in chapter V). All it is possible to affirm is that it has been increasingly counterbalanced by elements

---

[38] Carrera Andrade explains in a note that 'Los *quipos* eran cordeles de colores con nudos, utilizados por los Incas para consignar la memoria de los sucesos' (OPC 578). His own poetic adaptations are late equivalents of the *microgramas* (discussed in chapter III, III), but with emphasis on thought rather than image, a more flexible and slightly longer form, and usually a starting-point in the poet's 'yo' rather than in the world of creatures, elements, and objects.

of hope, one of which consists in the possibility that death
may be regarded as something meaningful rather than
absurd, acceptable rather than menacing, a beginning rather
than an end. The most characteristic aspect of this reconciled
view of death is that it is simply one of the natural laws
of the universe, a condition of life itself. Ultimately, it is
necessary for him to fall back on life itself in the hope of
finding a key.

Intense Experience. Love. Light. The Eternal Present

When Carrera Andrade acknowledges that he has not
encountered a religious faith that promises eternal life, in
'Sombra en el muro', it is not with a sense of failure:

> Yo sé que cuando muera
> dirán de mí: ardió como una brasa;
> fue ala, raíz, trigo,
> mas no encontró el camino de lo eterno.
> No se habrán dado cuenta
> de mi descubrimiento .... (OPC 531)

By interpreting the messages of the Universe he believes that
he has discovered a truth of a kind. Without stating categorically that eternal life is but a wishful dream, he discloses
that two things are certain: since his life on earth is fleeting,
he is an impermanent figure, lacking tangible, absolute reality
('una sombra en el muro'); but on the other hand, that
degree of reality is as much as he will ever achieve, and
it is living and fertile ('pero una sombra de árbol'). If no
key to his existence may be found outside this earthly life,
then that key — or a substitute — must lie within it. Although
he may still be searching, he has discovered that the key's
purpose is served by a rich, full existence. He is a mere
shadow, but the shadow of a tree that is 'constelado de
frutos'.

A notable comparison may be made between this poem
and 'Caudales' (OPC 537-8). The latter is another case of self-
assessment, but instead of a confident affirmation that he
has discovered the equivalent of lasting spiritual values he
now bases the poem on a regretful denial that he has en-

countered any durable values of a material kind. As though counting his earnings, he finds that his life has been a vain search, that he has constructed nothing, that he has accumulated no wealth, and that he has no concrete relics or permanence on earth. In compensation, however, he has read the signs of nature, enjoyed the delights of each day, and gathered emotional experience (especially human fellowship). The essence of his life's virtues is therefore precisely the same as in 'Sombra en el muro'. Whether he is able to assert it confidently as a justification of existence or is merely compelled to accept it as one of the few valid aspects of existence, intense experience clearly constitutes a vital solution to his ontological problems.

In a general sense, it may be said that Carrera Andrade's travels throughout the world have been his response to the need to accumulate rich experience. His observation of foreign lands (and his notes on the discoveries) have been a part of his attempt to draw as close as possible to the truth, to reality, to the meaning of existence. People, human relationships, countries, scenery, creatures, the elements, and objects all construct the very substance of life. One of the constant problems is that time relentlessly sweeps away even these things. As he admits in 'Cada objeto es un mundo', there is an inherent impossibility in rendering tangible and durable this intense experience of the world; but it must be attempted nevertheless:

> Apresa en tus dedos la brisa
> que pasa fugaz, indecisa. (OPC 435)

Indeed, with effort it is possible to achieve an effect similar to that of slowing the pace of time. It is a question of concentrating on each experience, of relishing it to the full:

> No veas el mundo de prisa. (ibid.)

One experience especially able to produce these results is love. It is among the three things which serve to make him not a mere shadow but a shadow of a full, rich tree — in the terms he uses in 'Sombra en el muro'. Despite the fact that Carrera Andrade has written but relatively few love

poems, he has made frequent reference to love in poems that
are based on other themes. It clearly constitutes an important
aspect of the solutions to his ontological problems. In poems
collected in *Rol de la manzana* (1935), such as those grouped
under the heading 'Mujeres y puertos' (ROL 61-76; OPC
201-9), love and woman are seen as one aspect of the theme
of adventure and discovery, like travel itself, and like visits
to new cities. A few years later, in 'Zona minada' (*País secreto*, 1939), sexual experience is shown to have a transcendental quality, as though it were the fulfilment of a sacred
ritual, obedient to the laws of the elemental life force:

> Cumplo la voluntad
> secreta de la tierra.   (OPC 282)

Later still, in 'Lección del árbol, la mujer y el pájaro' (*Aquí
yace la espuma*, 1950), in the third section of the poem
entitled 'Árbol de luz tu cuerpo' (OPC 334-5), Carrera Andrade finds woman capable of conquering his solitude. She
is, moreover, 'la excelsa forma humana', and this is where
her prime attraction lies, her main source of interest for the
poet. It is true that even when she is no longer youthful
she remains music, aroma, and light. But when her beauty
becomes 'derruida arquitectura' it is cause for lament and
constitutes yet another sign of the transitory nature of
delightful things. What makes woman especially valuable,
therefore, in this poem and others, is her physical form and
her capacity to provide sensual experience.

Turning now to the collection 'La visita del amor' (1958),
we find, in the title poem, a tentative version of the defi-
nitive view of love in Carrera Andrade's poetry. It awakens
him, revitalises him, cancels the effect of darkness, and
clothes the world with a new radiance:

> Pero el fuego revive a tu llegada
> y las cosas se visten de luz maravillosa.   (OPC 405)

Love transforms the world into a joyful place and the poet
into a happy man. Among its attributes one should not fail
to notice its essential similarity to the world of nature:

En tus ojos, Amor, cantan los pájaros;   (ibid.)

and:

Hoy, Amor, me conviertes en el dueño
de tus pastos de sol, tu gran reino de flores.   (ibid.)

In this poem there are signs that love possesses a supernatural quality, clearer signs than those of 'Zona minada'. For example, love is a source of life: 'me das la vida' (ibid.). It transforms stone into a spring, an orchid into an angel (OPC 406). Moreover, its powers pertain to the realm of mysticism; in his search for the meaning of his existence, and in his thirst for a way to eternal life, he discovers in love a possible solution: it is a 'ventana al infinito' (ibid.). Similarly, when expressing his attitude to love in 'Hombre planetario', VII, he evokes an impression of the sexual act as a way to infinity, thereby attributing to it a quasi-spiritual function:

Minero del amor, cavo sin tregua
hasta hallar el filón del infinito.   (OPC 443)

In various poems there are metaphorical references to love or to woman which broaden this idea. In 'Cuerpo de la amante' woman's body is not only a spring, but a god (OPC 408), a temple (OPC 410), a cathedral (ibid.), even Truth itself (ibid.). A wife's love, as it is seen in 'La esposa', has a religious power comparable to that of the Christian gospel:

Tu amor es como el pan del evangelio,
manantial que discurre en onda pura
abrevando mi sed de eternidad
en dones sucesivos de hermosura.   (OPC 496)

It will be noticed that in the last example, besides making deliberate use of Christ's own metaphors ('I am the bread of life: he that cometh to me shall never hunger; and he that believeth on me shall never thirst'), [39] Carrera Andrade spells out the fundamental symbolism by stating that a woman's love and beauty have the saving power of eternal

---

[39] St. John's Gospel, 6, verse 35.

life. In 'Hombre planetario', VII, love and woman, considered each in turn as complementary parts of a single whole,
are evoked in similarly Biblical language: love is resurrection
and rebirth; woman is the promised land of milk and honey
(OPC 442-3).

Carrera Andrade does not seek to suggest that woman
or sexual love are the exact equivalents of Christ. There is,
clearly, a vital difference in their function. While the Biblical
Saviour is the way to eternity of the spirit, Carrera Andrade's
love of man for woman is, ultimately, confined to the human
body and to this earthly life. Thus, in 'Hombre planetario',
VII, love is 'resumen de la tierra' (OPC 443). But the idea
is that a man's love for a woman is a means of achieving
some kind of spiritual need through physical experience.
Indeed, the great role played by woman seems to be her
capacity for providing intense experience for all Carrera
Andrade's senses; she is an anthology which he reads 'con
mis cinco sentidos' (OPC 409). In much the same way as
nature instils in the poet a zest for life, woman enables him
to live in plenitude. So full is the experience of love, so
sharply does it bring to life the five senses, that its value
seems infinitely greater than that of the daily routine. While
the colourless days of the week speed insipidly by, in 'Hombre planetario', III, there seems no point in measuring time
in the conventional way, for this would imply an absolute
quality to an interval such as an hour, in which the measure
would be invariable irrespective of how that hour is passed.
Far more constructive, to Carrera Andrade's mind, is the
process of assessing time in terms of human experience: the
hours of bitter or of joyful feelings, the minutes of silences
or of solitudes. In these terms, intense experience is able to
fill out time, as though multiplying the value of each interval.
At the supreme point of this experience time seems to cease
its flow, and the present moment assumes the semblance
of eternity. Love, in this sense, can bring eternity, as the
poet writes in 'Hombre planetario', VI:

> Yo viví sesenta años en un día
> y en una hora de amor
> sesenta eternidades.   (OPC 442)

One reason for the importance of love among Carrera Andrade's solutions to ontological problems is that it is a direct expression of man's natural instinct. Sexual love's connection with the idea of fertility and with the elemental life force draws it close to nature, and to all that nature represents for the poet. Another, however, is that love is a source of sheer delight and joy, the height of human happiness: 'la isla más dichosa', as he expresses it in 'La esposa' (OPC 497). It is not, clearly, the only source of this state. The presence of nature is capable of inspiring a sense of exaltation and joy in him when his faculties are attuned to it. The rose that represents nature in 'Hombre planetario', XV, is therefore compared to a kiss, proof of love (OPC 448). What brings life to nature and thus produces its overwhelming effect in Carrera Andrade is light. There is something divine in light, as there is saving power in love and woman. As light clothes nature like a tunic and makes the sky smile, its visual effect becomes equivalent to an uplifting spiritual experience. Light brings joy, and joy is the earth's substitute for God. In 'Dios de alegría':

> Todo era lenguaje
> divino.
> Cada ala era un viaje
>
> hacia el Dios de alegría,
> todo luz.
> El mundo ardía.   (OPC 530)

In 'Las armas de la luz' (OPC 372-8) the poet expresses the sense of being encircled by the blue of the sky, held within a physical boundary; but this is also a visual image for the feeling of being held within that moment in time when all the light seems to be focussed on every tree, rock, and insect around him. The light gives an impression not merely of reflecting from all these objects but of actually being present within them ('omnipresente en árbol, roca, insecto' — OPC 372), endowing them with special qualities. Since it provides them with a message, it is an 'idioma de luz'. Since without light objects are unseen, light gives them existence, is their creator, and therefore is the origin of the intense experience they afford:

La luz hace nacer todas las formas. (ibid.)

There is a parallel between its function and that of God, emphasised by reminders of its heavenly source ('venida de la altura') and transcendental significance ('palabra de lo eterno'). As the creator of intense experience, it is responsible for that which gives meaning to Carrera Andrade's existence, while as a source of messages communicated by objects, it provides him with a degree of understanding which is akin to new birth. Light is not, however, an aloof creator but an intimate, loving source of life, and for this reason it can inspire in Carrera Andrade the image of mother: 'madre del universo', provoking in every planet the response of love (OPC 373). There is an intentional or subconscious connection with the Roman Catholic religion of his childhood, as seems to be indicated in the line 'hasta el fin de los siglos siempre virgen' which closely precedes (and possibly gives rise to) the concept of mother. But it is unnecessary to pursue this point, for what is important is his clear intention to draw a parallel between light and divinity while at the same time maintaining the essentially empirical basis of his concepts. Once again we are confronted with the idea that an explanation of ontological problems and the satisfaction of his aspirations to eternity are to be encountered in the plenitude of physical sensation at a moment in time. For Descartes a proof of existence was found in the mind: 'Je pense, donc je suis'. [40] In the case of Carrera Andrade, who clearly recalls these well-known words, the intellect's self-awareness is not the vital proof, nor does that proof spring from any source within the individual mind. Rather, it comes from outside, from his physical experience, from the world of objects, and above all from the light which brings them to life:

---

[40] *Discours de la Méthode*, Quatrième Partie, Manchester University Press, 2nd ed., 1961, pp. 31 & 32. It should be added that Descartes was not primarily concerned with proving his existence, but with demonstrating the power of his thought in determining the truth of things. Thus, the notion that 'pour penser il faut être' (p. 32) — which for him was self-evident — served as a point of departure in proving that 'les choses que nous concevons fort clairement et fort distinctement sont toutes vraie ......' (ibid.).

La luz me mira: existo.   (ibid.) [41]

It is important to notice at this juncture that the role of light has certain repercussions in his poetic technique. In his most recent poetic credo, 'El combate poético' (OPC 596), he constructs his theme on the struggle between light and darkness. Poetry affords the armour of light (it is associated with images of 'arma', 'lo bello', 'el reinado del rocío', 'cristal', 'armadura transparente', 'el patrimonio de la luz') with which he may conquer all that is symbolised by the dark enemy ('enemigo oculto', 'la sombra', 'la injusticia', 'la noche', 'el estiércol', 'la fealdad', 'el Oscuro'). It is a credo with a double edge, for it alludes to poetry's social function, which does not concern us here, as well as to the form that poetic expression should take. But essentially it is the development of ideas expressed many years before. In 'El objeto y su sombra' (OPC 179) he stresses the supremacy of things over abstractions — things liberated from their shadows. In 'Invocación a la palabra' (OPC 383-4) he urges the poetic word to be the kernel, the essence, a mirror, a close-fitting form, and an exact measure of the world; there should be no phantoms, no mist, no shadows, and no ornaments.

These aesthetic principles have governed the bulk of his work. Even when expressing highly subjective impressions of the world, he leaves his meaning clear. When he uses objects as symbols, or when he creates metaphors, there is rarely great obscurity. The term 'hermetic', sometimes no more than an euphemism for 'obscure', is totally inapplicable to his verse. The symbolic function of the dewdrop in 'Vida del rocío' (OPC 526), for example, presents no problems because it has attributes directly corresponding to those of real dew; there is no incongruity, no illogical subjection of the object's essential physical qualities to the poet's whim. The dewdrop is fresh, crystalline, watery, quivering, full of light, and transparent. It poses delicately on a blade of grass

---

[41] Carrera Andrade is nearer to Jorge Guillén ('Soy, más, estoy. Respiro ......', *Cántico*, Ed. Sudamericana, Buenos Aires, 5a ed., 1962, p. 18) than to Descartes, though he introduces spiritual and religious connotations that are not included by the Spanish poet.

for a brief period, until under the dissipating effect of the sun it falls to earth and vanishes (lines 9-20). Even certain images are aptly based on the physical appearance: like a minute convex mirror it reflects a wide area of the countryside (4-5); its form is reminiscent of a tear-drop (6), and its quivering is like the pulsating of a heart (9-10). Without altering the recognisable outward properties of a dewdrop, Carrera Andrade endows it with a number of characteristics that inevitably introduce affective connotations and intellectual concepts. The beauty of the dewdrop is doomed to be ephemeral because it is imprisoned within the confines of a delicate physical substance which the elemental processes of nature are bound to destroy. The dew seems full of intense life (it contains a universe and a palpitating heart) but already it evokes a sense of fear ('tembloroso') and grief ('lágrima de la hoja') in the face of certain annihilation. An unmistakable universalising effect is achieved through the use of key terms: 'paisaje' and 'universo' suggest it is a microcosm of the world; 'lágrima' and 'corazón' connect its fate with that of human lives; 'gloria' and 'memoria' are abstract terms implying that it epitomises the transitory nature of all things. This kind of transparent technique seeks, therefore, to communicate fully, to avoid areas of uncertain meaning. It has, however, a disadvantage. While not precluding complexity (for indeed many of Carrera Andrade's poems are complex) it can endanger subtlety. When the poet exclaims, in 'Vida del rocío', '¡Oh efímera gloria!' he lends emphasis to his dismay, discarding all appearance of giving a pictorial impression and stressing his own emotional involvement in the fate of the dew. Yet it is unnecessary to the reader's understanding, and may even be felt a disappointing intrusion, denying the reader that sense of participation derived from the act of interpreting. This tendency towards a lack of subtlety occasionally manifests itself in prosaic lines. [42] In one of his major works, 'Hombre planetario', where the method is to dilate rather than to com-

---

[42] This impression coincides with a passing comment in Enrique Ojeda, *J.C.A. Introducción* ......, where one of Carrera Andrade's poems is being compared with one by Francis Jammes: 'Carrera Andrade coincidió con su maestro aun en aquel exagerado prosaísmo en que éste a veces consentía' (p. 71).

press, there are one or two passages of this kind. In two lines at the end of Canto V he resorts to straightforward statement, as though the preceding images were insufficiently clear:

> Eternidad, tus signos me rodean,
> más yo soy transitorio.   (OPC 442)

while in XX the enumeration of peoples and places from all over the world are deemed inadequate to evoke a sense of universal identity, so that he rounds the list off with an anticlimactic summary:

> y soy los demás hombres del planeta.   (OPC 451)

In defence against the criticism that his poetry is excessively lucid, he has argued as follows:

> Some criticism adduces that an obscure zone should exist in poetry which obliges the reader to search for the mystery it contains. I deem that the language itself has in it a sufficient dose of enigma, the metaphysical echo or the repercussions of darkness which make the deliberate use of obscurity unnecessary. In addition, one of the essential aims of what is poetical is communion with other men. If poetry cannot transmit its emotional or sensory content, it no longer accomplishes its mission, which is to interpret the world, to make it tangible. I do not regret that logic, an indiscreet lamp, has lighted my poetic world. On the contrary, its light symbolises the endless vigil, the permanent watchfulness of consciousness over my poetry.
>
> ('Poetry of Reality and Utopia', SAP 81)

His method of vindication is not to point out the error of writing in a manner different from his own, but to insist on the reasons for writing as he does. Of particular concern here is that he explicitly states the aim of making his verse readily comprehensible, so that the world may be 'interpreted' and made 'tangible'. To this end he advocates the exercise of intellectual control over sentiment and intuition. He interprets the objects of the world for other men by bringing light to bear on them within a poem. Unlike the poetry in gestation favoured by some surrealists, his own verse is the finished product. The reader is denied the degree of creative participation required of him by a surrealist poem, but is invited instead to derive sensory and intellectual delight from the lucid, fresh, and sometimes striking expression — in synthesis — of a mood and an idea, illuminated by the 'indiscreet lamp' of logic. There is, then, an indirect link between his vision of the world — a world which he considers susceptible to interpretation — and the poetic technique whereby he elucidates that interpretation. His attitude to light in general connects with his ideal of a clear, transparent technique.

This leads us to the last ramification of these ideas, or more precisely to their culmination, for it is the closest Carrera Andrade seems to have come to finding the ultimate solution to his ontological problems. Plenitude of experience, love and woman, nature and objects, and light have all been found to play a crucial role. The problem is how to realise the potential of these things. Until the period of *Poesía última* (1957-66) they seem often subject to the same laws of transitoriness which afflict the whole of Carrera Andrade's existence. Even in *Poesía última* this is occasionally the case. But *Misterios naturales* (1972) have, on the whole, suggested a more optimistic attitude.

In 'Apetito de realidad' (OPC 536) it was observed above how the poet expresses the power of nature to draw his attention to the plenitude of that moment, thus affirming the value and fertility of life. In 'Estaciones de Stony Brook' (OPC 587-91), particularly sections VI and X, this idea is developed to its natural conclusion: the moment is everything, even eternity itself. It is significant that section VI opens with a line sharply reminiscent of the first and fourth lines of 'Apetito de realidad':

El silbo de un pájaro despierta las semillas

('Apetito', line 1, OPC 536)

... un pájaro / que picotea en el tramo de la percepción

('Apetito', lines 3-4, ibid.)

Un ave roja picotea las semillas

('Estaciones', VI, line 1, OPC 589)

Although the precise development of thought in 'Estaciones de Stony Brook' is different, there is clearly an association of ideas, and this should be borne in mind as the later poem is discussed in the ensuing lines.

That Carrera Andrade should choose the framework of changing seasons implies that a sense of time's relentless progress (in a cyclic rhythm) underlies the other themes of 'Estaciones de Stony Brook'. With summer the poem begins, and with summer it ends; but there is always the knowledge that winter will arrive again. In sections II to IV summer's absence gives rise to feelings of nostalgia (II), desolation (III), and fear and withdrawal into oneself (IV), but signs of spring cause a renewed delight (V). In VI, therefore, when the poet evokes the sight of a bird and of seeds the idea is that of new birth, of the repeated (and eternal) beginning of life as revealed in the fertility of nature. What Carrera Andrade does is to attempt to exclude the idea of past and future, and to concentrate his full attention on that moment of fertility. It is the essence of life, the epitome of an eternal pattern and therefore it is itself of eternal significance:

> la eternidad está presa
> en este instante bajo el árbol.   (OPC 589)

Just as a sense of eternity may be thus captured within a moment in time, so it is possible for this moment, if it is spent in the fullness of sensual experience, to hold the transcendental value almost of eternal life. In face of a man's questions about his existence, the nearest he will approach to a complete answer is in receiving vividly all the sensory perceptions of nature, as light brings the objects to full existence and time seems to cease its flow. The present moment and eternity become one, past and future lose their reality, for they are mere pictures and ideas within the mind. Life itself is a succession of eternal presents. Hence the following line, first introduced in VI but repeated at the end of the poem, where it achieves its greatest significance:

> Ahora eterno ahora   (OPC 589 and 591) [43]

---

[43] The deliberate effect achieved by the omission of punctuation in this line is explained by Carrera Andrade in the quotation from a letter to the author below.

Needless to say, the mind persistently introduces the awareness that the present (together with the eternity it embraces) must end when life itself ends. This is indeed a source of great pathos within this poem. Winter will return, nature will continue its progress, but death will eventually hold back the poet, so that he asks poignantly:

¿van a partir sin mí todas las naves?   (OPC 589)

Death remains a threat, the solution expressed will be insufficient to conquer that culmination of the law of nature. Yet without overcoming the menace of death Carrera Andrade does seem to have found a meaning for life. Since the future holds emptiness the present contains everything. And it is on this note of affirming the transcendental importance of the present moment that the poem — almost triumphantly, but not quite so — comes to an end.

When it was suggested to Carrera Andrade that he had been arriving at a new emphasis on the eternal present, the poet replied:

> En efecto, el *ahora eterno ahora* (sin puntuación para significar la continuidad irrompible de dos términos que parecían contrapuestos) es un concepto de la inmovilidad del tiempo y de lo eterno como un presente prolongado. El momento en que el hombre tiene plena conciencia del ser es el *ahora*, ya que el pasado y el futuro son irreales, fantasmagóricos. La vida es un ahora más o menos largo. El pasado ya no existe y el futuro no existe todavía; pero en la dimensión del *ahora* puede caber toda una eternidad, "la eternidad en un minuto". [44]

He then indicated that this is a concept which he has been developing since 'Hombre planetario', where one finds not only the reference to love's ability to afford plenitude of experience and thus swell the length of an hour to eternity (as explained above) but also an allusion to time's being a perpetual, motionless present:

Tiempo cósmico, reinas
sin fin omnipresente,
pulpo gris
sin ayer ni mañana, siempre ahora,
dormido en el espacio.   (OPC 442)

---

[44] Letter to the author, 10 December, 1972.

It will be evident that topics discussed in chapters III and IV are closely associated with the theme of intense experience in an eternal present. There is a link between travel in foreign lands and discovery; there is also a link between Ecuador and nature. A further connection is that of Carrera Andrade's homeland with light, for Ecuador is regarded by the poet as the land of light.

III.   UNIVERSAL UNITY AND SOLIDARITY

One of the tragic circumstances of the individual, Carrera Andrade believes, is his constriction within limits imposed by his perishable body and his isolation in earthly environments. As was remarked earlier, the sense of being part of a transitory worldly existence presents an ontological problem partly resolved through the concept of enjoying to the full the eternal present. But another partial solution might be the idea that the individual's own death is of no significance in relation to the constantly repeated cycle of life. One aspect of such an idea is that the individual lives on, in a sense, in other men, even that he *is* other men besides being himself. Another writer attracted to this idea, Jorge Luis Borges, has expressed the concept succinctly as follows: 'Our destiny is tragic because we are, irreparably, individuals restrained by time and space; consequently, there is nothing more agreeable than a faith which eliminates circumstances and declares that every man is all men and that there is no one who is not the universe'. [45] Similarly, the individual's sense of imprisonment and solitude might be diminished if he were able to believe that everything in the world, including himself, is essentially a part of a single universal Being.

There are no grounds for suggesting the direct influence of Borges on Carrera Andrade. Various philosophers (including Berkeley and Hume) have dealt with the nullification of personality. Diverse forms of pantheism, and extensive literary and folkloric traditions have also covered similar

---

[45] Prologue to Emerson's *Representative Men*, quoted from Ana María Barrenechea, *Borges the Labyrinth Maker*, University of New York Press, 1965, p. 88.

ground. But such sources seem extremely nebulous. The names that it is most fruitful to link with Carrera Andrade's development of these thoughts are Schopenhauer, Whitman, and Montalvo.

Arthur Schopenhauer ('a quien leí en los años mozos como todos los jóvenes latinoamericanos de esa época')[46] is widely recognised as an important source of these ideas among modern poets. Alfredo Lozada, in his book *El monismo agónico de Pablo Neruda,* argues that certain basic concepts of Schopenhauer underlie the poetry of *Residencia en la tierra.* [47] In particular, Neruda reproduces Schopenhauer's view of the universe as ruled by a primordial cosmic energy: 'Wille', which is considered to be an irresistible force or impulse, a material which is eternal and unifying. [48] One consequence of this view is the acceptance that all men, all animals, plants, rocks, objects, the planets and stars themselves are part of a single substance; the various individual forms are in constant conflict with each other in the remorseless struggle for survival. As will be shown presently, a form of this monism is manifest in certain poems of Carrera Andrade's, in particular 'Hombre planetario'. [49]

Though doubting the impact of Schopenhauer, Carrera Andrade has acknowledged a debt to Walt Whitman's *Leaves of Grass:* 'Su sentimiento de universalidad ha tenido un eco profundo en mí, no hay duda'. [50] For Whitman, as one critic has recently observed, 'Body and soul are merged into an indivisible One'. [51] Whitman learned from the teaching of the phrenologists: 'The underlying assumption by the phrenologists ... is that the entire earth — its vast network of inhabitants, plant and animal life, and the universe as well — is an interconnecting network of correspondences testifying

[46] Letter to the author, 28 February 1974.
[47] Alfredo Lozada, *El monismo agónico de Pablo Neruda,* Costa-Amic Editor, Mexico, 1971, especially, pp. 113-6.
[48] See Arthur Schopenhauer, *Die Welt als Wille und Vorstellung,* Leipzig, 1819.
[49] There is no evidence of any direct influence of Schopenhauer on Carrera Andrade. 'No creo deber nada a Schopenhauer ...... El pesimismo de este filósofo ...... me impedía seguirle' (Letter to the author, 28 February 1974). It is suggested, however, that the philosopher's ideas have had such wide repercussions that the poet has absorbed some of them.
[50] Letter to the author, 10 December, 1972.
[51] Arthur Wrobel, 'Whitman and the Phrenologists: The Divine Body and the Sensuous Soul', *P.M.L.A.,* 89, 1974, p. 20.

to the essential unity throughout the whole universe. However complex and chaotic the universe may seem at times, it is basically ordered and unified, reflecting the same attributes of its Creator'. [52] It is indeed possible to argue that the link between Whitman and Carrera Andrade is at times close. Thus, the enumeration in 'Hombre planetario' XX, which will be discussed below, is strongly reminiscent of those of 'Song of Myself', particularly the section commencing 'One of the Nation of many nations, ...' [53]

A comparison of a rather different kind may be made with Juan Montalvo. It is clear from an essay of *Latitudes* that Carrera Andrade felt a spiritual affinity with this earlier master of Ecuadorian literature. [54] He has shared Montalvo's experience of exile, and his sense of solitude. Gradually he has come to mingle, like his predecessor, with people of many countries, and to admire Montalvo's concept of the universal oneness of the human race — his 'universalismo generoso que no creaba una discriminación entre los pueblos y entre las razas', as Carrera Andrade has more recently confessed. [55]

It is of little value to pursue the matter of influences, however, for although the ideas of these authors have impinged on Carrera Andrade's poetry, there is no doubt that the latter's concepts also arise naturally out of his own circumstances and preoccupations. [56] The origin of Carrera Andrade's sense of the oneness of everything may be found in his earliest poetry, where he expresses an impression of patterns in life-forms, patterns which imply that one creature embodies common characteristics, and that something of the world in general may be perceived in the particular. Hence his interest in the various forms of life in nature, even the smallest creatures, like the cicada, snail, cricket, or birds. He

---

[52] Ibid., p. 18.
[53] Walt Whitman, *Leaves of Grass*, D. Appleton & Co., New York & London, 1909, p. 42.
[54] 'Juan Montalvo y yo en París', LAT 113-22.
[55] Enrique Ojeda, 'Entrevista a J.C.A.', *Norte*, 3 + 4, 1968, p. 92.
[56] 'El origen de este concepto no es fruto de una influencia literaria ...... sino que ha existido profundamente arraigado en mi ser desde mi juventud' (Letter to the author, 28 February 1974).

tells us, for example, that 'Los pájaros son / las letras de mano de Dios'. [57]

It is in 'Hombre planetario' that Carrera Andrade reaches the clearest awareness of what arises out of his life-long attention to the messages of nature and objects, his constant communication with them, as though the very plants and rocks of our planet were alive. After expressing his anguish at a sense of lost identity, he blends self-assessment with critical meditation on the evils and ailments of contemporary civilisation. Throughout the poem it is clear that the discovery of his identity, the solution to his personal problems, and the answer to the world's predicament must be simultaneous. In 'Hombre planetario' XV the role of the rose is crucial in initiating his discovery. It will be noticed that he actually addresses the rose, just as he has addressed vegetable life, animals, and inorganic matter in all periods of his poetry. This flower helps the poet to establish an ontological fact. Some hidden life-force, some 'máquina secreta' or 'oculto motor verde' (OPC 447) gives the plant an appearance of self-sufficiency and of a passionate zest for life. Something in the rose suggests a relationship of love between the creatures of the earth, which are doomed to perish, and the earth itself:

> ¿O eres acaso el beso de la tierra
> a todo lo que vive,
> prueba de amor de un día
> a las cosas oscuras
> devoradas a medias por la muerte?   (OPC 448)

In this way he discovers that to be a human being does not mean to be mind or spirit as opposed to body, not abstract as opposed to tangible object, not aloof from or merely a visitor to this planet, but composed of the essential substance of the earth. Thus, in 'Hombre planetario' XVI he expresses the notion of this identification with the earth in the following words:

---

[57] 'Alfabeto', OPC 85. Borges coherently explains this view of the universe in 'El Zahir', El Aleph, Alianza/Emecé, Madrid & Buenos Aires, 1972, p. 115: 'Dijo Tennyson que si pudiéramos comprender una sola flor sabríamos quiénes somos y qué es el mundo. Tal vez quiso decir que no hay hecho, por humilde que sea, que no implique la historia universal y su infinita concatenación de efectos y causas. Tal vez quiso decir que el mundo visible se da entero en cada representación ......'.

Soy hombre, mineral y planta a un tiempo,
relieve del planeta, pez del aire,
un ser terrestre en suma.   (ibid.)

It will be noticed that this amounts to a form of monism. Unlike Schopenhauer, however, Carrera Andrade believes there to be, not conflict, but love between the constituent parts of the single whole. Indeed, the emphasis and purpose are quite peculiar to Carrera Andrade's own thought. What he realises — to put it in an exaggerated form — is that he is not of divine material but of dust. It is clear that this idea links with the importance of the eternal present, as examined in the preceding section. For man's aspirations to eternity must turn in on the earth itself: his destiny is in all respects bound up in the planet of which he is a part.

Simultaneous with this aspect of the poet's thought has been his persistent concern with social problems. In his own words, 'lo humano apareció en mi obra conforme yo fui descubriendo la realidad física del planeta'. [58] In the years 1926-8, when he was Secretary of Ecuador's Socialist Party, his eagerness to improve the conditions of the Indian population was the seed of his vision of a universal human brotherhood. As he travelled in Europe during the years 1928-33 [59] he quickly recognised that what he observed in the plight of Ecuador's Indians was evident in all other parts of the world he visited (the solitude of the individual, the hunger of the masses of common people). He could therefore write in a poem of those years:

El mundo es uno mismo, a pesar de sus formas.

('Tercera clase', OPC 224)

What began as a sense of solidarity with the underprivileged has developed into a broader feeling of solidarity with the whole human race. All men are bound by their natural condition to live in solitude (as is suggested in 'Soledad habitada', OPC 286), and to meet a death that reduces their life to

---

[58] Ojeda, 'Entrevista ......', p. 93.
[59] And, he says, as he read poets such as Rilke, Hölderlin, and Saint-John Perse (ibid.).

absurdity (as in 'Nada nos pertenece', OPC 284-5). As his compassion for the suffering of others has blended with his distaste for the violence and greed which he finds pervasive in modern civilisation, he has seen the hope for mankind lying in a universal brotherhood. Thus, in 'Aurosia' the inhabitants of his Utopian planet 'forman una sola familia, / una sola nación' (OPC 398), while in 'Hombre planetario' XIX the vision of a better era for our own world depends upon all men living in peace and harmony (OPC 450).

In this concept of the world national frontiers disappear, countries are not political entities but different fragments of the same earth. When assessing his planetary identity in 'Linaje' he alludes only briefly to his birth and childhood in Ecuador, and even then in such terms as to insist on the irrelevance of the political unit and the sole importance of the geographical features:

> Árboles de los Andes, yo crecí con vosotros.   (OPC 489)

His true lineage is not restricted to this area, however:

> Mi estirpe es del extremo de la tierra.   (OPC 490)

In 'Hombre planetario' this idea comes as a crucial discovery, returning to Carrera Andrade a lost sense of identity. Although he emphasises that his roots are in 'El suelo equinoccial' (not, it will be noticed, in a nation designated by the political term Ecuador), he indicates how different parts of him have originated in other parts of the world:

> Árbol del Amazonas mis arterias,
> mi frente de París, ojos del trópico,
> mi lengua americana y española,
> hombros de Nueva York y de Moscú.   (OPC 448)

It is probably intended that each aspect should correlate with an aspect of his experience: place of birth and youth, country whose culture has had most impact on him, countries whose social attitudes have most claimed his attention. Ultimately, however, he discovers that it is unimportant whether or not he is aware of any particular country having had

any impact on him, for in the final canto of 'Hombre planetario' he expresses the idea that he is not merely Jorge Carrera Andrade but all men. He refers to the whole planet,
including among his specific examples some places and peoples known to him personally and others virtually unknown:

> Soy el hombre de Tokio, que se nutre
> de bambú y pececillos;
> el minero de Europa,
> hermano de la noche;
> el labrador del Congo y de la arena,
> el pescador de ostiones polinesios,
> soy el indio de América, el mestizo,
> el amarillo, el negro,
> y soy los demás hombres del planeta.   (OPC 450-1)

One sense in which he is 'Hombre Planetario' is that all
men of the planet are one, and he is them all. Another is
that all men form part of the earth, and Carrera Andrade
with them.

In the poem 'Yo soy el bosque' he eliminates even the
idea of time as a barrier between men; all men of all periods
are represented in him:

> Yo soy un hombre-pueblo, un hombre sucesivo
> que viene desde el ser original
> hasta formar la suma: un hombre solo.   (OPC 492)

At the same time as being the embodiment of all mankind, he
is a single man; he is both all men and one individual. He
possesses both a plural identity derived from his containing
within him all other men, and a singular identity derived
from his own personal characteristics and experiences. In
his own words:

> Plural y a la vez único,
> soy el hombre del bosque y soy el bosque mismo.   (ibid.)

On the basis of this dual identity he constructs his notion
of the duty of a poet. As we observed in 'El condenado' (OPC
434) he is in a sense jointly responsible for the evils of modern
civilisation even though he condemns them. As a poet he is

able to act in two complementary ways. He is in part a prophet, privileged to have perceived truths to which most men are blind — a teacher whose duty is to inform people and advise them. On the other hand he also speaks on behalf of his fellow men, acting as their spokesman, their advocate. Both social functions have been explicitly mentioned by Carrera Andrade. As to the first, he has described the poet's mission as 'interpretar las apariencias del mundo y descifrar el lenguaje de las cosas para darles a entender a los otros hombres, contribuyendo de esa manera a que la vida humana sea digna de vivirse'. [60] And as to the other aspect, 'El poeta debe ser solidario de los destinos colectivos. Debe intentar ser el portavoz de su pueblo'. [61] 'Hombre planetario' thus combines the two. As one man representing all men he discovers on their behalf their universal identity — one which reduces the importance of their individual personalities and their countries of origin in order to stress their common features and their participation in the circumstances of the whole planet. As a poet, he writes to instruct the world concerning these facts. Also as a poet, however, he intercedes on behalf of all men to pledge them to peace and union:

> Sobre mi corazón firman los pueblos
> un tratado de paz hasta la muerte.   (OPC 451)

To these points must be added the effects of Carrera Andrade's life as a diplomat. This career has encouraged him to attend to the relations between his own country and other lands. Moreover, during the forty-eight years between his first departure from Ecuador and his return in 1976 he had undergone profound influences from exile and travel. With only short visits or periods of residence in his own country (a total of about 51 months, as stated in chapter I), and posts in Peru, France, Japan, the U.S.A., Venezuela, England, and Holland, it is clear that the exclu-

---

[60] Straub, 'Conversación ......', p 310. Similarly, he has said, in a different interview, 'En nuestras sociedades incipientes, el poeta debe servir a la construcción de la cultura, debe aportar sus conocimientos para ayudar a redimir a su pueblo de la ignorancia', *Alcor* (Asunción), 36, mayo-junio de 1965, p. 4.
[61] Rubén Bareiro Saguier, 'Entrevista a J.C.A.', *Alcor*, 36, mayo-junio de 1965, p. 4. To these points should be added the argument in chapter III, iv.

sive claim on him of his country of origin had been removed. This constant travel has helped to give him the sense of belonging to the whole planet. In his autocritical essay 'Poetry of Reality and Utopia' he traces the growing effect on his concept of the world caused by the discovery of different countries: 'Getting stronger in me', he writes, 'was the idea of universal unity' (SAP 75); 'My cosmovision was strengthened by my journey to Chile, Brazil, and Venezuela' (SAP 76). Meanwhile, though Ecuador continued to preoccupy him deeply for its social problems (as is revealed in his correspondence) he rarely expressed this aspect of his thought in his poetry. Ecuador became less relevant, as a poetic theme, for its present social realities than for its virginal landscape and its authentic life and indigenous heritage. Because of his exile, therefore, Ecuador became a vision of an ideal place, a Utopia. He explains how it is quite logical to reconcile his national themes with his planetary scope, his dream with reality, the small country to which he belongs as a political subject with the universe to which he belongs as a human being:

> My native country is exalted precisely as a part of the world as a whole, as a terraqueous fragment and not as a political entity. My native land with its varied vegetables and minerals taught me to love America first and then the whole planet. (SAP 83)

Finally, it is important to notice that Carrera Andrade's inner preoccupation with questions of identity, and his sense of universal unity, have a significant effect on the standpoint that he adopts in his poems. That is to say, poems that ostensibly refer merely to himself in fact refer, at times, to both private and collective experience. It becomes an essentially technical issue. When he uses the first-person standpoint (to adopt a terminology normally reserved for the study of novels), when he uses the word 'yo', he does not always mean to denote the individual case of Jorge Carrera Andrade. [62]

---

[62] A fuller treatment of this issue constitutes part of an article, 'Theme and standpoint in the poetry of J.C.A.', by the author, in *Iberoromania* (Munich), 3/4, 1971, pp. 348-56. The article deals with all three standpoints (first, second, and third persons).

In, for example, the love poems grouped under the title
'La visita del amor' (OPC 403-11), the thoughts and emotions
do indeed seem to arise directly from events in his own
life (apparently his second marriage, in 1951). But in a
poem such as 'La llave del fuego', 'yo' seems to lose this
purely private meaning, for he wishes to express his sense of
identification with Ecuador. The first-person subject is used
only initially in a personal sense: 'De nuevo oigo tus grillos
y cigarras' (OPC 353); a change in perspective soon occurs:
'Yo soy el hombre de los papagayos', where the pronoun
identifies the poet with all men of the land represented
by the idea of parrots. Then follow references to the discovery of the New World ('Colón me vio'), to the Wars of
Independence ('acompañé a Bolívar'), and to the formation
of a republic ('Yo fundé una república') to stress the poet's
feeling of participating in those historic moments, to express
the idea that his own self has been formed by Latin
America's past, and to show his role of mediator and spokesman for his ancestors and compatriots. There are, moreover, numerous poems where 'yo' represents the spirit of
the New World, expressing antipathy for the Old, or offering help to a withering society. Such is the use of the
first person in 'Se prohibe andar sobre el césped', which
begins:

> Castaño europeo: tiéndeme tu mano amarillenta
> que se desprende y vuela para morir.
> Yo conozco tu mundo de parques encarcelados.   (OPC 433)

Ultimately 'yo' loses not only its private identity but also
its connection with Ecuador and the New World. It speaks,
in fact, for the whole of mankind, as in the final section of
'Hombre planetario', where different peoples of the world
are listed in a series in which each item acts as complement
of the words 'yo soy' (OPC 450-1). Moreover 'yo' is sometimes
the voice of a prophet, like the supra-terrestrial being of
'Cuaderno del paracaidista' (OPC 305-6) who descends from
the sky (as though from heaven) as an emissary, to bring the
message of peaceful co-existence.

It is because Carrera Andrade believes himself to be both one man and all men, both the voice of virginal Ecuador and the spokesman of the modern age, that 'yo' assumes a plurality of meaning in his verse. It is clear, in fact, that he frequently makes conscious use of a first person standpoint in order to emphasise the common identity of self and others, or to give dramatic form to an idea. It is also because of his belief that the poet's task is to communicate the messages of the world to his fellow men that 'yo' should often be the fusing of his own voice with that of a prophet.

It has been argued that in recent years Carrera Andrade has drawn closer to discovering solutions to his ontological problems. These solutions, in their various forms, are major themes in his poetry. This does not mean, however, that they are ultimately successful in overcoming the poet's sense of solitude, his incomprehension of the mystery of life, and his anguish over the transitory nature of things. For it is clear from the verse discussed in chapter V — and it will be equally evident in chapter VII — that even his most recent poems reflect a continuation of those problems. As though they were delicately poised at opposite ends of a balance, both the anguish and the comfort are present in the poet, sometimes one and sometimes the other becoming predominant, the scales swinging according to his mood. One is inevitably led to conjecture that most of those ideas which seem to hold the potential of countering his problems are, ultimately, not full solutions but types of consolation. The plenitude of experience in the present moment, which is probably his main argument against the absurdity of existence, is unable to compensate the certainty of death. Only his recognition of human life as dependent on natural laws and his idea of the universal unity (and thus continuity) of all forms of life and matter possess the promise that his own death may not be a final negative blow but a moment of illumination.

VII

EXILE AS A POETIC THEME

ALTHOUGH it was not until 1970 that Carrera Andrade first made careful use of the term exile, and deliberately constructed poems on the theme — in 'Libro del destierro' — exile has from early years been an underlying factor in themes such as travel, alien environment, solitude, imprisonment, and loss of identity. The main purpose of this chapter is to analyse 'Libro del destierro'. But first I hope to indicate the ways in which the imagery and thought of that poem have been anticipated in previous verse.

As was remarked earlier, travel to foreign lands provided Carrera Andrade in the first place with an opportunity to discover new things. Distant horizons lured him, and a sense of adventure drove him on. It should be remembered that, according to one of his principles, the essence of making sense of one's existence is to observe and fully experience the objects of the world. It is significant that in the lines of 'El objeto y su sombra' where he expresses this advice, the image that he used is a prime means of transport: a ship:

> Que el ojo apareje su nave
> para un nuevo descubrimiento.   (OPC 179)

What the eye is to the man the ship is to the traveller. Similarly, since any view from a window reminds the poet that a whole world waits to be discovered, 'La ventana es continua invitación al viaje' ('Las amistades cotidianas', OPC 253). The poetry of *Boletines de mar y tierra,* though dealing with experiences after departure from the homeland, does not express any sense of journey into exile or loss of 'patria'; it is rather a question of discovery and search. If anything,

Carrera Andrade feels himself not so much an exile as an envoy. Hence the lines:

> Hombre del Ecuador ...
> ... yo te mando el saludo de los puertos
> desde estos países manufacturados.
>
> ('Saludo de los puertos', OPC 190)

and:

> Estoy en la línea de trenes del Oeste
> empleado en el Registro del Mundo. (OPC 191)

There are already glimpses of other senses in which life may be represented in the image of a journey. Gradually, for example, travel is associated with the idea of passing time. In 'Escala' (OPC 204) a romantic experience is treated as a brief interlude in the relentless progress of the poet's life, and it is now found to have been left in the past; this temporal sense is conveyed, however, through a spatial image, for the experience belongs to the Azores, islands from which Carrera Andrade is now separated by a stretch of ocean. 'Temperaturas' (OPC 192) mixes notions of travel across the earth with those of changing seasons of the year, a procedure well illustrated by the first line: 'La tierra viaja en invierno al polo'.

In some poems of this period the flow of time, expressed, for example, as a river or as the blood in the poet's veins, holds not only a threat but also a promise. The river in 'Promesa del río Guayas' (OPC 160) is 'cargado de horizontes' and offers a 'promesa líquida': it provides fertility and has an air of self-sufficiency, permanence, and progress. By *Biografía para uso de los pájaros* (1937) this has led to an anguished sense that he has, simultaneously, travelled to a distant land and reached an age when youth is past. Thus, in the title poem, his past is expressed in terms of being engulfed in a sea over which he has sailed:

> Todo ha pasado ya, en sucesivo oleaje,
> como las vanas cifras de la espuma.
> Los años van sin prisa enredando sus líquenes
> y el recuerdo es apenas un nenúfar

que asoma entre dos aguas
su rostro de ahogado.   (OPC 252)

The sea is clearly beginning to assume antagonistic characteristics, being the barrier between himself and his youth.
It is also, of course, the distance which separates him from
his homeland. And youth and Ecuador, as was noted previously, are essentially synonymous in his ˋpoetry; [1] the
memory of himself as a young man therefore travels to visit
him from ʿun país de fechas y retratos' (ʿEl visitante de niebla', OPC 290). The sea which exiles him also separates him
from his youth. It will now be seen that there is a link
between the ideas of exile and transitory existence.

Besides being a barrier and a symbol of the distance
covered (the time that has passed), the sea also represents
the course taken by Carrera Andrade's journeys, or, in other
words, the image of daily life. A number of poems express
the idea of life's hardships and perils through imagery based
on a rough sea. The waves that swell and come tumbling
down in foam in ʿViaje' (OPC 268) remind him of the eternal
rhythm of life, which is a journey over the tumultuous seas
of infinity, a journey from which he is able to find respite,
in ʿDefensa del domingo' (OPC 255), on the islands of peace
and repose, the function of Sunday in the remorseless tide
of time being represented spatially. Things that help him to
endure his existence or guide him in how to live are attributed faculties that would assist travel. In ʿSegunda vida
de mi madre' his mother, symbol of his childhood's secure
and guided course, of the way his past may be adapted to
aid him in the present, and of the spiritual presence within
each aspect of nature, is compared to a compass:

Brújula de mi larga travesía terrestre.   (OPC 278)

The Oakland Bridge, near San Francisco, in 1939 the longest
in the world, becomes for him a symbol of triumph over
time and death, a substitute for man's own failure to achieve
those aspirations, and inspires his ʿCanto al puente de
Oakland' (OPC 293-7).

---

[1] See chapter III, viii.

The idea of an enigmatic, vainly-sought destination enters many poems. The journey of life becomes, not only a daily-renewed attempt to discover objects and experiences which are in themselves the purpose of travel, nor the constant hardships of routine existence, but a great quest, a search for a distant Absolute that gives ultimate sense to the journey. In 'Viaje infinito' Carrera Andrade finds quest to be a characteristic of every creature in the world:

> Todos los seres viajan
> de distinta manera hacia su Dios.   (OPC 323)

Man's own journey, if the object of search is encountered, may be seen as a quest for light; but if no goal is discovered, it is a journey to the void. Therefore, in this poem, death looming at the end of the voyage acts as a stimulus for the poet to find some form of light.

Gradually the impression grows that the object of Carrera Andrade's quest is remote, nebulous, and even unreal; an aura of improbability surrounds the cherished goal. For this reason it is comparable to the myth of El Dorado. In 'Jornada existencial', a poem dating from 1966, when Carrera Andrade is assessing the course of his life, he exclaims in despair:

> ¡Oh reino inencontrable, Florida o Eldorado!   (OPC 483)

His travels have been in vain: the countries discovered and the time consumed have also been in vain. The nearest he has come to finding any absolute is his own person:

> El país de Eldorado está en nosotros mismos.   (OPC 484)

It is an 'Imperio de las flores y delicias', for it offers the delightful experiences of the senses; but it remains ultimately a 'reino efímero sin nombre', since it lies within his own transitory body, while around him lurk the menacing and mysterious forces and infinite spaces of emptiness. In the whole of the cosmos the only kind of haven, reward, or goal seems to be his own self, though clearly he would like it to

be Heaven, as these lines from another poem, 'La mina más
alta', suggest:

> Cielo, en vano cada día
> me revelas tu secreto:
> Eldorado inalcanzable,
> mina de nubes y sueños.   (OPC 485)

Ultimately, of course, it is a case of needing to discover the
existence of a Heaven to which he will finally travel after
death, and indeed something approaching this concept will
be discussed later in relation to 'Libro del destierro'. But
more immediately he has sought some kind of heaven on
earth, some place on this planet with the features of paradise
— he has made a vain journey

> en busca de un ansiado paraíso
> terrenal y de luz, siempre lejano.   ('Caudales', OPC 537)

If travel abroad has led to no desired destination, if the
ultimate aim and explanation of life lie within himself, if
he has sought a paradise on earth, the possibility arises
whether the solution might be a return to the place of
origin. Ecuador, we know, represents light, virginal territory,
authentic living, and his youth. It must be admitted that in
the poem 'Viaje de regreso' he is not far from expressing
the view that his own country fulfils the needs which gave
rise to his journey. [2] His life has been dream-like; his return
to Latin America serves to awaken him from the dream,
drawing from him the kind of response expected from a
man who reaches his promised land: he kneels humbly,
reverentially on the soil of his country. All that is left for
him now, he wonders, may be simply to die:

> ¿Hay tres escalas en mi viaje:
> soñar, despertar y morir?   (OPC 348)

But he has not found the complete answer to his needs,
for once he is revitalised by the Latin American ambience,
the yearning for further exploration returns:

---

[2] Strictly, since Ecuador is not named in the poem, the thoughts apply to
Latin America as a whole.

Mas, de nuevo arde en mi garganta
sed de vivir, sed de morir.   (OPC 350)

It is clear from later poems, moreover, that going back to his homeland fails to answer his quest. This is made particularly evident in 'Estación penúltima', where he likens his plight to that of Ulysses, having travelled fruitlessly in distant lands only to encounter disillusionment on each homecoming. What he longs for, he recognises, is unobtainable both in exotic countries and in his own land; it is as remote as the stars, as mythical as Ithaca:

Inútil viaje. Vuelta inoportuna:
suspiro como Ulises
por la Itaca celeste de la luna.   (OPC 495)

This, it will be seen below, is a vital point to emerge also in 'Libro del destierro'.

It was demonstrated earlier that Carrera Andrade's solitude and anguish have close connections with his actual residence in foreign countries dominated by cities and machines. [3] This fact clearly has an important bearing on the matter now under discussion. It is useful to extend the scope of the material discussed at that juncture in order to show how consistently the poet expresses his suffering through imagery based on the feelings of a foreigner in a strange country. We are not now dealing with his allusion to specific lands or areas of the world, but to the more abstract idea of exile.

Carrera Andrade's withdrawal into the loneliness of his thoughts gave rise to a collection of poems whose title suggests a journey to an inner country: *País secreto*. Solitude itself is often treated as though it were a country: e.g. 'País de soledad' (OPC 539), and 'única patria humana' ('Soledad habitada', OPC 286). It is particularly a place like a prison, such as an island, as in 'Soledad y gaviota' (OPC 277), or a city, imposing walls as though they were frontiers, as in 'Soledad de las ciudades' (OPC 221). The traveller, moreover, is treated as a key image of solitude in this last-mentioned

---

[3] See chapter I, and chapter V, I and II.

poem. One aspect of solitude is nostalgia for the homeland, causing the poet to reminisce about the merits of things connected with his childhood in Ecuador. In 'El extranjero' (OPC 266-7) and 'Moneda del forastero' (OPC 389-90) his loneliness is intensified by the unfamiliarity of the countries in which he finds himself, countries whose language is unintelligible, whose customs are alienating, and whose landscape is an encircling desert — 'Un territorio helado me rodea' (OPC 266) — or a vast wasteland with remnants of dead civilisations and inanimate products of the new civilisation — 'forastero perdido en el planeta / entre piedras ilustres, entre máquinas' (OPC 389) —. Even Carrera Andrade's loss of identity is inherently connected with his absence from Ecuador. As we read in 'Hombre planetario', it is inadequate to regard himself as one individual; it is equally inadequate to think of one country alone as his homeland. He has lost the sense of complete belonging to his land of origin, and in the void he has created the concept of belonging to the whole planet. This may well have its advantage in his philosophy of universal brotherhood, as expressed in 'Hombre planetario', but it also has its drawbacks, for it leaves him as a figure dwarfed by the immensity of the planet, as he puts it in 'Moneda del forastero': 'perdido en el planeta' (OPC 389), 'solo en medio del mundo' (OPC 390).

In his journey across the hostile seas and in his solitude in a desert, Carrera Andrade finds a haven and solace with woman and love. It is quite predictable that for this idea also he should often resort to images of countries or landscapes. For the lost stranger, therefore, love is a refuge like an island. In 'La visita del amor' it is 'Isla de las Delicias' (OPC 405); in 'La esposa' (OPC 496-7) it is both an island and a continent. The body of the woman he loves is referred to in 'Cuerpo de la amante' as a spring in the desert (OPC 408), an island for which the swimmer may head (OPC 411), a nuptial paradise (ibid.), and a pure homeland (ibid.). It is clear from the last two images that he associates the effect of longing for love with that of exile, while the woman's ability to satisfy and to comfort is linked with his youth and with Ecuador.

Even when the issue is man's relation to the cosmos and to eternity Carrera Andrade tends to express things in terms of travel by sea between continents and between islands. Thus, in 'Linaje', after tracing the various respects in which he descends from and is a part of the whole human race, he ends with the impression that the whole of our planet is one island (or country) in an infinite sea, the 'Oceanía del cielo', with distant stars enticing like islands of refuge and Eldorados, 'Islas del paraíso' (OPC 490). The great enigma of life is expressed not so much through reference to the stars in the sky (though this does occur from time to time) as through the image of the sea; one complete poem, 'Enigma del mar' (OPC 516) is dedicated to the theme.

Two poems from the collection *Floresta de los guacamayos* are vital to this discussion. 'In this last little book', Carrera Andrade has explained, 'the utopia of earthy happiness and of love is suggested, represented by the symbol of the bird with showy plumage, a compendium of the American tropics but also of a false paradise'. [4] It is clear from the poem 'Teoría del guacamayo' (OPC 456-9) that Carrera Andrade is thinking on two levels simultaneously: the macaw is a 'Maravilla del Nuevo Mundo' because it helps to establish Latin American reality as a wonder in comparison with other lands of the world; but the bird is at the same time a 'promesa o paraíso' because it represents all men's aspirations beyond the limits of this earth. That is to say, the tropical land [5] seems to be paradise on earth, and in this appearance lies its great attraction and ultimate deception. At the end of the poem Carrera Andrade is ready to make a kind of pilgrimage to 'las Islas del Eterno Domingo', and the journey is envisaged as 'el más prodigioso de los viajes'. Clearly he is alluding not merely to that land on this earth but to the broader sense of going to the paradise after death.

---

[4] 'Poetry of Reality and Utopia', SAP 77.
[5] Nicaragua was the direct inspiration of this collection of poems: 'La naturaleza de Nicaragua, fértil y acogedora, me fue propicia para la creación poética. Sin plan preconcebido se entretejieron en mi mente las imágenes de "Floresta de los Guacamayos" ......' (VC 280).

The tropical Latin America of this poem, therefore, is the apparent goal, but in the final analysis it proves to be one more reminder of man's temporary existence on earth. This point should be borne in mind when 'Comarcas ignotas' is read, a few pages later. [6] An even clearer idea is given here of the symbolic nature of the Latin American lands, whose characteristics are transferred to imaginary territories with utopian names such as 'Aurosia', 'Aurelia', 'Islas de la Felicidad'. For almost the first time in his poetry the longing that the poet feels is explicitly described as a sense of exile:

> ¡oh nombres que repite
> mi corazón en el exilio!   (OPC 462)

If this separation from utopia or paradise may be expressed as a form of exile, then clearly those ideal places are associated with Ecuador, from which he is also separated. Indeed, the fantastic regions named in this poem are also called homelands:.

> ¡oh patrias suspiradas de mi ser verdadero!   (OPC 460)

To extend the idea, it may be said that in his exile the homeland offers prospects of an earthly paradise, but that he is aware that there is a degree of falseness in the impression — for he has briefly alluded to it in 'Teoría del guacamayo'.

All the various ideas and images examined above are brought together in 'Libro del destierro' (OPC 541-53), and a number of innovations are introduced. This poem of twenty-five cantos is as important and as successful, in its own way, as 'Hombre planetario' (which Carrera Andrade has, perhaps erroneously, called his best work). [7] Like 'Hombre planetario' it begins with a negative position or a question mark and progresses toward something positive, some form of answer. It develops, like the earlier work, from an an-

---

[6] In PU this poem, like 'Teoría del guacamayo', has a page missing.
[7] W. J. Straub, 'Conversación con J.C.A.', *Revista Iberoamericana*, 79, 1972, p. 307. Rather than 'best', the present writer finds 'most representative' to be the appropriate assessment. 'Hombre planetario' reiterates many of his well-worn themes, and lacks the tautness and density of some of his works.

guished sense of being lost, through stages of gradually-increasing awareness, to the discovery of the poet's position. Both works, moreover, are crucibles in which ingredients of many other poems are melted down and blended into an overall structure. Where the basic difference lies is not in the underlying theme — for the two themes are ultimately rather similar — but in the focus of attention on the private anguish of the individual in exile.

Cantos I to III of the poem concern Carrera Andrade's exploration of the notions of fleeting life, old age, and death. Though he is coming alive again to the messages of nature, he has a persisting sense of the transitory existence of all things (I). Despite his old age there is a need to be fertile (i.e. productive, rich in experience) (II). In face of the vastness of the cosmos, death seems near, and life appears a journey (via the oceans of Space, and via the stars) from nothing back to nothing. A humble, diminutive, and earthbound creature (the glow-worm) is of more spiritual value to him than these cosmic dimensions. Having introduced the idea of life as a journey, he proceeds to develop it in IV, as he sums up his life as though it were already complete. (The use of a preterite tense in the first two lines will be seen to give an air of finality, an effect which is repeated in XVI where, again, he is considering an aspect of his life (love) in its totality.) The course of his life has responded to a quest for something elusive; he expresses this variously as 'patria', 'ser libre', 'morada', and 'refugio', four terms which contain the paradox underlying the whole of his attitude to Ecuador and exile. As he travelled, he drew the basic needs for existence from the discovery of different countries, he relished intense experience, and he treated nature and his fellow man with love. He characterises these activities as follows:

> era la libertad buscando patria,
> era la patria andando hasta ser libre.   (OPC 542)

The crux of the matter lies in these two lines, in the attitudes to 'patria', one of which implies that Carrera Andrade, as the embodiment of freedom, needed to look outside Ecuador

for a homeland capable of accommodating liberal ideas, while
the other takes Ecuador as his homeland, but treats it as a
land which is not free and which seeks its freedom vicarious-
ly through the medium of the poet. Ecuador therefore *is*
and *is not* the homeland. The poet implies, moreover, that
he has found freedom ('hasta ser libre') but that he has not
discovered his other goal: a dwelling and refuge. Already
it is evident that what Carrera Andrade really requires is
a place combining freedom with refuge, or in other words
a free homeland. His exile is therefore both separation from
Ecuador and the inability to reach the homeland that his
imagination has substituted for Ecuador.

From cantos V to XIII Carrera Andrade expresses the
different aspects of his anguish, uniting them in the image
of a man in exile. The exile has originated in a mission of
quest (as was revealed in IV), a quest that has remained
unfulfilled. Since the poet's present position is, therefore,
essentially the same as the whole of his life of travel, the
image now chosen to express his plight — that of exile —
is applicable retrospectively. The poet certainly realises that
it is not a new experience:

> Te reconozco viento del exilio.   (OPC 543)

For it is essentially an experience of anguish:

> Te reconozco viento de la angustia.   (ibid.)

In canto V the image of a wind is extended: exile destroys
order and beauty, the place where Carrera Andrade feels
at home (nature, a garden); exile bears with it the signs of
transitoriness and death (dust) and it removes traces of the
path his life has followed. The fierce violence introduced
by the image of a wind leads to an alternative image of
savage animals, to express the sense of relentless and furious
guardians impeding his progress to a refuge, while the link
between the wind and the sky develops into an impression
that exile is of cosmic proportions. In VII the poet turns
his attention to expressing visual impressions of the expe-

rience of exile, imagining it to be a country, and thus drawing close to the literal truth of his life in foreign lands:

> El país del exilio no tiene árboles. (OPC 544)
> El país del exilio no tiene agua. (ibid.)
> El país del exilio no tiene aves. (OPC 545)

These parallel lines reveal that exile is associated with the negation of all that Carrera Andrade needs and loves; lacking trees and birds it prevents his contact and communication with nature, and lacking water it leaves him in vain longing. In exile he is doomed to live in solitude: 'Es una inmensa soledad' (OPC 544). He must suffer his ontological anguish, while death looms near:

> Es desierto poblado por los buitres
> que esperan el convite de la muerte. (OPC 545)

Canto X continues the treatment of exile as a geographical location. It is an island, the imprisoning condition of his life on earth surrounded by infinity. The enormous expanses surrounding the island of his earthly existence are increasing day by day with the passage of time and the approach of death. In this aspect of the image he has drawn from a temporal idea expressed already in VIII:

> Es el desierto vasto como el tiempo. (ibid.)

While in XI and XII exile as a form of imprisonment and as the rule of time are two ideas expressed simultaneously:

> Lo fugaz, la extensión, el tiempo, el número:
> Son los cuatro barrotes de mi cárcel
> metafísica . . . (OPC 546)

Since it means separation from the country of his youth, exile means nostalgia and age itself. But the vast time that perplexes him is not merely the past years of his life ('El rastro de mis pasos', OPC 545) but ultimately the expanse of cosmic time, which, according to the concept expressed in XII, is static and infinite, and within which each man's life moves a minute distance. In this respect, therefore, exile combines the senses of being lost both in time and in space. It is an insignificant moment of existence in relation to eternity, and it makes the poet an insignificant figure dwarfed by the infinity of the universe. Finally, in IX and XIII exile is linked with the poet's loss of self, loss of identity. As he moves further into exile, he leaves behind his true self (and his youthful self):

> Cada día me alejo de mí mismo,   (OPC 545)

until, finally:

> Me busco y no me encuentro.
> Ya no estoy en mí mismo.   (OPC 547)

In the first half of 'Libro del destierro', then, Carrera Andrade has constructed an impression of exile as a wind-swept desert island in which the poet is a lost and solitary figure, haunted by the sense of life's fleetingness, and longing for a refuge and spiritual refreshment which there seems no hope of finding. Exile is the essence of life itself (X); although it begins with a desire to search for freedom and refuge (IV), it is a condition from which there seems no escape on this earth, for life ends with a return to nothing (III). It will be quickly evident that this picture is completely consistent with the interpretation of Carrera Andrade's attitudes to travel in foreign lands and absence from Ecuador given in earlier chapters.

At this point mid-way through the poem comes a transitional stage (XIV-XVI) which introduces a mood of hope and of solace. Nature brings mental peace and gives Carrera Andrade the message that travel offers the prospect of joy and freedom. But the journey to be undertaken does not have as its destination the homeland on earth that he has previously sought in vain. This journey ends in a place where he will hear 'la caracola del sueño del olvido' (OPC 548), and his means of transport is 'mi nave anclada en el ocaso' (ibid.). There can be no mistaking the allusion to the destination of death.

For the moment, however, he rejects a purely introspective and self-centred frame of mind, in which he has been dwelling on his private preoccupation with death. From XVII onwards 'Libro del destierro' takes into account his humanitarian and socialist views. Obsessed with visions of human suffering and of man's brutality to his fellows through war, and in undisguised horror at U.S. military involvement in South-East Asia, [8] he reaches the conclusion that his duty is to protest. It is a profoundly emotional attitude, temporarily obliterating both his ontological anguish and his usual belief that one should enjoy the things of this world:

> Aparta la mirada del ocaso florido,
> del teatro de las cosas.
> Tú no puedes callar mientras los mártires
> combatan por tu paz y por las golondrinas.   (OPC 549)

Although he now proceeds to adopt a non-political stance, and surveys human suffering as a feature of the universal condition of mankind, he never loses sight of the basic necessities which have just dawned on him.

Canto XVIII is crucial to this development of his ideas. In the last two lines a summary is given:

> En la hogaza de pan hallo mi patria
> en un lugar cualquiera del planeta.   (OPC 550)

At once it seems that Carrera Andrade has at last encountered the object of his quest; that his journey is finally made meaningful; that he has arrived at his homeland. First, however, it should be noted that the word 'patria' is used in a completely metaphorical sense: it does not refer to any specific country, for it may be found anywhere on earth. 'Patria' here means that which he has sought and needed, the refuge, freedom, and spiritual refreshment mentioned in IV. At the same time it is clear that a deeply-loved but inadequate Ecuador, and an imaginary utopian world inevitably underlie the metaphorical meaning. The loaf of bread which now epitomises the ideals contained in the word 'patria' seems to symbolise a number of confluent ideas. The most important is that carried over from the previous

---

[8] At this time U.S. troops were heavily engaged in Vietnam.

canto of the poem: bread is a basic need of every man, and
in the provision of this essential commodity, in the human
solidarity implied in sharing it, Carrera Andrade finds an
expression of his ideal. Hence the bread's 'perfume solar
igualitario / repartido en blandura protegida / por las manos
del pueblo' (OPC 549). In the canto's imagery there are
also associations of the loaf with his childhood, family, home,
and own country. Something equivalent to his homeland
(which is lost) may be discovered in things symbolised by
bread. But such associations are extended beyond the private
context to embrace an ideal vision of the whole world in
which there is provision, childlike innocence, security, and
love. This reverential attitude to bread is reminiscent, moreover, of the idealisation of corn that is to be found in
poems such as 'Alabanza del Ecuador' (OPC 415), 'Hombre
planetario' XIX (OPC 450), 'Ocaso de Atahualpa' (OPC 459),
and 'Los antepasados' (OPC 463). In every case corn is
associated with the concept of an Ecuador close to nature
and authentic in its traditional, pre-Columbian way of life.
Bread also symbolises, therefore, the essential life force and
the authentic, innocent, pure form of existence close to
nature.

If Carrera Andrade had now discovered his long-sought
homeland it would be expected that as a logical result his
exile should have come to an end. But this, it transpires, is
not the case. The loaf of bread may seem to be one form
of 'patria', but it is insufficient to satisfy the poet's quest.
In XIX he expresses the desire to be free of the human
condition, to be given a life somewhere 'fuera del tiempo y
del espacio' (OPC 550). In XXII and XXIII time and solitude
again perplex him, and man's life is seen (through the symbol
of the first space flight to the moon) as a barren journey in
exile. And in XXI the desert landscape, previously seen in
VII, returns to give the idea that exile extends into old age,
where there lies a frontier to an unknown land which may
be a dark desert or a fertile garden. Death, then, has returned
to cause him anguish, and it is of death that he is thinking
when, in XXIV, he sees signs of a general exodus to various
types of 'patria' in August:

Los hombres van en busca de la patria del trigo
la patria del descanso en las playas ardientes.
El éxodo es la luz detrás del horizonte.
Es la gran travesía del hombre en su destierro.
¡Oh frescor! Surge el cacto
absorbiendo la vida del desierto
en sus frágiles formas retorcidas
por el fuego solar.
       El verde signo
anuncia su camino al viajero extraviado.   (OPC 552)

There is a tension between the first two lines and the remainder of the quotation. First Carrera Andrade expresses his impression of the human activity he witnesses in August; then he interprets it, inferring from this general scene a meaning related to his ontological preoccupations. August appears to be a time when men are able to find the things they need: food, fellowship (suggested by the harvest of the corn), [9] rest and refuge. Consistent with its use in other parts of this work, the word 'patria' is used loosely to represent the idea of 'goal' or 'ideal'. It retains, however, its more literal sense of homeland in relation to that land from which the exodus takes place. For the poet himself, the exodus in August, when the cycle of life begins to close (with the harvest), leads out of exile, across the frontier of life's end, into the land of death. If the obvious and deliberate Biblical connotations are taken into account it will be realised that death is being envisaged here as something not dreaded but welcome, for Exodus implies a long-awaited journey out of exile to the promised land. [10] In the two senses, therefore, of (a) release from exile, and (b) deliverance to a land that has been longed for, death itself is a kind of 'patria'. Hence the parallel between his own exodus into death and the departure of men to their 'patria del trigo' and 'patria del descanso'. Moreover, images used here to evoke his impressions of death suggest a place of light (and for Carrera Andrade light is a form of the Absolute), a place of freshness, and the idea of guidance to a goal and refuge. Although canto XXV

---

[9] The link of 'trigo' with 'hogaza de pan' (poem XVIII) should be noted.
[10] Cf. the Israelites' crossing of the Red Sea from slavery in Egypt into freedom, in the Book of Exodus, 14.

ends the poem on a note of great pathos, when Carrera Andrade feels that all the wealth of the earth's beauty and all
the intense experiences of his existence are memories in
remote countries to which there is no return, there can be
no erasing the supreme effort to come to terms with death in
order to accept it as a welcome destination of his earthly
journey, a refuge from his exile on earth. [11]

There remain, however, certain incongruities. One of the
main difficulties is the fact that cantos XVII and XVIII imply
a sense of social commitment and human solidarity that for
the moment seem to fulfil the role of 'patria', yet Carrera
Andrade continues to explore beyond this discovery. The
problem appears to be that these things are a goal only
for his life on earth; they do not provide a solution to the
great enigma of death. Ultimately one has the impression
that they are incomplete, that the loaf of bread which can
save the poet from his sense of exile wherever he is on earth
is only a substitute found for 'patria' in the absence of any
ideal homeland, utopia, or paradise. It must not be forgotten
that in the previous chapter, this kind of incomplete and
earthbound solution was found to be the full enjoyment of
the experience of the five senses. In canto XVII of 'Libro del
destierro' there are — as was noted above — lines which suggest that the solution of human fellowship and care for the
world must supplant that other self-centred one. If this were
consistently stated in recent poems it would constitute a
fundamental shift of emphasis in the poet's quest for meaning; it would signify, also, a change in his poetic creed.
But however sincerely he believes in this 'patria del hogazo'
it does not seem to have taken the place of intense experience,
but simply to have combined with it. Indeed, the theme of
the eternal present reaches its culmination in 'Estaciones de
Stony Brook', a poem written shortly after 'Libro del destierro'.

Similarly, he does not prove to be completely satisfied
with death as 'patria'. He allows a sign of fear at death's
approach to slip into the final canto of 'Libro del destierro'

---

[11] Cf. the senses in which his coming to terms with death is examined in
chapter VI, II.

(the brackets suggest stealth, and perhaps his unwillingness fully to reveal his fear):

> (Un hombre de ceniza me acompaña
> a medias en la sombra sumergido) (OPC 553)

There are echoes of 'La alquimia vital', written in 1937, during the poet's darkest phase:

> Un viejo vive en mí fabricando mi muerte. (OPC 263)

Clearly, Carrera Andrade is not in a position to accept death entirely as a refuge and a response to all his yearning, for he is unable to remove a fundamental doubt about its nature:

> Es límite o comienzo
> madrugada o poniente. (OPC 551)

Death could be truly 'patria' only if it were paradise. Since it is all that he can perceive at the end of his quest, however, and since it will inevitably lead him out of exile, death must be made to assume the character of homeland. It is a stoical measure that enables Carrera Andrade to face death with dignity.

Despite certain anomalies, a complex structure of inter-related images grows out of the poems examined in this chapter, culminating with 'Libro del destierro'. Carrera Andrade's life is represented essentially as a journey across the sea of distance and time, in whose depths lies the great enigma. Among the islands discovered as he travels, some provide refuge, but others imprison him and create an intense solitude. The journey proves to be a quest for an ideal land, a country which Carrera Andrade would like to call his homeland. At times the answer seems to be a return to the country of his birth, but this fails to fulfil all his needs. At other times he regards the whole world as his homeland, but this leaves him lost in the vast expanses, which seem infinite and eternal. He is left to seek an ideal land that is enveloped in an aura of myth: an Eldorado, Utopia, or paradise. The journey leads him into a great desert, where the distances from the land of his origin and the inability to discover a permanent alternative homeland induce an anguished sense of exile. One final frontier remains, beyond which may lie the promised land, or an utter void. Travel has represented his search for meaning, while exile has symbolised the ultimate vanity of that quest. When he contemplates the course of his life retrospectively, therefore, if the poet envisages his life as a quest for a homeland, he must also recognise it as exile. The human condition is itself a form of exile.

CONCLUSION

C A R R E R A Andrade's various poetic themes have a special interrelationship, determined by the interplay of his private circumstances and his universal preoccupations. Ecuador has remained one of his constant sources of inspiration as a writer; apart from some early expression of disapproval and disenchantment the tendency has been, on the whole, towards admiration and affection. But he has focussed not so much on the internal social problems or the external political affairs as on the more abstract and philosophical significance of his country's relation to the world at large and to his own ontological inquiry (though the unjust treatment of the Indians and the repression of the proletariat are occasional themes of his poetry and quite frequent topics in his prose).

In the course taken by his life we have suggested an ambivalence that provides the key to an understanding of his written work. Expressed in crude terms, this is the contrast between his allegiance to Ecuador and his residence in foreign lands. In Carrera Andrade's poetic vision of the twentieth century world Ecuador and foreign lands tend to stand at opposite poles. The overall picture is one of the false, materialistic, technological world of cities and man-made objects (i.e. Europe) *versus* the land close to nature (Ecuador, or Latin America as a whole). Clearly, when this is considered in relation to the climate of thought among Spanish American writers it looks extremely conventional. What makes it of especial significance is the manner in which it corresponds to Carrera Andrade's ontological thought. For here too there are two poles — problems and solutions — and they relate closely with the poles of Europe and Ecuador. Intense human solitude, man's loss of innocence, the loss of identity, the inability of man to fathom the meaning of his existence, and his perplexity when confronted with the remorseless flow of time, which transforms

all things into transitory forms and brings him to old age
and to the prospect of death — all this is associated with
technological, urban Europe. The possible solutions are in-
timately linked with Ecuador. Nature as the elemental life
force, as a host of guiding signs, and as a world with which
to commune is epitomised by virginal Ecuador; Carrera Andrade's pre-Columbian ancestors, also, are his guides; and
he perceives the necessity of grasping the present moment
and living it intensely with the help of nature (particularly
the nature of virginal Ecuador, which is bathed in overhead
light). To these ontological problems, Ecuador acts as a
kind of key. So consistent is this pattern of thought that it
appears to have become quite deliberate, however subconscious it may have been in the early stages.

These are essentially private solutions, however. Carrera
Andrade also has a collective solution, which inherently links
the ontological issues with practical considerations. All men,
belonging to a universal human brotherhood, must live in
harmony and solidarity. An ambivalence in his poetic vision
is discernible here, essentially the same ambivalence as may
be detected in the course taken by his life. For although the
concept of a world-wide fellowship might be expected to
bring a sense of being at home wherever he travels, and a
concomitant feeling of serenity, what in fact usually happens
is that he seems left to his solitude, imprisoned in an alien
environment. It is, then, the position of an exile. The ideal
of universal solidarity and the belief in the oneness of ev-
erybody and everything in the world, though genuine, ultimately fail to provide the complete answer to the poet's
inner anguish. Exile is the outward manifestation of that
frustration.

As Chapter VII attempts to evince, the experience often
expressed in terms of solitary man in alien surroundings,
burdened with existential preoccupations, is essentially that
of exile. Most of the imagery of travel abroad in relation to
homeland — which forms the ingredients of verse in all
periods of Carrera Andrade's life — is precisely that of the
exile's sufferings and perplexities. Only at times — and especially before 1936 — has there been an air of optimism;

only at times has the eagerness for the discovery of new things outweighed the sense of tragedy. A term more complete than 'journey' (which Carrera Andrade himself has preferred), is therefore 'exile', since it gives the necessary emphasis to the despair and the failure to arrive at the desired destination, or 'patria'. Although his homeland symbolises solutions to the ontological problems epitomised by exile; although Ecuador, when named, is given a favourable and even an idealised portrayal; and although it counters the effects of foreign lands, it is not, ultimately, equal to 'patria'. It falls short of being 'patria' in the combined senses of 'ideal', 'solution', and 'home', just as the ontological problems ultimately prevail, answered only incompletely. Left without the true 'patria' that he seeks, whether a paradise on earth or in Heaven, Carrera Andrade attempts to find substitutes.

While serving as Ecuador's delegate at the United Nations during the forming of the Universal Declaration of Human Rights in 1948, he intervened personally in order to include the right of man not to be exiled (VC 200). The reasons that he gives for this intervention are highly significant:

Intervine en la discusión de los diferentes artículos de la Declaración Universal de Derechos Humanos movido por un ideal humanitario. Me pareció que la Declaración debía contener la respuesta a las aspiraciones del hombre moderno, en lo referente a su libertad. En el proyecto constaban los derechos del hombre a no ser perseguido ni encarcelado, pero no se decía nada del destierro. Sin embargo, el mundo acaba de salir de una guerra espantosa, en la que se utilizaron todos los medios de exterminación, inclusive la expulsión del hombre de su suelo natal. En un campo más reducido, el destierro ha sido un arma tradicional de los déspotas en América Latina. Más concretamente, en el Ecuador los gobiernos se han servido del destierro a los hombres de oposición para librarse de ellos. Casi todos los escritores más notables han sido desterrados, en una o en otra época. Juan Montalvo — gran pensador y artista de la prosa — murió en el destierro, en París. También no regresaron nunca al país Federico Proaño, Miguel Valverde, y otros muchos. Personalmente, creo que privarle al hombre del contacto con la patria, de la vida de su tierra, es una de las mayores torturas que se le puede infligir. Es como mutilarle a un árbol arrancándole sus raíces y condenándole así a una muerte lenta. El destierro es una pérdida de la libertad, tan terrible como el encarcelamiento. [1]

---

[1] Letter to the author, 13 July 1973.

As one might expect, the motivation was both humanitarian and personal. Carrera Andrade was first considering the universal significance of banishment: the Second World War had seen many cases; it was frequent in Latin American politics, and it was a recurring plight of writers. (Indeed, this and other interventions at the Assembly earned him the approval of the President of the Third Commission for his attitude of 'alto idealismo'.) (VC 200). But it is clear that he was also prompted by something more personal: by his own preoccupation with exile. It is not that he himself was ever formally banished, but that he knew the desolate experience of separation from the homeland. It is significant that the private feelings of exile are expressed, in this letter, in terms that are reminiscent of images in his poetry: suffering (torture), a life that is slow death, and the loss of freedom.

In a study of poets driven into exile by the Spanish Civil War, [2] I.R. Warner finds that among the effects of exile on these Spanish poets are initial despair and disillusion and a 'highly pessimistic notion of the human historical condition in general' (p. 27), the development of an interest in the 'character and historical evolution of the Spanish people and their culture' (p. 57), a nostalgia for the homeland of their childhood years, and a sense of being in a living death. Moreover, when Birute Ciplijauskaite considers these effects, in *La soledad y la poesía española contemporánea,* she remarks that 'la pérdida de la patria terrestre induce a algunos entre ellos a buscar una patria más amplia: sentirse partícipes en el orden cósmico o añorar la admisión en el reino divino'. [3] The close similarity of such effects to those exerted on Carrera Andrade by his life in the diplomatic service substantiates our view that 'exile' is an appropriate term to epitomise his life. [4] Support for this argument may also be

---

[2] I. R. Warner, *The Theme of Exile in Spanish Poets of the Guillén-Alberti Generation, from the Civil War to 1965,* unpublished Ph.D. Thesis, University of Leeds, 1969.

[3] Birute Ciplijauskaite, *La soledad y la poesía española contemporánea,* Ed. Insula, Madrid, 1962, p. 189.

[4] Admittedly, the comparison between his poetic vision and that of the Spanish poets in exile has its limits. Carrera Andrade lacks their tendency to regard their position as 'eradication' (Warner, op. cit., p. 45): far from Domenchina's reiteration of the notion of uprooting, for example (in poems such as the 'Segunda

found, moreover, by comparing the thoughts, emotions, and images discussed in chapter VII with those of a poet who is a clear-cut case of an exile. It is generally acknowledged that the Venezuelan poet Juan Antonio Pérez Bonalde, in political exile most of his life, captures the quintessence of the exile's feelings in 'Vuelta a la patria', which was inspired by a brief return to the homeland in 1877. [5] The homeland is a shore sighted from the sea (stanza 1), an image of happiness (1), a reminder of childhood and innocence (2), light (4), harmony (6), maternal love (9, 22, and the whole of Part II), a reminder of the passing years (11-14), and a land of nature (2, 16, 21, etc.). Exile, on the other hand, is a cold, grey land (32), suggestive of travel across oceans and through towns (35), and the cause of constant suffering (36).

It is worth observing, finally, that in his profound concern with exile, both in the literal sense of banishment or absence from his homeland and in the metaphorical sense of alienation from the human condition, Carrera Andrade clearly has much in common with many other Spanish-American writers. To some extent he may be considered one specific case exemplifying certain recurrent characteristics of their psychology and circumstances. It gives historical perspective to his case if we remember the dual heritage of the Spanish-American writer (Spain and the Old World/ the New World), which has often tended to create a dual allegiance. After three centuries of colonial rule and cultural dependence on Spain, the concerted attempt to achieve intellectual as well as political independence was hardly a complete success. The Americanist aspects of literature during the nineteenth century, represented by voices such as those of the gauchesque poets, were balanced by the continuation of a fundamental cultural subservience to Europe, Spain usually yielding to other countries, particularly to France. In the twentieth cen-

---

elegía jubilar'), he can write of his roots being firmly planted in the soil of Ecuador ('Hombre planetario', XVI, OPC 448. In his letter quoted above he does indeed make use of the image of uprooting.). Nor is there an impression, in the Ecuadorian's poetry, of the feeling shared by Spanish poets in exile that a return home would amount to self-betrayal: in his life there has been no destruction of his links with his homeland, no complete closing of the door.

[5] *Antología de la poesía hispanoamericana*, ed. Julio Caillet Bois, Aguilar, Madrid, 1965, pp. 517-20.

tury this dualism has continued: *mundonovismo,* regionalism, *indigenismo,* literature of social realism and other literary trends associated with exploration or illustration of the realities of the Spanish American countries have run parallel with the Parnassian and Symbolist facets of *modernismo,* with the avant-garde, surrealism, and other movements with their source in Europe. It should be noted that there have been few instances where clear classification of individual authors under any one of the headings used above has been possible, for balancing or conflicting trends have tended to coexist within each writer. It is under such circumstances that an ambivalent attitude to homeland and foreign countries comes into existence.

To this it should be added that Carrera Andrade belongs to an extensive tradition of Spanish-American poet-diplomats. Among those whose career included diplomatic service abroad on behalf of their country the most notable are: José Joaquín Olmedo (Ecuador, 1780-1847); Andrés Bello (Venezuela, 1781-1865); Rafael Pombo (Colombia, 1833-1912); Juan Zorrilla de San Martín (Uruguay, 1855-1931); Rubén Darío (Nicaragua, 1867-1916); Ricardo Jaimes Freyre (Bolivia, 1868-1933); Amado Nervo (Mexico, 1870-1919); Enrique González Martínez (Mexico, 1871-1952); Guillermo Valencia (Colombia, 1873-1943); José Santos Chocano (Peru, 1875-1934); Gabriela Mistral (Chile, 1889-1957); and Pablo Neruda (Chile, 1904-73). Clearly, one reason for this phenomenon is the countries' legitimate and astute use of their poets' international reputation, cultural knowledge, and cosmopolitan outlook. At the heart of the matter, however, is something within the poets themselves: the obvious fact that most of them have preferred — at least temporarily — to reside abroad while still serving their country. In other words, they all suggest, to some degree, the ambivalent attitude to the homeland and to exile which is held by Carrera Andrade. They are, in fact, barely distinguishable from the numerous Spanish-American writers who live in voluntary exile without a diplomatic career.

Some deficiency in their own country — its society, its political system, its cultural facilities or traditions — leads

to the disenchantment of these Spanish-American writers
and prevents a total sense of belonging; some persisting
element of their dual heritage combines with this disenchantment to entice them to Europe. Yet they remain, at
the same time, remorselessly drawn to the homeland and
constantly preoccupied with its problems. Jean Franco writes
of the *modernistas* that they 'appeared to expect little from
their own societies, tending to seek recognition from abroad'. [6]
But Mario Benedetti — a Uruguayan writer who is much
opposed to the idea of voluntary exile — while recognising
the unfavourable cultural environment in Latin America
(until the mid-1950s), insists that poets such as Darío always
have their own country, or Latin America, at the back of
their minds: 'Si el poeta se siente postergado y no suficiente-
mente reconocido en Nicaragua, si se queja de la asfixia
latinoamericana, y aun si en cierta etapa piensa crédulamente
que Europa compensará de algún modo esas carencias, todo
ello sirve para confirmar que a Darío, como a todo artista
latinoamericano que se instala en París, le preocupa especial-
mente la repercusión de su obra en América Latina'. [7] To
take as another example a writer more recent than the
modernistas, Julio Cortázar is an Argentinian who has lived
for many years in Europe while writing and thinking about
Argentina and Latin America. His compatriot, Ana María
Barrenechea, has captured the essence of the situation: 'Cortázar ha llamado la atención sobre una característica de los
argentinos (¿y por qué no de los americanos?) que parecen
desterrados en su patria, viven añorando la cultura europea
y nunca dejan de ser hombres de dos mundos aunque reali-
cen su sueño. El mismo Cortázar es en la vida un hombre
dividido entre dos mundos. Nunca se sintió contento en su
tierra y fuera de ella sigue recreándola en sus obras. . .'. [8]

In recent years Spanish-American writers have become
conscious of the need to justify their choice of residence in
Europe. The "Padilla Affair" helped to bring to a head the

[6] Jean Franco, *The Modern Culture of Latin America. Society and the Artist*, Pelican Books, Harmondsworth, 1970, p. 50.
[7] Mario Benedetti, *Letras del continente mestizo*, Arca, Montevideo, 1967, p. 34.
[8] Ana María Barrenechea, 'La estructura de *Rayuela*', in J. Lafforgue (ed.) *Nueva novela latinoamericana*, Editorial Paidós, Buenos Aires, vol. II, pp. 228-9.

opposition between those living at home and those prefer-
ring exile. [9] Although the central issue concerned the internal
affairs of Cuba, an increasingly important side-issue became
that of a writer's commitment to his country's social causes
and the question whether voluntary exile in Europe permits
such commitment. In the interchange of published letters
a good deal of scorn was shown for the émigrés by those
who remained in what they considered to be the front line.
A letter signed in Uruguay by Juan Carlos Onetti and Mario
Benedetti, among others, alludes to the 'actitud poco menos
que *elitista* de ciertos latinoamericanos, casi europeos, que
parecen creer que un intelectual siempre es inocente. . .', [10]
while a declaration signed by eleven Peruvian intellectuals
denies the involvement of the European residents in Latin
America's social struggle: 'Como escritores que vivimos en
los avatares de la revolución latinoamericana, desde dentro y
no desde "capitales de la cultura occidental", debemos ma-
nifestar a la opinión pública mundial que la "línea" de Var-
gas Llosa y de algunos otros "exiliados voluntarios" no es
ni ha sido nunca una línea de combate'. [11]

   J.M. Oviedo has succinctly and frankly put the case on
behalf of the exiles as follows: 'Ocurre que los escritores
quieren, sencillamente, ser escritores, antes que nada, y que
Europa es el medio que les garantiza mejor el ejercicio
profesional de su arte. . . .' [12] He adds that in Europe they
can avoid political pressures and also achieve a greater universality. Such an attitude, he insists, does not imply a lack
of involvement in their countries' affairs; they go into exile
'sin sentirse menos comprometidos con sus países que cual-

   [9] Many Latin Americans in Europe denounced Cuba's approval of the Russian
invasion of Czechoslovakia in September 1968. The imprisonment of the Cuban
poet Heberto Padilla in 1971 led to a letter of protest to Fidel Castro about
repressive measures, signed by expatriot Latin-American writers (plus European
intellectuals and Latin Americans resident in their own countries) many of whom
had previously implied moral support for Cuba's Revolutionary government. When
Padilla recanted and was released, another letter was sent accusing Castro's regime
of the use of 'Stalinist' methods to achieve the poet's 'autocrítica'. (Carrera
Andrade was not among the signatories of either letter.) Meanwhile, Cuba was
taking countermeasures, which included the decision to have only resident authors
on the panel of judges for the Casa de las Américas prizes, and a speech by
Fidel Castro accusing expatriot authors of supporting Cuba for the sake of their
own prestige, and of furthering the cause of colonialism by a kind of cultural
colonialism.
   [10] *Indice* (Madrid), 292-5, 1971, p. 75.
   [11] Ibid., p. 77.
   [12] Ibid., p. 41.

quier otro ciudadano'. [13] To these arguments, which aptly cover some of the key interpretations given in the course of this work of Carrera Andrade's own position, might be added the fact that it is precisely when in Europe that many intellectuals have best seen their country on the Latin American continent in perspective. Just as Carrera Andrade spent several years of his exile in Paris at work on the study of Ecuador's pre-Columbian history, so Alejo Carpentier spent much of his eleven years of exile in France (1927-38) reading in order to discover America, and developing, with the help of the surrealists, his concept of Latin America as a continent of magic. [14] Miguel Ángel Asturias — to take another example that comes readily to mind — while in Europe during the years 1923-33, devoted a good deal of his energy to research, in the British Museum and at the Sorbonne, on the Maya civilisation.

But these cultural-political considerations are only part of the issue of exile, however fundamental they may appear to many. As this study has sought to demonstrate, Carrera Andrade's ambivalent attitude toward his own country and the question of residence abroad, on the one hand, becomes inextricably linked with his sense of dissatisfaction with modern civilisation, his visions of a utopia, and his preoccupation with the ontological issues of fleeting experience, death, and the quest for meaning. In this respect too, Carrera Andrade's specific case illustrates a more general phenomenon. A broadly similar fusion of themes seems to underlie some of the poetry of Pablo Neruda, for example. In a work such as 'Alturas de Macchu Picchu' (to take one of his best-known poems), Neruda identifies his inadequate private experience and inner anguish with the petty daily death of urban society, from which he is alienated; his solution, the collective struggle, is identified with the Latin American continent. Neruda's alienation from a materialistic world is thus combined with an ontological anguish, while his

[13] In her article 'Writers and Exile', *Bulletin of the Society for Latin American Studies*, No. 22, 1975, p. 9, Nissa Torrents suggests that some *émigrés* of the generation of writers since 1971 'are not interested in revolution or politics as their disillusion is total; thus the problem of commitment is alien to them'.
[14] See Luis Harss, *Los nuestros*, Ed. Sudamericana, Buenos Aires, 1968, pp. 53-4.

attraction to a virginal land is combined with a solution to that anguish. Carrera Andrade's alienation was shown to be ultimately a sense of estrangement within the human condition, leading to the formula: exile = life on earth. In this concept he shares a mood widely held, and often even expressed through the image of exile. James Higgins has shown, for instance, that the interlinked preoccupations of alienation and exile are typical of modern Peruvian poetry: 'la nota más característica de la poesía peruana de este siglo: una vivencia de enajenación, de destierro. No es casual que César Vallejo y César Moro hayan vivido literalmente en el exilio ni que José María Eguren y Martín Adán hayan dado la espalda a la sociedad para vivir como reclusos en su propio país. Los mayores poetas peruanos son seres marginados que se sienten extranjeros en el país y en el mundo donde les ha tocado nacer'. [15]

Carrera Andrade's treatment of exile, his homeland, alienation, and ontological enquiry reflects an ingrained characteristic of Ecuador without completely typifying the country's poetic production. He is certainly an example of the Ecuadorian who feels his own land to be a prison from which escape is a constant dream, the kind of man of whom César Andrade y Cordero is thinking when he writes: 'El prisionero ama la fuga. El precito ecuatoriano quiere dejar la cárcel verde ... los ecuatorianos estamos siempre en actitud fugitiva'. [16] But once Carrera Andrade has escaped, of course, Ecuador begins to assume the air not of a prison but a haven. Other Ecuadorian poets too have treated life as a journey, and suggested the change that absence brings to one's attitude to the homeland. Thus Galo René Pérez, in a meditation in poetic prose entitled 'La nostalgia de los viajes', echoes Carrera Andrade's voice in lines such as the following: 'A la vida se le ha comparado con un viaje, ineluctable viaje por la corriente de los años. Todos nos hallamos de tránsito, rumbeando hacia la misma orilla....'. [17]

[15] James Higgins, 'Los poetas enajenados', *Insula*, 332-3, 1974, pp. 7 and 9.
[16] César Andrade y Cordero, *Ruta de la poesía ecuatoriana*, Casa de la Cultura Ecuatoriana, Quito, Quinta edición revisada, 1971, p. 378.
[17] In Augusto Arias, *Panorama de la literatura ecuatoriana*, Casa de la Cultura Ecuatoriana, Quito, Quinta edición revisada, 1971, p. 378.

He refers to precisely the kind of allurement of foreign lands
to which Carrera Andrade at first succumbed: '... Pero sola-
mente el viajero que ama las lontanías y cede a la atracción
de extrañas ciudades, de países remotos, siente profundos
cambios en su alma, pues que experimenta el verdadero mi-
lagro del viaje, su deslumbramiento y sus desengaños'. And
he then expresses the idea, already found to exist in Carrera
Andrade's poetry, that search abroad will not bring the
discovery desired, since the dissatisfaction is essentially not
with the homeland but with the human condition: 'Herido
por la basteza, la incomprensión o las ruindades de la ciudad
nativa, cree que hallará lenitivo para su mal en lugares dis-
tantes, pero tal vez no ha reparado en que las imperfecciones
que ha aborrecido y que le han desterrado de su patria son
la condición de todo lo humano. El viaje conlleva, así, una
doble experiencia: la del frenesí gozoso y la de una desilu-
sión a veces tristísima'. Then, as in Carrera Andrade, the
homeland (which loses its original disadvantage) is thought
of with nostalgia. Despite such cases of similarity, however,
Carrera Andrade is seen by his fellow countrymen as an
extreme case rather than as a typical example. The writer
and critic Augusto Arias finds him 'el del viaje más extenso
entre los poetas ecuatorianos de todas las épocas'. [18] César
Andrade y Cordero sees him as one whose departure enabled
him to rise above the others of his group and to achieve a
degree of poetic skill and a moderation which is not found
at home; he is 'esta isla, este continente de la lírica ecuatoriana'. [19] When Isaac J. Barrera refers to him as 'el más
representativo de los poetas ecuatorianos de hoy', [20] he is
not alluding strictly to his typical qualities but to his importance, as is suggested when he continues: '... y el más
conocido en los círculos intelectuales del mundo'.

There is indeed no doubting Carrera Andrade's prestige
as a poet in his own country. With few exceptions histories
of Ecuadorian literature regard him as one of the country's

[18] Arias, *Panorama* ......, p. 275.
[19] Andrade y Cordero, *Ruta* ......, p. 120. The poets remaining in Ecuador
are seen as unbridled revolutionaries.
[20] Isaac J. Barrera, *Historia de la literatura ecuatoriana*, Casa de la Cultura
Ecuatoriana, Quito, 1960, p. 1138.

greatest twentieth-century poets. In his book *La literatura ecuatoriana*, for example, Agustín Cueva calls him 'El poeta más famoso del Ecuador contemporáneo', [21] while — to take an even more enthusiastic opinion — Raquel Verdesoto de Romo Dávila, in *Lecciones de Literatura* believes that 'Sin lugar a dudas, Jorge Carrera Andrade es el poeta de más altos valores, dentro del Ecuador literario contemporario'. [22] What most earns him such acclaim is the degree of universality that he alone of Ecuador's writers has achieved: that is, the expression of eternal human themes combined with the international recognition that he has received. Augusto Arias calls him 'un poeta universal. El poeta ecuatoriano universal'. [23] Although only his exile has made this possible, there is no feeling that Carrera Andrade belongs anywhere but in Ecuador; Arias adds: 'Con los pies fijos en su tierra nativa'. The poet's constant desire to serve his country in exile has been manifestly successful, not only in the diplomatic field but also in the domain of literature. His own international reputation has made a vital contribution to the prestige of Ecuadorian letters. Hugo Alemán sums up this view: 'Hombre de nuestra tierra, la enaltece, como pocos, dentro y lejos de las fronteras. . . . Su nombre mismo es un defenso de los valores espirituales de la Patria'. [24]

In terms of international as opposed to national prestige, however, his success is still incomplete. From time to time he has been acknowledged in Europe and the U.S.A. as one of the representative Latin American poets, but Latin America as a whole has not yet begun to treat him as an indispensable figure. The countries where he is best known are, not surprisingly, those where he has served as a diplomat; his personal presence has given an impetus. If this wide travel has afforded him a special advantage, other factors have possibly presented an obstacle to fuller recognition: factors such as the influence of Ecuador's own limited

---

[21] Agustín Cueva, *La literatura ecuatoriana*, Centro Editor de América Latina, Buenos Aires, p. 57.
[22] Raquel Verdesoto de Romo Dávila, *Lecciones de literatura*, Segunda edición, Editorial Universitaria, Quito, 1965, p. 507.
[23] Arias, *Panorama* . . . . . ., p. 295.
[24] Hugo Alemán, *Presencia del pasado*, Casa de la Cultura Ecuatoriana, Quito, Vol. II, 1949, p. 140.

cultural and political significance, and the relative inaccessibility of his texts. Interest in his work has not been assisted, moreover, by the fact that he has tended to stand apart from the internationally famous trends. Of particular significance is his uninvolvement, since the early 1930s, in social protest poetry; to some he has perhaps seemed — erroneously as we have argued — to belong to the highly-developed world rather than to the underdeveloped Latin American nations. In a different aspect, his deliberate search for transparency of technique, sometimes leading to a relatively simple type of verse, constitutes an aesthetic problem for readers accustomed to mystery, hermeticism and obscurity. One of the aims of this book has been to suggest the complexity underlying the apparent simplicity of his poetic vision, and to stimulate appreciation of his delight in the objects and experiences of this world and his tragic concern with eternal human issues.

APPENDIX

CHRONOLOGICAL SUMMARY OF CARRERA ANDRADE'S CAREER

1903   J.C.A. born in Quito on 18 September.

1908   Began formal education in Catholic boarding school founded by the priest, Dr. Pedro Pablo Borja.

1911   Profoundly impressed by violent street scenes on 11 August during the uprising against President Eloy Alfaro, and by the latter's subsequent downfall.

1915   Entered Colegio de la Merced for religious instruction.

1916   Transferred to the Liberal lay-school, the Instituto Nacional Mejía.

1917   With Augusto Arias and Gonzalo Escudero founded the journal *El Crepúsculo* (which lasted one year), and contributed to the school's journal *Vida Intelectual*. Began to publish first poems in newspapers and magazines. Helped to found *La Idea*, a journal later recognised as marking a new departure in Ecuador's literature.

1921   Editor of *Vida Intelectual*. Finished secondary education and entered University to study law.

1922   Published first book of poetry, *Estanque inefable*. Participated in student socialist groups and campaigns. Moved to Guayaquil as journalist.

1923   Returned to Quito. Abandoned university studies. Appointed chief editor of new 'leftish' magazine *Humanidad*. Imprisoned for subversive activities with *Humanidad*.

1924   Editor of socialist magazine *La Antorcha*. Employee of Ministry of Education.

1925   Military revolution brought new momentum to socialism in Ecuador.

1926   During first conference of Partido Socialista Ecuatoriano J.C.A. named Secretary of the Party. Wrote his first social poems. Published *La guirnalda del silencio* (verse). Living in bohemian style.

1928   Sailed to Europe as delegate of Ecuador's Socialist Party at Fifth International Congress in Moscow. Penniless in Hamburg and Berlin. Barred entry to Russia. Became Secretary of Asociación General de Estudiantes Latinoamericanos. Completed the collection of verse influenced by Baudelaire: *Los frutos prohibidos* (subsequently lost and never published).

1929   First visit to Paris. Met César Vallejo and Gabriela Mistral. Visited Le Havre and Marseilles. Settled in Barcelona.

1930   Published *Boletines de mar y tierra*. Journalism, translating, and editorial work.

1932   Obtained doctorate in Filosofía y Letras at University of Barcelona. Enquired about possibility of foreign service.

1933   Returned to Quito. Published *Cartas de un emigrado* (letters written previous year). Named Prosecretario del Senado in Quito. Taught literature at the Instituto Nacional Mejía.

1934   Appointed Cónsul Interino del Ecuador in Paita (Peru). On return to Quito published *Latitudes* (essays). Won competition for entry into Ecuador's diplomatic service. Appointed Cónsul del Ecuador in Le Havre.

1935   Published *Rol de la manzana* (verse) and *El tiempo manual* (verse). Married Paulette Colin Lebas.

1937   Published *La hora de las ventanas iluminadas* (verse) and *Biografía para uso de los pájaros* (verse). Appointed Cónsul General del Ecuador in Yokohama (Japan).

1938   Brief visits to New York and San Francisco on the way to Yokohama.

1939   Death of J.C.A.'s mother. Published *Guía de la joven poesía ecuatoriana* (essays).

1940   Published *Microgramas* (verse) and *País secreto* (verse). Returned to Quito. Interim appointment as Director General de la Sección Consular del Ministerio de Relaciones Exteriores. Published *Registro del mundo. Antología poética 1922-39*. Appointed Cónsul General del Ecuador in San Francisco.

1941   Peru gained possession of one third of Ecuador's territory. Published *Canto al puente de Oakland. To the Bay Bridge* (verse).

1943   Published *Mirador terrestre* (historical).

1944   Appointed Encargado de Negocios del Ecuador in Caracas.

1945   Published *Poesías escogidas, Lugar de origen*, and *Canto a las fortalezas volantes. Cuaderno del paracaidista* (verse). Worked for Ecuador's participation in the Flota Mercante Grancolombiana.

1946   Resigned from consular post, but remained in Caracas. Editorial work with *Revista Nacional de Cultura* (Caracas), journalism, lecturing.

1947   Returned to Quito. Member of Comisión Política which negotiated on behalf of Socialist and Civic Parties for Ecuador's new President and Cabinet. Death of J.C.A.'s sister, Lucrecia, and his mother-in-law. His wife sought (and later obtained) a divorce. His father was ill. Published *El visitante de niebla y otros poemas.* Appointed Enviado Extraordinario y Ministro Plenipotenciario del Ecuador in London.

1948   Member of Ecuador's delegation at 3rd General Conference of United Nations Organisation in Paris. Participated on behalf of the clause on the individual's right not to be exiled. Drafted the Spanish text of the Declaration of Human Rights. Published *Rostros y climas* (essays).

1950   Returned to Quito as Ministro Plenipotenciario de los Departamentos Consular y Diplomático de la Cancillería. Later resigned and became Vice-President of the Casa de la Cultura Ecuatoriana and editor of the journal *Letras del Ecuador*. J.C.A.'s father died. Published *Aquí yace la espuma* (verse).

1951   Published *Poesía francesa contemporánea* (translations). Married Janine Ruffier des Aimes. Appointed Permanent Delegate of Ecuador at UNESCO in Paris.

1952   With Velasco Ibarra returning to power in Ecuador for the third time, J.C.A. resigned UNESCO post and became editor of publications in Spanish at UNESCO and Editor of *El Correo de la Unesco*. Began period of research on history of Ecuador.

1953   Published *Familia de la noche* (verse).

1955   Published *La tierra siempre verde* (part of history of Ecuador).

1958   Published *Moneda del forastero. Monnaie de l'étranger* (verse). Visited Quito for two months, returning to Paris. Published *Edades poéticas (1922-56)* (verse).

1959   Published *El camino del sol* (part of history of Ecuador), *Hombre planetario* (verse), and *Galería de místicos y de insurgentes* (essays). Suffering from poor health, resided with relatives on Long Island (U.S.A.).

1960   Appointed Delegate of Ecuador, with rank of Ambassador, at United Nations in New York. After interview with Velasco Ibarra in Quito, named Embajador en Misión Especial en Chile, Argentina y Brasil, with duty of explaining Ecuador's views on the nullity of the 1942 pact conceding territory to Peru.

1961   Appointed Embajador Extraordinario y Plenipotenciario del Ecuador in Caracas. Published *Viaje por países y libros* (essays).

1962   Published *Mi vida en poemas* (verse) and *Los primeros poemas de J.C.A.* (verse).

1963   After Venezuela suspended relations with Ecuador, J.C.A. returned to Quito. Lost manuscript of *La República de los Generales* (continuation of history of Ecuador) in the move. Published augmented edition of *Hombre planetario* (verse), *Presencia del Ecuador en Venezuela* (essays), and *El fabuloso reino de Quito* (history).
        Uncertain whether to enter politics in opposition party or to continue serving as diplomat. Finally chose latter course and

after four and a half months in Quito, was appointed Embajador Extraordinario y Plenipotenciario del Ecuador in Managua.

1964 Published *Floresta de los guacamayos* (verse), *Radiografía de la cultura ecuatoriana* (essays), and *Interpretación de Rubén Darío* (a speech). Appointed Embajador Extraordinario y Plenipotenciario del Ecuador in Paris.

1965 Published *Crónica de las Indias* (verse) and *Retrato cultural del Ecuador* (essays).

1966 Head of Ecuador's delegation at UNESCO. After political reshuffling in Ecuador, returned to Quito to take up appointment in the government as Ministro de Relaciones Exteriores.

1967 Internal political pressures led to his resignation after six months. Published *Interpretaciones hispanoamericanas* (essays), and *Relaciones culturales entre el Ecuador y Francia* (essays). Appointed Embajador Extraordinario y Plenipotenciario del Ecuador in The Hague.

1968 Participated in International Poetry Conference in New York. Published *Poesía última* (verse; includes a new work: *El alba llama a la puerta*). Special number of the journal *Norte* (Amsterdam) dedicated to him. On commencement of Velasco Ibarra's 5th term in office resigned and moved to Paris.

1969 Took up a two-year appointment to teach Spanish-American Literature at the State University of New York at Stony Brook, Long Island, U.S.A.

1970 Published *Libro del destierro* (verse) and *El volcán y el colibrí* (autobiography).

1971 Returned to Paris. Translating work with UNESCO.

1972 Published *Vocación terrena* (verse), *Misterios naturales* (verse), and *Reflections on Spanish-American Poetry* (essays).

1973 Published *Selected Poems of J.C.A.* (Ed. and Transl. H. R. Hays).

1976 Returned to Quito. Published *Obra poética completa*. Appointed Director of the Biblioteca Nacional. [1]

---

[1] This summary is based on Carrera Andrade's autobiography, VC, with the support of Enrique Ojeda, *Introducción. . .*, and unpublished correspondence.

BIBLIOGRAPHY

1. WORKS OF JORGE CARRERA ANDRADE

(a) Poetry (including important anthologies)

El estanque inefable. Universidad Central, Quito, 1922.

La guirnalda del silencio. Imprenta Nacional, Quito, 1926.

Boletines de mar y tierra. Prólogo de Gabriela Mistral. Editorial Cervantes, Barcelona, 1930.

Rol de la manzana (1926-1929). Introducción de Benjamín Jarnés. Espasa Calpe, Madrid, 1935.

El tiempo manual. Ediciones Literatura, Madrid, 1935.

Biografía para uso de los pájaros. Cuadernos del Hombre Nuevo, París, 1937.

La hora de las ventanas iluminadas. Ediciones Ercilla, Santiago de Chile, 1937.

Microgramas. Ediciones Asia-America, Tokyo, 1940.

País secreto. Edición del autor. Talleres Bunsh-Sha, Tokyo, 1940.

Registro del mundo. Antología Poética. 1922-39. Ediciones del Grupo "América", Imprenta de la Universidad, Quito, 1940.

Canto al puente de Oakland. To the Bay Bridge. Original Text in Spanish, English Translation by Eleonor L. Turnbull, Stanford University Press. Office of Pan-American Relations, Hoover Library on War, Revolution and Peace, 1941.

Poesías escogidas. Prefacio de Pedro Salinas, Ediciones Suma, Caracas, 1945.

Lugar de origen. Ediciones al Servicio de la Cultura, Caracas, 1945.

Canto a las fortalezas volantes. Cuadernos del paracaidista. Ediciones Destino, Caracas, 1945.

Registro del mundo. Segunda edición. Editorial Séneca, México, 1945.

El visitante de niebla y otros poemas. Casa de la Cultura Ecuatoriana, Quito, 1947.

El visitante de niebla y otros poemas. Segunda edición. Casa de la Cultura Ecuatoriana, Quito, 1947.

Aquí yace la espuma. Editorial Presencias Americanas, Paris, 1950.

Lugar de origen. Segunda edición aumentada. Casa de la Cultura Ecuatoriana, Quito, 1951.

Familia de la noche. Librería Española de Ediciones, Paris, 1953.

Familia de la noche. Segunda edición. Colección Hispanoamericana, Paris, 1954.

Edades poéticas (1922-1956). Editorial Casa de la Cultura Ecuatoriana, Quito, 1958.

Moneda del forastero. Monnaie de l'étranger. Traduction de Jean Mazoyer. Collection Terres Fortunées, Dijon, 1958.

Hombre Planetario. Ediciones de la revista Mito, Bogotá, 1959.

Mi vida en poemas. Ediciones Casa del Escritor, Caracas, 1962.

Los primeros poemas de Jorge Carrera Andrade. Lírica Hispana, XX, no. 234, Caracas, 1962.

Hombre Planetario. Segunda edición aumentada, Casa de la Cultura Ecuatoriana, Quito, 1963.

Antología poética. Selección y estudio por Giuseppe Bellini, La Goliardica, Milan, 1963.

Floresta de los guacamayos. Editorial Nicaragüense, Managua, 1964.

Crónica de las Indias. Centre de Recherches de l'Institut d'Etudes Hispaniques, Paris, 1965.

Poesía última. Las Américas Publishing Company, New York, 1968.

Prosa y poesía de J. C. A. In *Norte* (Holland), Año IX, Nos. 3 + 4, 1968.

Libro del destierro. In *Papeles de Son Armadans,* CLXIX, 1970, pp. 35-48.

Libro del destierro. Bilingual edition (Spanish and French), University of Dakar (Senegal), Dakar, 1970.

Vocación terrena. In the collection *Árbol de Fuego,* No. 51, Caracas, 1972.

Misterios naturales. In *Cuadernos Americanos,* CLXXXI, 1972, pp. 167-71.

Misterios naturales. Centre de Recherches de l'Institut d'Etudes Hispaniques, Paris, 1972.

Selected Poems of J. C. A. Bilingual edition (Spanish and English). Edited and Translated with an Introduction by H. R. Hays, State University of New York Press, Albany, 1973.

Obra poética completa. Casa de la Cultura Ecuatoriana, Quito, 1976.

(b) *Prose*

Cartas de un emigrado. Editorial Elan, Quito, 1933.

Latitudes (Hombres, viajes, lecturas). Editorial América, Quito, 1934.

Guía de la joven poesía ecuatoriana. Ediciones Asia-América, Tokyo, 1939.

Latitudes. Segunda edición, corregida. Editorial Perseo, Buenos Aires, 1940.

Mirador Terrestre (La República del Ecuador, encrucijada cultural de América). Las Américas Publishing Company, New York, 1943.

Rostros y Climas (Crónica de viajes, hombres y sucesos de nuestro tiempo). Ediciones de la Maison de l'Amérique Latine, Paris, 1948.

Poesía Francesa Contemporánea. Editorial Casa de la Cultura, Quito, 1951.

La Tierra siempre verde (El Ecuador visto por los Cronistas de Indias, los corsarios y los viajeros ilustres). Ediciones Internacionales, Paris, 1955.

El Camino del Sol (Historia de un reino desaparecido). Ediciones Casa de la Cultura Ecuatoriana, Quito, 1958.

Galería de místicos y de insurgentes (La vida intelectual del Ecuador durante cuatro siglos: 1555-1955). Casa de la Cultura Ecuatoriana, Quito, 1959.

Viaje por países y libros. Ediciones Casa de la Cultura Ecuatoriana, Quito, 1961.

El Fabuloso Reino de Quito (Historia del Ecuador desde los tiempos más remotos hasta la conquista española). Ediciones Casa de la Cultura Ecuatoriana, Quito, 1963.

Presencia del Ecuador en Venezuela (Entrevistas, artículos, discursos). Editorial Colón, Quito, 1963.

Interpretación de Rubén Darío. Ediciones Cuadernos Darianos, Managua, Nicaragua, 1964.

Radiografía de la cultura ecuatoriana. Ediciones del Ministerio de Educación Pública, Managua, Nicaragua, 1964.

Retrato cultural del Ecuador. Publicaciones del Institut d'Etudes Hispaniques de la Universidad de Paris, 1965.

Retrato cultural del Ecuador. Cultural Portrait of Ecuador. Portrait Culturel de l'Equateur. Segunda edición trilingüe, Gulf Oil Corporation, Pittsburg, 1966.

Interpretaciones hispanoamericanas (Crítica). Ediciones Casa de la Cultura Ecuatoriana, Quito, 1967.

Las relaciones culturales entre el Ecuador y Francia. Edición del Ministerio de Educación Pública, Quito, 1967.

El volcán y el colibrí (Autobiografía). Editorial José M. Cajica, Jr., Puebla, México, 1970.

Reflections on Spanish-American Poetry. Translated by Don C. Bliss and Gabriela de C. Bliss, State University of New York Press, Albany, 1973.

(c) *Other works*

Antología poética de Pierre Reverdy. Ediciones "Asia-América", Tokyo, 1940.

'Selección de hai-kais japoneses'. In *Microgramas,* Ediciones "Asia-América", Tokyo, 1940.

Cementerio marino. Cántico de las Columnas. Otros poemas de Paul Valéry. Translation and Notes by J.C.A., Ediciones Destino, Caracas, 1945.

Poesía francesa contemporánea. Anthology, Translations, and Biographical Notes by J.C.A., Casa de la Cultura Ecuatoriana, Quito, 1951.

Pierre Reverdy, Antología. Versión libre, selección y notas de J.C.A., Librería Clan, Madrid, 1951.

The extensive bibliography of Enrique Ojeda, in *J.C.A. Introducción al estudio de su vida y de su obra,* Eliseo Torres & Sons, New York, 1971, includes poems and articles published separately in newspapers and magazines, translations of his works, speeches and unpublished works.

2. LETTERS BY CARRERA ANDRADE CITED IN THIS WORK

(Bound volumes of the poet's correspondence between 1929 and 1968 are held in the Special Collections Library at the State University of New York at Stony Brook, Long Island, U.S.A. When the author consulted this material in 1972 the letters had not been clearly ordered, though some attempt had been made to arrange them in periods. Box 8 covers 1929-49; Boxes 12 and 13: 1950-64; and Box 14: 1964-68. In the following list the appropriate Box number will be given; letters with no Box number are in the possession of the author.)

1. No place. Date 1929. To Juana de Ibarbourou. (Box 8)
2. Marseilles, 4 November 1929. To Manuel Salguero. (Box 8)
3. Marseilles, 26 November 1929. To Alex Gastelú. (Box 8)
4. Barcelona, November 1931. To General Leonidas Plaza. (Box 8)
5. Barcelona, 7 July 1932. To Enrique Teñón. (Box 8)
6. Quito, 1933. To the Editor of *El Día.* (Box 8)
7. Le Havre, 8 October 1935. To Luis Alberto Sánchez. (Box 8)
8. San Francisco, 28 February 1941. To José Camacho Lorenzana. (Box 8)
9. San Francisco, 2 May 1941. To Bolívar Paredes. (Box 8)
10. San Francisco, 13 November 1942. To Lloyd Mallan. (Box 8)
11. San Francisco, 20 June 1944. To his father. (Box 8)
12. Caracas, 14 May 1946. To Raúl Andrade. (Box 8)
13. London, 14 February 1949. To Galo Plaza, President of Ecuador. (Box 8)
14. La Garenne - Colombes, 5 May 1955. To Ricardo Descalzi. (Box 13)

15. Paris, 20 April 1956. To Mariano Picón Salas. (Box 13)
16. Paris, 9 January 1957. To Mariano Picón Salas. (Box 13)
17. Paris, 28 February 1957. To Dorothy Eve Harth. (Box 12)
18. La Garenne, 3 May 1972. To the author.
19. La Garenne, 3 August 1972. To the author.
20. La Garenne, 10 December 1972. To the author.
21. La Garenne, 27 February 1973. To the author.
22. Périgueux, 13 July 1973. To the author.
23. La Garenne, 28 February 1974. To the author.

3. SELECT LIST OF CRITICAL STUDIES ON CARRERA ANDRADE

ALEMÁN, Hugo. *Presencia del pasado.* Casa de la Cultura Ecuatoriana, Quito, Vol. II, 1953, pp. 88-140.

ANDRADE Y CORDERO, César. *Ruta de la poesía ecuatoriana contemporánea.* Casa de la Cultura Ecuatoriana, Núcleo del Azuay, Cuenca, 1951, pp. 115-28.

ANON. 'South American Poet', *The Times Literary Supplement* (London), 21 July 1950, p. 454.

ARIAS, Augusto. *Panorama de la literatura ecuatoriana.* Casa de la Cultura Ecuatoriana, Quito, 1971, pp. 275-81.

BACIU, Stefan (Editor-Publisher). *MELE* VIII/24 (International Poetry Letter), Organisation of American States, Honolulu, Hawaii, June, 1973.

BAREIRO SAGUIER, Rubén. 'Entrevista a J.C.A.', *ALCOR* (Asunción), No. 36, May/June, 1965, p. 4.

BARRERA, Isaac J. *Historia de la literatura ecuatoriana.* Casa de la Cultura Ecuatoriana, Quito, 1960, pp. 1138-1141 et al.

BEARDSELL, Peter R. 'Theme and Standpoint in the Poetry of J.C.A.'. *Iberoromania* (Munich), 3/4, 1971, pp. 348-56.

―――. 'Hombre planetario and Alturas de Macchu Picchu: Two types of collective identity', *Bulletin of Hispanic Studies* (Liverpool), vol. XLIV, 1977, pp. 21-8.

BELLINI, Giuseppe. 'Etapa actual de la poesía de J.C.A.', *Revue l'Interprète,* No. 3 (Milan), 1957, reproduced in *J. C. A., sus primeros poemas,* Lírica Hispana, XX, No. 234, Caracas, 1962, pp. 75-99.

―――. 'La poesía de J.C.A.', *Ínsula* (Madrid), Nos. 152-3, 1959, p. 28, reproduced in:

―――. *J.C.A. Antología poética, selección y estudio.* Biblioteca di Studi e Testi Universitari, I, La Goliardica, Milan, 1963.

BELLINI, Giuseppe. *La letteratura ispano-americana dalle letterature precolombine ai nostri giorni*. Sansoni, Firenze, 1970, pp. 326-32.

BENÍTEZ VINUESA, Leopoldo. 'J.C.A.: El sensualismo poético', *Revista Nacional de Cultura*, (Caracas), 1963, pp. 150-62.

CARRASQUER, F. 'Jorge Carrera Andrade. Equinoccio de la poesía hispano-americana', *Norte* (Amsterdam), IX, nos. 3 and 4, 1968, pp. 49-54.

CASARES CARRERA, Fanny. *J.C.A. y la nueva orientación poética en las letras ecuatorianas.* Tesis presentada previa a la obtención del grado de Bachiller. Colegio de los SS. Corazones de Rumipamba, Quito, 1962.

CORRALES EGEA, José. 'Carta de París. J.C.A.' *Ínsula* (Madrid), No. 96, 1953, p. 5.

COULTHARD, G. R. Introduction to *Visitor of Mist*. Williams and Norgate Ltd., London, 1950, pp. 7-9.

CUADRA, José de la. 'J.C.A.' in *Doce siluetas* in *Obras Completas*, Casa de la Cultura Ecuatoriana, Quito, 1958, pp. 829-35.

DURAND, René L. F. *J.C.A.* Présentation, choix de textes, traduction, bibliografie. Portraits, facsimilés. Poètes d'Aujourd'hui (156), Ed. Pierre Seghers, Paris, 1966.

GUEREÑA, Jacinto Luis. 'J.C.A. y Europa', *Norte* (Amsterdam), IX, 3 and 4, 1968, pp. 85-9.

HAYS, H. R. 'J.C.A., Magician of Metaphors', *Books Abroad* (Oklahoma, U.S.A.), XVII, 1943, pp. 101-5.

———. Introduction to *Selected Poems of J.C.A.*, State University of New York Press, Albany, 1973.

HEALD, W.F. 'Soledad in the Poetry of J.C.A.', *Publications of the Modern Language Association of America*, LXXVI, 1961, pp. 608-612.

LEAL, Luis. 'Una nueva edición de la poesía de J.C.A.', *Revista Hispánica Moderna* (New York), XXVI, 1960, pp. 118-20.

LISCANO, Juan. 'Americanos en Europa. País y poesía de J.C.A.', *Cuadernos Americanos* (Mexico), XV, 1956, pp. 232-55.

LUCIO, Francisco. 'J.C.A. y "El hombre planetario"', *Cuadernos Hispanoamericanos* (Madrid), 235, 1969, pp. 201-219.

MARTÍN, C. 'J.C.A. en Holanda', *Norte* (Amsterdam), IX, Nos. 3 and 4, 1968, pp. 59-60.

MISTRAL, Gabriela. 'Explicación de J.C.A.', Prologue to *Boletines de mar y tierra*. Editorial Cervantes, Barcelona, 1930, pp. 7-17.

OJEDA, Enrique. *J.C.A. Introducción al estudio de su vida y de su obra*. Eliseo Torres & Sons, New York, 1971.

———. 'Entrevista a J.C.A.', *Norte* (Amsterdam), IX, 3 and 4, 1968, pp. 90-6.

PALLEY, Julián. 'Temática de J.C.A.', *Hispania* (Baltimore & Wisconsin), XXXIX, 1956, pp. 80-3.

REQUENI, A. 'J.C.A., cronista del cosmos', *Norte* (Amsterdam), IX, Nos. 3 and 4, 1968, pp. 54-59.

REYES, Alfonso, *et al. J.C.A. y la crítica.* Espasa-Calpe, Madrid, 1935. (Extracts from newspaper reviews, etc.).

RODRÍGUEZ CASTELO, Hernán. *Gangotena, Escudero y Carrera Andrade. Tres cumbres de nuestro postmodernismo.* (2 vols.). Clásicos Ariel, Guayaquil/Quito, 1972.

RUMAZO GONZÁLEZ, Alfonso. 'J.C.A.' in *Siluetas líricas.* Editorial Bolívar, Quito, 1932, pp. 187-95.

SALINAS, Pedro. 'Registro de J.C.A.', *Revista Iberoamericana* (Pittsburgh), Vol. V, No. 10, 1942, pp. 285-94 (also as preface to *Poesías escogidas de J. C. A.*, Ediciones Suma, Caracas, 1945).

SÁNCHEZ TRINCADO, José, 'J.C.A.' in *Literatura Latinoamericana Siglo XX*, A. Peña Lillo, Editor, Buenos Aires, 1964, pp. 107-9.

SERRANO AGUIRRE, Ángel. 'Jorge Carrera Andrade', *Cuadernos Hispanoamericanos* (Madrid), 85, 1957. 7 pp. (unnumbered).

——. 'J.C.A.', *Cuadernos Hispanoamericanos* (Madrid), 142, 1961, pp. 1-21.

STRAUB, William John. 'Cosmovisión de J.C.A.', *Cuadernos Americanos* (México), CLXXXI, 1972, pp. 172-89.

——. 'Conversación con J.C.A.', *Revista Iberoamericana* (Pittsburgh), XXXVIII, 79, 1972, pp. 307-315. Reproduced as 'Conversation with J.C.A.', *Latin American Literary Review*, Vol. I, No. 1, 1972, pp. 71-8.

UNDURRAGA, Antonio de. 'La órbita poética de J.C.A.', *Revista Iberoamericana* (Pittsburgh), Vol. IV, No. 8, 1942, pp. 293-303.

VANDERCAMMEN, Edmond. 'Profil lyrique de J.C.A', *Adam International Review* (London), XVI, 1948, pp. 27-29.

VERDESOTO DE ROMO DÁVILA, Raquel. *Lecciones de literatura.* Editorial Universitaria, Quito, Segunda edición, 1965, pp. 506-9.

4. OTHER WORKS CITED IN THIS BOOK

ADOUM, Jorge Enrique. 'Las clases sociales en las letras contemporáneas de Ecuador' in *Panorama de la actual literatura latinoamericana*, Editorial Fundamentos, Madrid, 1971, pp. 208-24.

BARRENECHEA, Ana María. *Borges the Labyrinth Maker.* University of New York Press, 1965.

——. 'La estructura de "Rayuela" de Julio Cortázar', in *Nueva novela latinoamericana*, compilación de Jorge Lafforgue, Editorial Paidós, Buenos Aires, Vol. II, 1972, pp. 222-47.

BENEDETTI, Mario. *Letras del continente mestizo.* Arca, Montevideo, 1967.

BERDYAEV, Nicolas. *Solitude and Society*. Transl. George Reavey, Geoffrey Bles: The Centenary Press, London, 1938.

BORGES, Jorge Luis. 'El Zahir' in *El Aleph*. Emecé, Madrid & Buenos Aires, 1972, pp. 105-16.

CAILLET BOIS, Julio (ed.). *Antología de la poesía hispanoamericana*. Aguilar, Madrid, 1965.

CARRIÓN, Benjamín. *Índice de la poesía ecuatoriana contemporánea*. Ediciones Ercilla, Santiago de Chile, 1937.

CIPLIJAUSKAITE, Birute. *La soledad y la poesía española contemporánea*. Ínsula, Madrid, 1962.

CUEVA, Agustín. *La literatura ecuatoriana*. Centro Editor de América Latina (Col. Enciclopedia Literaria, 29), Buenos Aires, 1968.

DESCARTES, René. *Discours de la Méthode*, Manchester University Press, 2nd edition, 1961.

DEHENNIN, Elsa. *La Résurgence de Góngora et la génération poétique de 1927*, Didier, Paris, 1962.

Diccionario de la lengua española. *Decimoctava edición*. Real Academia Española. Madrid, 1956.

Enciclopedia Universal Ilustrada Europeo-Americana. Hijos de J. Espasa, Editores, Barcelona, 1925.

FRANCO, Jean. *The Modern Culture of Latin America. Society and the Artist*, Revised edition. Penguin Books, Ltd., Harmondsworth, 1970.

GUILLÉN, Jorge. *Cántico*. Ed. Sudamericana, Buenos Aires, 1962.

HARSS, Luis. *Los nuestros*. Ed. Sudamericana, Buenos Aires, 1968.

HIGGINS, James. 'Los poetas enajenados', *Ínsula* (Madrid), 332-3, 1974, p. 7.

————. *César Vallejo. An Anthology of his Poetry*. Pergamon, Oxford, 1970.

ICAZA, Jorge. *Huasipungo*. Losada, Buenos Aires, tercera edición, 1965.

JACKSON, R.L. 'Apuntes sobre la lengua greguerística en la poesía contemporánea hispanoamericana', *Hispanófila* (Madrid & Illinois), XXVIII, 1966, pp. 49-58.

LOZADA, Alfredo. *El monismo agónico de Pablo Neruda*. B. Costa-Amic Editor, México, 1971.

MORENO MORA, Vicente. *La evolución de la literatura americana*. Casa de la Cultura Ecuatoriana, Cuenca, 1948.

NERUDA, Pablo (Neftalí Ricardo Reyes). *Obras completas*. Losada, Buenos Aires, tercera edición, 1967.

RAYMOND, Marcel. *De Baudelaire au Surréalisme*. José Corti, Paris, 1940.

REYES, Oscar Efren. *Breve historia general del Ecuador*. Editorial "Fray Jodoco Ricke", Quito, quinta edición, 1955.

SHIPLEY, Joseph T. (ed.). *Dictionary of World Literary Terms*. Allen & Unwin, London, third Edition, 1970.

The Shorter Oxford English Dictionary. Clarendon Press, Oxford, 1933.

TORRENTS, Nissa. 'Writers and Exile', *Bulletin of the Society for Latin American Studies* (Southampton), 22, 1975, pp. 7-13.

WARNER, I.R. *The Theme of Exile in Spanish Poets of the Guillén-Alberti Generation, from the Civil War to 1965*. Unpublished Ph.D. Thesis, University of Leeds, 1969.

WHITMAN, Walt. *Leaves of Grass*. D. Appleton & Co., New York & London, 1909.

WROBEL, Arthur. 'Whitman and the Phrenologists: The Divine Body and the Sensuous Soul', *Publications of the Modern Language Association of America*, 89, 1974, pp. 17-23.

INDEX OF POEMS AND WORKS BY JORGE CARRERA ANDRADE

Abril, 52, 53.
Agua germinal, 145, 165.
Alabanza del Ecuador, 63-4, 73, 77, 79-81, 82-3, 87, 90, 92-4, 218.
Alfabeto, 196n.
Apetito de realidad, 155-6, 190.
Aquí yace la espuma, 163, 182.
Aurosia, 168, 169, 177, 198.

Biografía para uso de los pájaros, 58, 105, 205.
Biografía para uso de los pájaros, 83, 86-7, 205-6.
Boletín de viaje, 99-100, 109, 114.
Boletín del mal tiempo, 109-10.
Boletines de mar y tierra, 24, 108, 204-5.

Cada objeto es un mundo, 157, 181.
Campanas del Havre, 101.
Campanas del Kremlin, 17.
Canción breve del espantajo, 50.
Canción del continente negro, 101.
Canto al puente de Oakland, 73, 81, 90, 206.
Caracol, 61-2.
Carta al General Miaja, 113n.
Cartas de un emigrado, 24, 25, 36, 40, 41-2.
Caudales, 180-1, 208.
Color de La Habana, 105-7.
Comarcas ignotas, 212.
Corte de cebada, 52, 53, 60-1.
Crónica de las Indias, 63, 67-8, 72, 73-5, 77n.
Cuaderno de poemas indios, 60-3.
Cuaderno del paracaidista, 202.
Cuerpo de la amante, 183, 184, 210-11.

Chopo, 56.

De nada sirve la isla, 129, 133, 164.
Defensa del domingo, 206.
Destino, 103.
Dibujo del hombre, 113-4, 116, 131.
Dios de alegría, 185.
Dolor vegetal, 129.
Domingo, 52, 53, 61.

250 WINDS OF EXILE

Edad de sombra, 70-1.
Edades poéticas, 10-11.
El alba llama a la puerta, 146-9, 153.
El alba llama a la puerta, 146, 148-9, 156, 173.
El camarada parte de la tierra natal, 49-50, 99.
El camino del sol, 36, 37-8, 40, 76, 161, 164, 166.
El canto diminuto, 129.
El combate poético, 187.
El condenado, 132-3, 134, 199.
El estanque inefable, 21, 50-1.
El extranjero, 125, 210.
El fabuloso reino de Quito, 36, 37.
El libro de la bondad, 175-6.
El objeto y su sombra, 104-5, 187, 204.
El pasajero del avión, 117.
El reino de las cosas, 138-9, 141, 156.
El río de la ciudad natal, 73, 77, 87, 89, 93.
El tiempo manual, 46, 47, 105, 108, 109, 110-13, 117-8, 128n.
El visitante de niebla, 144-5, 206.
El volcán y el colibrí, 15-35, 36, 103n, 108n, 149-50, 171-2, 211n, 225-6.
Enigma del mar, 211.
Epílogo, 50-1.
Episodio, 54, 150.
Escala, 102-3, 205.
Estación penúltima, 145, 209.
Estaciones de Stony Brook, 174, 190-2, 220.
Estrofas del alba, see El alba llama a la puerta.
Evangelio de la Sor, 16n.
Evasión del lunes, 117-8.
Expedición al país de la canela, 77.

Familia de la noche, 73, 87-9, 90.
Fantasma de las granjas, 149.
Fiesta de San Pedro, 53, 61.
Floresta de los guacamayos, 211-2.

Galería de místicos y de insurgentes, 36, 38, 42.
Golondrina, 56.
Guía de la joven poesía ecuatoriana, 36.

Ha llovido por la noche, *see* Noticias de la noche.
Han cerrado la escuela, 51.
Historia contemporánea, 110-11.
Hombre de cualquier tierra, 85-6, 91.
Hombre planetario, 64, 67, 112n, 115, 116, 118-9, 126-7, 134-5, 141-4, 145, 146, 162, 168-9, 175, 176-7, 183-5, 188-9, 192, 195, 196-7, 198-200, 202, 210, 212-3.
Hombres en marcha, 40-1.

Imagen entera, 135.
Indiada, 61-2.
Interior, 177-8.
Interpretación de Rubén Darío, 36.
Interpretaciones hispanoamericanas, 36, 43-5, 162.
Invitación a la paz, 64-5.
Invocación a la palabra, 187.
Invocación al aire, 165, 168.
Islario, 167-8.
Islas niponas, 119n.
Isolina, 16n, 172.

Jornada existencial, 207.
Juan sin Cielo, 130-1.

Klare von Reuter, 102.

La alquimia vital, 142, 176, 221.
La Coruña, 102, 107.
La esposa, 183-4, 185, 210.
La extrema izquierda, 65-6.
La guirnalda del silencio, 21, 51n.
La Habana, 107-8.
La hora de las ventanas iluminadas, 172-3.
La llave del fuego, 89-90, 93, 94-7, 159, 202.
La mina más alta, 208.
La Pallice, 107.
La tierra siempre verde, 36, 37.
La vida perfecta, 52, 53, 156, 163-4, 167.
La visita del amor, 182-3, 202, 210.
Las amistades cotidianas, 204.
Las armas de la luz, 91-2, 185-7.
Latitudes, 24, 42, 45-8, 108, 195.
Lección del árbol, la mujer y el pájaro, 138, 141, 157-8, 162, 182.
Lenguas vivas, 156.
Lenin ha muerto, 17.
Les Halles, 114.
Levantamiento, 61-3, 66-7, 72.
Libro del destierro, 9, 143, 145, 204, 208, 209, 212-22.
Linaje, 198, 211.
Lo que es el caracol, 56.
Los amigos del paseo, 53, 129, 160-1.
Los antepasados, 63, 76, 83, 93, 169n, 218.
Los terrícolas, 131.
Lugar de origen, 73, 78.

Mal humor, 50, 51.
Mecanografía, 56.
Mediterráneo, 139.

Microgramas, 52, 55-8, 179.
Mirador terrestre, 36, 38, 39.
Misterios naturales, 155, 176, 179, 190.
Moneda del forastero, 91, 210.
Morada terrestre, 140-1, 178.
Museo universal, 118.

Nada nos pertenece, 133-4, 174-5, 198.
Niña de Panamá, 102.
No hay, 134.
Noticias de la noche, 154, 156.
Nueva oración por el ebanista, 172.

Obra poética completa, 10-11.
Ocaso de Atahualpa, 63, 75-6, 83, 169*r*, 218.

País de soledad, 209.
País secreto, 182, 209.
Paraíso de los ancianos, 145-6.
Poemas de pasado mañana, 111-2.
Poesía francesa contemporánea, 45, 47.
Poesía última, 10, 159, 176, 190, 212*n*.
Polvo, cadáver del tiempo, 137-8, 142, 176.
Presagios, 136.
Presencia del Ecuador en Venezuela, 36, 39, 42.
Primavera & Compañía, 52, 172-3.
Prisión humana, 158-9.
Promesa del río Guayas, 73, 77, 205.
Provincia, 129.
Puerto a las ocho, 101.
Puerto en la noche, *see* Puerto a las ocho.

Quipos, 179.

Radiografía de la cultura ecuatoriana, 36, 40.
Reflections on Spanish-American Poetry, 36, 37, 43-5.
Registro del mundo, 10, 103-4, 159.
Retrato cultural del Ecuador, 36, 38-9.
Rol de la manzana, 69, 101, 108, 167, 182.
Rostros y climas, 36, 42, 43-5.

Saludo de los puertos, 84, 101-2, 103, 113, 117, 205.
Se prohíbe andar sobre el césped, 114-6, 118, 202.
Segunda vida de mi madre, 206.
Señas del Parque Sutro, 116*n*.
Sierra, 52, 53, 61.
Soledad de las ciudades, 125-7, 209-10.
Soledad habitada, 128, 197, 209.

Soledad y gaviota, 127-8, 209.
Sombra en el muro, 180-1.

Taller del tiempo, 146, 147-8, 164.
Temperaturas, 205.
Teoría del guacamayo, 165-6, 211-2.
Tercera clase, 99, 117, 128, 197.
Tiempo de golondrinas, 73, 83.
Tierras, bosques, 61-2.
Torre de Londres, 139.
Tres estrofas al polvo, 137-8, 142.
Tribulación de agosto, see Episodio.
Tormenta, 52.

Viaje, 206.
Viaje de regreso, 84-5, 208-9.
Viaje infinito, 207.
Viaje por países y libros, 36, 42, 45, 47-8.
Vida del grillo, 52, 53, 156.
Vida del rocío, 140, 141, 187-8.
Vocación terrena, 160.

Yo soy el bosque, 199.

Zona minada, 182, 183.